Just Memos

Just Memos

Second Edition

Laurel Currie Oates
Director, Legal Writing Program
Seattle University School of Law

Anne Enquist
Associate Director, Legal Writing Program
Seattle University School of Law

ASPEN
PUBLISHERS

76 Ninth Avenue, New York, NY 10011
http://lawschool.aspenpublishers.com

Aspen Publishers
Attn: Permissions Department
76 Ninth Avenue, 7th Floor
New York, NY 10011-5201

Printed in the United States of America.

2 3 4 5 6 7 8 9 0

ISBN 0-7355-6232-6

Library of Congress Cataloging-in-Publication Data

Oates, Laurel Currie, 1951-
   Just memos / Laurel Currie Oates, Anne Enquist. — 2nd ed.
      p. cm.
   Includes index.
   ISBN 0-7355-6232-6 (pbk. : alk. paper) 1. Legal composition. I. Enquist, Anne, 1950- II. Title.

   KF250.O178 2007
   808′.06634—dc22

                                                          2006031099

About Aspen Publishers

Aspen Publishers, headquartered in New York City, is a leading information provider for attorneys, business professionals, and law students. Written by preeminent authorities, our products consist of analytical and practical information covering both U.S. and international topics. We publish in the full range of formats, including updated manuals, books, periodicals, CDs, and online products.

Our proprietary content is complemented by 2,500 legal databases, containing over 11 million documents, available through our Loislaw division. Aspen Publishers also offers a wide range of topical legal and business databases linked to Loislaw's primary material. Our mission is to provide accurate, timely, and authoritative content in easily accessible formats, supported by unmatched customer care.

To order any Aspen Publishers title, go to *http://lawschool.aspenpublishers.com* or call 1-800-638-8437.

To reinstate your manual update service, call 1-800-638-8437.

For more information on Loislaw products, go to *www.loislaw.com* or call 1-800-364-2512.

For Customer Care issues, e-mail *CustomerCare@aspenpublishers.com*; call 1-800-234-1660; or fax 1-800-901-9075.

Aspen Publishers
a Wolters Kluwer business

To my parents, Bill and Lucille Currie,
my husband, Terry,
and my children, Julia and Michael.
Thank you.

To my family, Steve, Matt, and Jeff Enquist,
for their love, support, and patience.

Summary of Contents

Contents xi
Preface xvii
Acknowledgments xix

Part I : Introduction 1

Chapter 1:   Making the Transition 3
Chapter 2:   Understanding the United States Legal System 23
Chapter 3:   Understanding Statutes 39
Chapter 4:   Understanding Judicial Opinions 61
Chapter 5:   Reading Statutes and Cases 97

Part II: Objective Memoranda 109

Chapter 6:   Drafting Memos 111
Chapter 7:   Drafting the Statement of Facts 153
Chapter 8:   Drafting the Issue Statement and Brief Answer 163
Chapter 9:   Drafting the Discussion Section Using a
             Script Format 175
Chapter 10: Drafting the Discussion Section Using an
             Integrated Format 215
Chapter 11: Drafting the Discussion Section for an Issue of
             First Impression 243
Chapter 12: Drafting the Formal Conclusion 265
Chapter 13: Revising, Editing, and Proofreading 271

Index 297

Contents

Preface xvii
Acknowledgments xix

Part I : Introduction 1

Chapter 1: Making the Transition 3
1.1   Understanding the Purpose of an Office Memo 4
1.2   Knowing What Your Readers Want and Need from an
        Office Memo 6
1.3   Understanding Your Role as the Writer of an Office Memo 10
1.4   Learning the Specific Conventions of a Legal Office Memo 11
1.5   Advice for Specific Groups 12
        1.5.1   English Majors 13
        1.5.2   Philosophy Majors 13
        1.5.3   Journalism Majors and Journalists 14
        1.5.4   Science Majors and Scientists 15
        1.5.5   Chinese Writers 15
        1.5.6   Japanese Writers 17
        1.5.7   Korean Writers 17
        1.5.8   French Writers 18
        1.5.9   Spanish Writers 19
        1.5.10   Slavic/Polish Writers 19
        1.5.11   Brazilian Writers 20
        1.5.12   Arabic Writers 20
        1.5.13   Russian Writers 21
        1.5.14   Ugandan Writers 21
        1.5.15   Indian Writers 22

Chapter 2: Understanding the United States Legal System 23
2.1   A Short History 23
2.2   The Federal System 25
        2.2.1   The Federal Legislative Branch 26
        2.2.2   The Federal Executive Branch 26
        2.2.3   The Federal Judicial Branch 26
2.3   The State Systems 28
        2.3.1   The State Legislative Branch 28
        2.3.2   The State Executive Branch 29
        2.3.3   The State Judicial Branch 29
2.4   Other Court Systems 30
2.5   The Relationship Between the Federal and State Systems 30

2.5.1   The Relationship Between Laws Enacted by
Congress and Those Enacted by the
State Legislatures 31
2.5.2   The Relationship Between Federal and
State Courts 31
2.5.3   The Relationship Among Federal, State, and
Local Prosecutors 32
2.6   Types of Law 33
2.7   Mandatory and Persuasive Authority 34
2.7.1   Determine Which Jurisdiction's Law Applies 34
2.7.2   Determine What "Law" Is Binding 35
2.8   Exercise 36

Chapter 3: Understanding Statutes 39
3.1   How Statutes Are Enacted 39
3.1.1   Federal Statutes 40
3.1.2   State Statutes 42
3.2   How Regulations Are Promulgated 42
3.3   The Relationship Among Statutes, Regulations, and Cases 43
3.3.1   Federal Statutes Govern 44
3.3.2   State Statute Governs 45
3.3.3   Both Federal and State Statutes Govern 45
3.3.4   Party Argues that a Statute Is Unconstitutional 46
3.3.5   Party Argues that Agency Exceeded Its Authority in
Promulgating a Particular Regulation 47
3.4   Reading and Analyzing Statutes 48
3.4.1   Finding Statutes Using the Citation 49
3.4.2   Distinguishing Between the Text of the Statute and
Other Material Provided by the Publisher 50
3.4.3   Making Sure You Have the Right Version
of the Statute 55
3.4.4   Identifying the Elements or Requirements 55
3.5   Exercise 58

Chapter 4: Understanding Judicial Opinions 61
4.1   Which Cases Are Binding on Which Courts 61
4.1.1   Issue Governed by State Statute and Cases
that Have Interpreted and Applied that Statute 62
4.1.2   Issue Governed by a Federal Statute and
Regulations and Cases that Have Interpreted that
Federal Statute and the Federal Regulations 65
4.1.3   Issue Governed by Common Law 68
4.2   How Attorneys Use Cases 68
4.2.1   Case as Authority for Rule 68
4.2.2   Using Analogous Cases to Illustrate How Courts
Have Applied a Statute or Common Law Rule 70
4.3   Reading and Analyzing Cases 71
4.3.1   Finding Cases Using the Citation 71

4.3.2   Distinguishing Between the Text of an Opinion and Material Added by Publisher 73

4.3.3   Reading the Opinion 79

4.4   Exercise 87

Chapter 5: Reading Statutes and Cases 97

5.1   Good Lawyers Are Good Readers 97

5.2   Good Legal Readers Read and Reread Material Until They Are Sure They Understand It 99

5.3   Good Legal Readers Synthesize the Statutes and Cases They Read 101

5.4   Good Legal Readers Place Statutes and Cases into Their Historical, Social, Economic, Political, and Legal Contexts 102

5.5   Good Legal Readers "Judge" the Statutes and Cases They Read 103

5.6   Good Legal Readers Read for a Specific Purpose 105

5.7   Good Legal Readers Understand that Statutes and Cases Can Be Read in More than One Way 105

5.8   Exercise 106

Part II: Objective Memoranda 109

Chapter 6: Drafting Memos 111

6.1   Audience 112

6.2   Purpose 112

6.3   Conventions 112

6.4   Sample Memos 113

6.4.1   Informal Memo in Which the Writer Sets Out but Does Not Apply the Law 113

6.4.2   Formal Memo in Which the Writer Sets Out the Facts First and Organizes the Discussion Section Using a Script Format 117

6.4.3   Formal Memo in Which the Writer Sets Out the Issue Before the Statement of Facts, Does Not Include a Brief Answer, and Organizes the Discussion Section Using an Integrated Format 123

6.4.4   Formal Memo Involving Three Issues, the Last of Which Is an Issue of First Impression 129

6.4.5   Bench Memo Involving an Issue of First Impression 137

Chapter 7: Drafting the Statement of Facts 153

7.1   Decide What Facts to Include 155

7.1.1   Legally Significant Facts 155

7.1.2   Emotionally Significant Facts 157

7.1.3   Background Facts 157

7.1.4   Unknown Facts 157

7.2   Select an Organizational Scheme 158

7.3   Present the Facts Concisely but Clearly 160

7.4   Present the Facts Accurately and Objectively 160
7.5   Checklist for Critiquing the First Draft of the
       Statement of Facts 161

Chapter 8: Drafting the Issue Statement and Brief Answer 163
8.1   The Issue Statement 163
8.2   The "Under-Does-When" Format 164
       8.2.1   Reference to the Applicable Law 164
       8.2.2   Statement of the Legal Question 165
       8.2.3   The Key Facts 166
8.3   The "Whether" Format 168
8.4   Readibility 170
8.5   Checklist for Critiquing the Issue Statement 170
8.6   The Brief Answer 171
8.7   Checklist for Critiquing the Brief Answer 173

**Chapter 9: Drafting the Discussion Section Using a
Script Format** 175
9.1   The Script Format 176
9.2   The Introductory, or General Rule, Section 180
       9.2.1   Decide What Information You Need to Include 180
       9.2.2   Order the Information 180
       9.2.3   Prepare the First Draft 181
       9.2.4   Include a Citation to Authority for Each Rule 184
9.3   The Undisputed Elements 185
       9.3.1   Decide Where to Put Your Discussion of the
                Undisputed Elements 185
       9.3.2   Prepare the First Draft of Your Discussion of the
                Undisputed Elements 186
9.4   The Disputed Elements 187
       9.4.1   Set Out the Specific Rules 188
       9.4.2   Describe the Analogous Cases 189
       9.4.3   Draft the Arguments 200
       9.4.4   Predict How the Court Will Decide the Element 211
9.5   Checklist for Critiquing a Discussion Section Written
       Using a Script Format 212

**Chapter 10: Drafting the Discussion Section Using an
Integrated Format** 215
10.1   The Integrated Format 215
       10.1.1   Inductive Reasoning vs. Deductive Reasoning 217
       10.1.2   Script Writer vs. Judge 217
       10.1.3   Advantages and Disadvantages 218
10.2   The Specific Rule Section 218
10.3   The Analogous Case Section 220
10.4   The Mini-conclusion or Prediction 222
10.5   The Arguments 224
10.6   Common Problems 227
       10.6.1   Give Appropriate Weight to Each Side's
                Arguments 227

10.6.2   Write Sentences that Are Easy to Read 229
10.7   Another Example 231
10.8   Checklist for Discussion Section Written Using an
       Integrated Format 240

**Chapter 11: Drafting the Discussion Section for an Issue of
First Impression** 243
11.1   Organizational Plans for Issues of First Impression 244
11.2   The Introduction 246
11.3   Identifying, Setting Out, and Evaluating the Arguments 249
       11.3.1   Identify the Arguments 249
       11.3.2   Identifying and Presenting Plain Language
                Arguments 250
       11.3.3   Identifying and Presenting Legislative History
                Arguments 255
       11.3.4   Identifying and Presenting Arguments Based on
                Case Law 259
       11.3.5   Identifying and Presenting Arguments Based on
                Policy 262
11.4   Checklist for a Discussion Section Involving an Issue of
       First Impression 263

Chapter 12: Drafting the Formal Conclusion 265
12.1   Formal Conclusion in a One-Issue Memo 265
12.2   Formal Conclusion for a Multi-issue Memo 267
12.3   Advice 268
12.4   Checklist for Formal Conclusion 269

Chapter 13: Revising, Editing, and Proofreading 271
13.1   Revising 271
       13.1.1   Content 272
       13.1.2   Large-Scale Organization 273
       13.1.3   Roadmaps, Signposts, Topic Sentences,
                Transitions, and Dovetailing 277
13.2   Editing 281
       13.2.1   Sentences 282
       13.2.2   Writing Concisely 288
       13.2.3   Writing Precisely 289
       13.2.4   Grammar and Punctuation 292
13.3   Proofreading 293
13.4   Citations 294
13.5   Some Final Thoughts About Revising, Editing, and
       Proofreading 294

Index 297

Preface

This book, the second edition of *Just Memos,* sets out the materials that were published in Books I and II of the fourth edition of *The Legal Writing Handbook*. It contains the chapters on the American legal system, on legal reading, and on researching, analyzing, and writing objective memoranda. In addition to updating the sample memos in the first edition, the second edition includes both a new opening chapter, designed to help students transition from the writing they were doing before law school to legal writing, and Practice Pointers, designed to help students apply what they are learning to the practice of law.

As you work through the materials in this book, keep in mind that writing a memo is a complex task. To do a good job, you must understand our legal system; you must know how to locate, select, and read the applicable statutes and cases; and you must be able to construct and evaluate each side's arguments. In addition, you must be a good writer. You must be able to use the conventional organizational schemes to present the law, the arguments, and your predictions clearly, precisely, and concisely. Finally, writing a good memo requires the exercise of judgment. You must exercise judgment in deciding when to stop researching, in determining which information the attorney needs, and in evaluating each side's arguments.

Instead of presenting each of these skills in isolation, *Just Memos* presents them in context. Chapter 6 shows four sample memos. Later chapters walk you through the process of writing a statement of facts, an issue statement and brief answer, a discussion section using different organizational schemes, and a conclusion. As you read through these chapters, keep your goal in mind. Instead of working to get an "A" on a particular assignment, use your assignments to learn how attorneys think and write about legal issues. By learning how to think and write as a lawyer, you will not only be a good student but you will also develop the skills that you need to be a good attorney.

Acknowledgments

In writing this book, we have been fortunate to have had the critiques and counsel of numerous colleagues who have taught legal writing. A heartfelt thank you to our longtime colleagues Lori Bannai, Mary Bowman, Janet Chung, Lucas Cupps, Janet Dickson, Connie Krontz, Susan McClellan, Chris Rideout, and Mimi Samuel. We would also like to thank Patrick Brown for his guidance on the section about the writing of philosophy majors, Eric Easton for his insights about journalism majors, and Theo Myhre for his invaluable help on the section about the writing of science majors and scientists.

Perhaps the most important collaborators in this project have been our students. Their writing appears throughout the book, and they were our first readers. So many made recommendations and allowed us to use their writing that we cannot mention them all, but we want them to know how much we appreciate their part in what we think of as "their book."

Some students made substantial contributions and deserve special recognition. Thanks to Donald Miller for his help on this edition and to Elaine Conway and Chad Kirby for allowing us to reproduce their memos in the book.

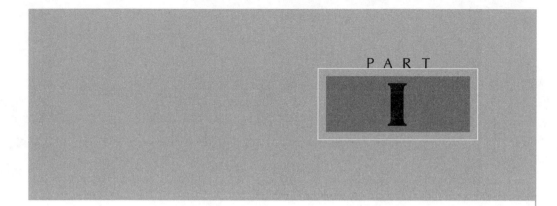

PART

I

Introduction

1

Making the Transition

Everyone comes to law school with some writing experience. Whether you were an undergraduate or graduate student at a university, a business person, scientist, poet, paralegal, student, or attorney from a country other than the United States, you have come to a U.S. law school with a range of writing skills and experience that shape who you are as a writer.

For example, if you are coming to law school immediately after receiving your undergraduate degree, you have undoubtedly been shaped as a writer by the expectations of your undergraduate professors, particularly those in your major. Consciously or subconsciously you have absorbed some of the customs and conventions of academic writing and the specific conventions of your major's discipline.

Similarly, if your most recent writing experiences have been from work, whether it was as a business person, social worker, police officer, or other professional, you too have absorbed the writing conventions of your field. The various writing projects and reports you wrote and read for work have shaped your beliefs about "good writing" and how it is done.

Even if you wrote for a living—as a novelist, journalist, poet, technical writer—or perhaps we should say, *especially* if you wrote for a living, you have been shaped as a writer by the work you did before law school. As a writer, you are more likely to be consciously aware of the conventions of the genre in which you were writing before entering law school, and you have undoubtedly honed the writing skills necessary to write successfully in that genre. The challenge, of course, will be to adapt those writing strengths to a new genre, legal writing, and to new readers, lawyers and judges in the U.S. legal community.

Whatever you were doing before law school, you were part of a specific culture—the world of health care, the world of school children, the world of wildlife biologists—and the writing that was done in those cultures was tailored for specific purposes and specific readers. The change to legal writing will require an adjustment.

Those of you who are coming to a U.S. law school from another country may have a more obvious cultural adjustment to make when it comes to writing. In some cases it will include the challenge of learning the writing conventions of another language, but even in cases in which the language of your home country is English, there will undoubtedly be cultural differences in what your new readers will expect from your written work.

In short, everyone coming to law school is making a transition from the writing he or she did before law school to the writing of the U.S. legal community. The trick, of course, will be to figure out what are the obvious and subtle similarities and differences between the writing culture you are coming from and the writing culture you are joining. Even if you were a paralegal before law school, you will have to figure out what was specific to the firm or legal setting in which you worked and what is generally true about writing for the larger, more generic legal community. At the very least, your specific role as a writer will have changed from paralegal to attorney, and that change alone will make a difference in the expectations your readers will have for your writing.

This chapter is designed to help law students make the transition to legal writing as smoothly and painlessly as possible. Several concepts are the keys to a successful transition: (1) understand the purpose of the new type of writing you are learning; (2) know what your new readers want and need from the writing; (3) understand what your role as the writer is in this genre; and (4) learn the specific conventions of the new type of writing you are adding to your writing repertoire, in this case, office memos.

§ 1.1 Understanding the Purpose of an Office Memo

If you are coming to law school from the world of business, you know what an office memo is in that context—a written internal communication between employees in the same company. For the most part, this definition applies in the law office setting as well. Like other businesses, a law firm uses a form of the office memo, often called an objective memorandum (or objective memo, for short) for internal communication about the cases the firm is handling. The main similarity between memos in other businesses and objective memos in a law firm, then, is that the writer and reader(s) of these memos are "on the same team"; they are members of the same firm sharing information about one of the firm's cases.

The most noticeable differences between the typical business memo and an objective memo for a law firm tend to be the format, content, and length. The format starts off looking like a standard business memo with "To," "From," "Date," and "Re" lines, but as you will see in Chapter 6, the format and structure of an objective memo becomes quite law-specific from there on and, if anything, the content of an objective memo has more in common with a business report than it does with a business memo. However, unlike either a business memo or a business report, an objective memo is unlikely to contain bullet points, charts, or other such features. The preferred form in the objective memo is to set out all information in paragraphs and sentences.

When you read Chapter 6, you will see that most memos begin with the facts of the client's case (journalists and short story writers will feel at home here), followed by a statement of the legal issue and a brief answer, a discussion section that sets out the governing law, including both statutes and relevant cases; the arguments each side is likely to make; and a conclusion that predicts what a court is likely to do in the case. The latter four sections—issue, law, arguments, conclusion—have some parallels to a sophisticated undergraduate research paper. The issue and brief answer frame the discussion in much the same way a good thesis statement does in an undergraduate research paper. The law and argument portions of the discussion section set out the writer's research. The argument section shows how both sides will debate the issue. The conclusion summarizes the analysis and predicts how the case will turn out.

All of these sections mean that an objective memo may be considerably longer than a typical business memo and more like the length of a research paper or a business report. The length of any given objective memo will vary, of course, depending upon the complexity of the facts and law and the number of cases and arguments that need to be described. As you will see in the chapters and examples of memos that follow, some objective memos may be as short as two or three pages while others may require twenty pages to get the job done.

What is important to realize, though, is that writing longer memos is not the goal; in fact, quite the opposite is true. The readers of these memos will want their writers to tell them what they need to know in as few words as possible. Why? Virtually everyone in a modern law firm feels overworked and overloaded with reading. By writing concise objective memos, you will save your readers' time and patience. This point is important to remember, particularly if you have developed the common undergraduate habit of "padding" your writing to meet assignment page requirements. Unnecessary pages will not impress busy legal readers, and they will not help your firm.

Another obvious difference between undergraduate research papers and objective memos is that one is an academic exercise and the other has a "real world" job to do. This difference will affect the writing in one very important way: unlike undergraduate research papers, objective memos are not about impressing a professor with how much you know or how much work you did. They are about making sure the readers in one's own firm have a clear understanding of the case so that they can do whatever comes next, whether it be to advise the client about his or her options, do more discovery, file a motion, or decline to take the case.

Notice too that these memos are called "objective" memos. Unlike many other types of legal documents that are written for external readers (such as a judge or opposing counsel) and are therefore advocacy pieces, objective memos are just what the word "objective" implies: they lay out the strengths and weaknesses of the case so that attorneys in the firm can better assess how to represent the client. Unfavorable facts, rules, analogous cases, and weaknesses in the client's case are dealt with openly. Objective memos include the arguments both for and against the client's position so that internal readers in the firm know what arguments they will be able to make, as well as those their opponents are likely to make.

Given the purpose of an objective memo, then, and how the memo works in a firm setting, it is not surprising that the most important "writing virtues" for memos are accuracy, brevity, clarity, and organization. Other writing virtues such as creativity and eloquence are nice-to-have extras, but they are relative luxuries in objective memo writing. Conveying what the reader needs to know in an accurate, brief, clear, and organized fashion increases the efficiency of the firm and facilitates the goal of representing clients effectively.

§ 1.2 Knowing What Your Readers Want and Need from an Office Memo

In the previous discussion about the purpose of an office memo, we emphasized that the memo's reader is someone else in the firm who is also working on the case. Invariably that person in the firm is someone who is higher up in the firm structure than the writer. He or she is someone who is in a position to assign research and writing tasks and who supervises the work of the writer.

Given the position of these supervising attorneys in a firm, the memo's reader will almost certainly be an experienced attorney. That experience will determine to some extent what he or she wants and needs from an office memo. Depending upon the reader's circumstances, he or she may have anywhere from no background in the specific area of law in the memo to an extensive background with years of experience handling similar cases.

Obviously if the reader has little or no experience with the type of case the memo discusses, the writer should provide a brief overview of the area of law. Any historical discussion of the law, though, should be succinct, hitting only the high points and moving rapidly toward the current state of the law. Giving some context for understanding the policy underlying the law is also common, but these discussions should be short and to the point. Long preambles that take pages or even paragraphs to get to the specific applicable law will not be well received. If, on the other hand, the reader is highly experienced in the area, the writer should adjust the memo accordingly, omit background basics, and dive right into the specific relevant statutes and cases. In general, then, memo readers want only enough background and context to deal with the case before them.

COMMON MISTAKE #1   Some students in legal writing courses mistakenly assume that their legal writing professors will be reading and evaluating their papers as though they, the professors, are the real readers. Consequently, these students leave things out of the memo on the assumption that "my professor already knows that." While it is true that your professor undoubtedly researched the problem and knows the analysis inside out, he or she will be evaluating your writing from the point of view of a "real world" reader—someone who is depending on the writer's research and analysis and who was not in class and participating in the class discussions on the issues.

Because the supervising attorney is sometimes the writer's source for the facts or the writer assumes the supervising attorney is already well versed in the facts, it may be tempting to assume that the supervising attorney does not need a statement of facts in the memo. This is generally not a good assumption. Including a clear and coherent statement of facts ensures that writer and reader are working from the same set of facts. Keeping the facts front and center in both the writer's and reader's mind also helps ensure that the arguments will be more tightly connected to the facts. In addition, many attorneys handle numerous cases at once. Having a well-written statement of facts in the memo can help a harried attorney keep the facts in many different cases straight. A well-written statement of facts is also useful if someone else in the firm who is new to the case steps in at some point to help out.

Once you are part of a firm and receiving assignments from your supervising attorney, you will have no problem picturing who it is you are writing for and what it is that reader wants and expects. You will undoubtedly learn his or her pet peeves and stylistic preferences. Some readers will be annoyed by what may seem to you to be a small mistake, such as missing apostrophes or confusing "affect" with "effect." Some may insist on a certain writing style, such as always using active voice or short, declarative sentences. Adjusting to individual readers, once you know them, is an expected part of law firm life.

In the meantime, while you are still in law school and learning how to write objective memos, assume your supervising attorney reader is a "friendly reader" (not an adversarial reader—after all you are in the same firm) who is very busy and consequently somewhat demanding and impatient with verbose writing. He or she hired you for your excellent research and analytical skills, as well as your legal judgment. What this reader wants from you in any given memo is just what he or she needs to understand the case—no more, no less.

Naturally you will be doing extensive research for your memo assignments and, at times, that research may take you in a fruitless, unproductive direction. Your reader, however, will not want to know every twist or turn in your research journey, nor will the reader need every scrap of information that you gathered. Before including something in your memo, ask yourself, "does my reader need to know this?" Notice that this question is different from "did *I* need to know this in order to analyze the problem?" Your reader will expect you to be selective about what you include in the memo and to synthesize the relevant material.

COMMON

MISTAKE #2

Some new legal writers make the "under-graduate mistake" when they are writing their first office memos: they want to make sure their legal writing professor or their supervising attorney knows how much work they did and how thoroughly they researched the problem. Consequently, they include far more cases than are necessary to understand the analysis or make the arguments. This mistake often comes directly from their undergraduate experience. As undergraduates, many of us were rewarded for writing papers that showed how much work we had done. Length often translated into high grades. Law school and law firm writing are different. Legal writers should adopt the real world readers' points of view about length, which is "I'm busy. Tell me what I need to know and then stop writing."

As you write a memo, remember that clear communication between you and your reader is your responsibility, not the reader's responsibility. Be explicit about how you are organizing the material. Use roadmaps, signposts, topic sentences, and transitions (see Chapter 13) to reveal the organizational structure to your reader and guide your reader through the sections and paragraphs. Do not worry that these structural signals will make your writing seem unsophisticated. Legal readers expect overt structures because they help them understand complex material more easily.

Similarly, when it comes to sentence structure and word choice, keep it simple. Your reader will not want to puzzle over any sentence or word in your writing. The test for whether a sentence is well written is whether it can be understood the first time it is read. The well-chosen word is one that the reader already knows. If an unfamiliar word is required in a given instance, define it immediately within the writing. Do not worry about "dumbing down" the writing. Clear communication is the goal, not dazzling the reader with your vocabulary or convoluted sentence structure.

COMMON
MISTAKE #3

Some new legal writers make the mistake of "dressing up their ideas." They fear that if they state things simply they will seem unsophisticated. Here again, the mistake may be the result of an undergraduate writing experience that rewarded students for making simple ideas seem complex. The opposite is true in legal writing: you will be rewarded and appreciated if you can make complex ideas seem simple.

In addition to being explicit about the organizational structure of the memo, be explicit about how you are analogizing or distinguishing your client's case and the key analogous cases. Here again you may be initially concerned that you are "dumbing down" the writing if you spell out exactly how the cases are similar or different, and you may be tempted to make a vague comparison like the following:

EXAMPLE   **Vague Comparison**

As in *Smith,* the defendants in the *Patel* case allowed their family friend to use the family car to drive to work.

The problem is that the sentence above leaves too much of the work for the reader to do. What exactly in *Smith* is analogous to *Patel*? Legal readers will want you, the writer, to do the work and spell it out for them, as the writer did in the sentence below:

EXAMPLE   **Explicit Comparison**

Like the defendant in *Smith,* who allowed his daughter's boyfriend to use the family car to drive to a dance, the defendants in *Patel* allowed their family friend to use the family car to drive to work.

The fact that experienced attorneys would want such explicit analysis may come as a surprise to some new legal writers. After all, not all cultures value such explicit explanations in the same way the legal culture does. In fact, leaving things unsaid and for readers to figure out is a mark of sophisticated writing in some academic fields and in some Asian and Middle Eastern cultures. Stating one's point so directly may be considered not just unsophisticated but also brash and even rude. For writers coming from these backgrounds, it may feel unnatural at first to spell out points so explicitly, but over time it will become second nature as these writers better understand how office memos and their readers work in the legal culture.

To summarize, then, what your reader wants and needs from the office memo is a well-organized, easy-to-read, concise document with the following parts:

- An accurate account of the relevant facts told as a story so that it is easy to understand who did what and when (Chapter 7)
- A focused issue statement that includes the applicable law, legal question, and legally significant facts (Chapter 8)
- A description of the relevant law and key cases (Chapters 9, 10, and 11)
- The arguments both sides are likely to make (Chapters 9, 10, and 11)
- A conclusion that objectively assesses how the case is likely to turn out (Chapter 12)

Some legal readers will also want a "brief answer" immediately following the issue statement. Brief answers will be discussed in Chapter 8. Other readers may want the writer to include strategic advice in the conclusion, which will be discussed in Chapter 12.

§ 1.3 Understanding Your Role as the Writer of an Office Memo

When a junior associate or a legal intern is assigned to research and write an office memo, the expectation is that the associate or intern will spend many hours researching and analyzing the legal problem and then write up that work in an office memo that will take the assigning attorney approximately fifteen minutes to read and understand.

An underlying assumption of the U.S. legal culture, then, is that the reader's time is more valuable than the writer's time. Legal readers, including supervising attorneys and partners in law firms, tend to have positions of authority over the writers of legal memos. Consequently, writers are expected to expend their time and energy writing clearly so that readers do not have to spend extra time and energy understanding what they are reading.

This does not mean, however, that the writer's role is unimportant. Far from it. As the writer, your role is to become the expert on a given case. Through careful study of the facts and thorough research, you will be the one who knows what law is the controlling law and which cases are the key cases. In addition, after reading the arguments set out in the cases and the courts' evaluation of those arguments, you will be the one who is in the best position to determine what each side can argue and how the court will view those arguments. Ultimately, your role is to give your educated opinion about what the court is likely to do in this case. In short, your role is to exercise judgment, and in fact, that is exactly what you are paid to do when you are assigned to write a memo.

Exercise judgment

- about what are the legally significant facts,
- about what statute(s) or common law doctrine will govern,
- about which cases are the key analogous cases,
- about which arguments the court will find persuasive, and
- about how the case will turn out (your prediction).

As new attorneys or law students, many find the memo writer's role a bit intimidating. It can be hard enough to be confident that you have found the right law and key cases without trying to create brand new, never-seen-before arguments, or worse, predicting what a court will do. Take heart, though. Many of the arguments will be variations of ones you see in the cases (no one is expecting you to make all of this up from scratch), and law school is exactly the right place to learn and practice these skills.

The chapters that follow will offer guidance on all these tasks, and you will note when you get to Chapter 12 that the task that you may find most daunting—predicting what a court will do—has some "wiggle room." You will be framing your conclusions as "likely" or "unlikely." In other words, you will be writing conclusions as predictions, not guarantees.

A key part of your role as well will be to cite authority to support each of the points you make. The citations show that you have the support of the law, other courts, and other legal minds behind your analysis. Furthermore, by including the source for the facts and correctly citing statutes, cases, treatises, law review articles, and other secondary sources, you create a document in which everything about the case comes together. Through your office memo, anyone in the firm working on the case can assess all the key components of the case.

Two final points about your role in writing an office memo: first, even though the memo is an internal document, keep the tone of the memo professional. This means that the language tends to be more formal than spoken language without becoming stilted or stuffy. An office memo is not the place for informality or a cocky or sarcastic tone. If, based on your research and analysis, you are confident that your client will win the case, phrase that prediction as "the court is highly likely to find that" and not "our case is a slam dunk" or "opposing counsel does not have a prayer." Second, remember that your role is to be an objective assessor of the case; you are not in an advocate role yet. Even though you will be thinking about how each side will set out its arguments and actually setting out those arguments as an advocate would, ultimately you will be objectively assessing the strengths and weaknesses in those arguments so that your readers can evaluate the case.

§ 1.4 Learning the Specific Conventions of a Legal Office Memo

In the earlier discussion of the purpose, readers' expectations, and writer's role in an office memo, a number of the specific conventions of memo writing were mentioned:

1. The standard format, including the "To," "From," "Date," and "Re" lines
2. Major sections, including the facts, the statement of the issue and brief answer, the discussion section, and the conclusion
3. Writing in paragraphs and sentences, not bullet points
4. Legal writing's emphasis on brevity
5. Objective handling of facts, statutes, cases, and both sides' arguments
6. Explicit roadmaps, signposts, topic sentences, and transitions
7. Easy-to-read sentences and paragraphs
8. Citations to authority

9. Conclusions phrased as predictions, not guarantees

10. Professional tone

In addition, new writers of office memos will be struck by a number of other conventions of office memos. For example, the format for issue statements, which are sometimes called "questions presented," seems to be an artifact from an earlier time. Because they include a reference to the relevant rule, the legal question, and the legally significant facts, *all in one sentence*, issue statements tend to be long and somewhat unwieldy. (See Chapter 8.) They alone seem to be immune to the trend toward shorter, readable sentences, which applies to all other sentences in an office memo.

Yet another convention that seems to go against the grain of all the other advice to "be brief" and "write concisely" is the common practice in memo writing to include your conclusions in several different places. Novice memo writers are often surprised to find, for example, that many memos contain both a Brief Answer after the Issue and a formal Conclusion at the end of the memo, both of which sum up the writer's answer to the legal issue. Others are surprised by the penchant for "mini-conclusions" at the end of each section of the discussion section. The usual rationale for what may seem like excessive summing up in memo writing is that the summaries ensure that readers can easily track the analysis and see how the points and sub-points are adding up.

Less surprising is the convention to set out a rule before applying it to the facts or making an argument using the rule. Also not surprising, at least for some, is the custom of setting out general rules before more specific rules. (See Chapters 9, 10, and 11.) In fact, throughout legal writing the convention is to organize material from general to specific.

Writers of academic prose may be immediately comfortable with another convention—the use of third person rather than the first person "I" or "we" or the second person "you." The practice of staying in third person means that language such as "I think," "I believe," or "I feel" is not typically used in office memos even when the writer is predicting how a court will decide a case. Rather than write "I think the court is unlikely to find" most lawyers write "the court is unlikely to find." Some firms do make an exception and use the first person "our" when referring to "our client" or "our case," but others maintain the more formal "the client" or the client's name when referring to the case, for example, "the Olsen case" or "the present case."

§ 1.5 Advice for Specific Groups

Even though it can be a bit risky to generalize about the customs and conventions of any given community of writers, knowing about some of these can ease a writer's transition into legal writing. Making that knowledge more explicit can help a writer look at his or her assumptions about "good writing" and see which assumptions apply and which do not apply to legal writing.

Below is a list of different communities of writers and some of the common assumptions those communities have about writing and how those assumptions are similar to or different from the underlying assumptions that inform legal writing. In creating this list, however, we do not mean to suggest that legal writing is somehow "right" in its assumptions about what makes good writing and these other fields or cultures are somehow "wrong." In fact, we would argue that the differences make sense given the differences in readers, purpose, and culture. Nor do we mean to suggest that writers need to erase and replace what they know about how to write for the communities they were part of before joining the legal community. Instead we would suggest that writers think of the experience of learning to do legal writing as adding a new category or genre of writing to their writing repertoire.

One final point: Not every undergraduate major, previous profession, or country or culture is discussed in the list below. Unfortunately, the experts in languages, their conventions, and stylistic preferences still have more work to do before we have a complete comparative picture of all types of writing in all languages and cultures.

§ 1.5.1 English Majors

Most English majors come to law school believing that they will do exceptionally well in their legal writing classes. In most cases, this proves to be true, but their success tends to happen more toward the end of the course rather than the beginning. Early in the course, English majors may resist what they consider the formulaic and restrictive nature of legal writing. They complain that it "stifles their creativity," and they are frustrated because they cannot show off their vocabularies and sophisticated writing style. Once they buy into the idea that they are learning a new genre, in much the way a poet would adapt when learning to write screenplays, they stop resisting, start adapting, and then gradually see how they can channel some of their earlier skills into legal writing. Their storytelling ability helps them write the facts; they apply their creativity to constructing arguments; and they bring the close reading skills they developed for literature and poetry to their reading of statutes and rules.

§ 1.5.2 Philosophy Majors

Like English majors, philosophy majors are likely to feel that their creativity is stifled and their analytic ability tightly restricted by the standard modes of legal analysis. In their doctrinal courses, they may be initially surprised by the heavy emphasis on precedent and the layers of doctrine, as well as disappointed by what may appear to them to be the law's emphasis on rhetoric.

As they learn to write office memos, philosophy majors are likely to find the construction of rules paragraphs to be arbitrary; their natural instinct will be to think about the validity of the rules rather than simply lay them out for the readers. Once they get to the arguments, philosophy majors are likely to feel at home, and it is here that their background in logic can give them an edge.

§ 1.5.3 Journalism Majors and Journalists

Like their "cousins" the English majors, journalism students and journalists bring an interesting combination of advantages and disadvantages with them to legal writing. Perhaps most important of all is the simple fact that they are not rusty as writers. They come to law school and the practice of law with their writing skills honed by lots of practice. In addition, journalists are already well-schooled in the concept of writing for a specific audience. Many of them have learned to adjust their style to the varying demands of straight news reporting to the specific conventions of the sports page, the op-ed page, and the lifestyle and feature sections. Initially some journalists may resent having to tone down their style a bit for legal writing, particularly if they have grown accustomed to writing "zinger" sentences or writing with vivid language and extended metaphors for the sports page.

Yet another advantage that journalists bring to legal writing is their completeness and accuracy with the facts. They are used to answering the questions "who," "what," "when," "where," and "how," and they are also used to being required to state the source for the facts.

Organization and paragraph length are usually the two areas in which journalists will have to adjust. The typical journalism piece is written in an inverted-pyramid, front-loaded style so the editors can cut the piece from the end to fit space limitations and, if a reader loses interest and stops reading midway in a story, he or she still will have gotten the key ideas in the opening sentences. While much of legal writing also puts key points (rules, the best cases, and arguments) up front, the organizational structure is shaped by very different considerations and reader expectations. A threshold issue will almost always be treated first, even if it is relatively easy to resolve. Even though legal readers are busy, most will read a memo through to the end and not treat the last pages or lines as optional. For the most part, true paragraphs do not exist in journalism. Because of the narrow width of many newspaper columns, the convention in journalism is to write mostly one-sentence paragraphs. Journalists transitioning into writing about law have to learn to write longer paragraphs.

Finally, most journalists have learned to be extraordinarily careful with spelling, particularly the spelling of proper names, which is an asset that carries over nicely into legal writing. Punctuation, however, may be a different matter. Journalism prefers "open punctuation," which means using as little punctuation as the rules will allow; legal writing, by contrast, tends to used "closed punctuation," which means that lawyers lean in the other direction and use commas when the rules give them the option to do so. The serial comma, for example, is generally omitted in journalism (no comma before the "and" in "red, white and blue"), but it is included in legal writing ("red, white, and blue").

§ 1.5.4 Science Majors and Scientists

Science majors and scientists bring a strong set of skills in critical thinking and formal analysis that individuals in many other professions or disciplines may lack. The ability to evaluate evidence, make logical connections, and draw plausible conclusions forms the very basis of substantive legal analysis. However, legal writing diverges from scientific writing in several ways that may prove challenging or even frustrating.

In terms of writing style, legal writing favors active voice sentences, not the passive voice sentences used as the professional standard in scientific writing. Formal organization of various legal writing projects requires a different organizational structure than scientific writing (e.g., title, hypothesis, materials, methods, observations, results, conclusion), although experience working with any formal structure will be of help in legal writing.

In terms of substantive analysis, deriving governing rules and tests from case law precedent or statutory language is similar to formulating the hypothesis and methods sections of a scientific paper. However, on a practical level jurisprudence has little in common with scientific laws and validity studies. Science majors and scientists may find their experience similar to the frustration experienced by philosophy students. "Law" is not created by systematic application of the scientific method in order to discover logically necessary, objective truths with universal application that can be repeated and verified by any scientist in a variety of conditions. Rather, "law" is created by a combination of individual circumstances, public policies, concepts of fairness, tradition, emotion, credibility, economic realities, political considerations and persuasive argument, among other factors.

In fact, legal reasoning and persuasive argument may represent the greatest challenges to science majors and scientists engaged in legal writing. Although persuasive argument skills have a subtle use in the results and conclusion parts of a scientific paper, the rhetorical strategies and skills necessary for legal writing will likely draw on a legal writer's experience in non-scientific areas of life. Consequently, science majors and scientists transitioning into writing about law should be prepared to merge an "objective" approach with a more subjective "relational" approach because legal writing bases itself on applying law to the facts of either specific or general circumstances, where human interactions create dynamic complications.

§ 1.5.5 Chinese Writers

Experts in contrastive rhetoric believe that modern Chinese (Mandarin) is shifting from a reader-responsible to a writer-responsible approach to written communication. In the meantime, many Chinese writers are influenced by the tradition of a reader-responsible language. In reader-responsible languages, the reader quite literally has the primary responsibility for the communication between the reader and the writer. If there is misunderstanding between the two, it is the reader's fault for not understanding better what the writer is saying. Writers are allowed to be, even expected to be, obscure at times; being explicit is considered unsophisticated. For example, a Chinese writer may give concrete examples to support a point, but the cultural preference is to stop after listing the examples and allow the reader to make the connection and draw the inevitable conclusion. In contrast, English is a writer-responsible language. The primary responsibility for clear communication lies with the writer. Hence, writers in English are admonished to be clear and explicit. While some types of writing in English may encourage writers to stop before explicitly making a connection and drawing a conclusion, writers of legal English are expected to complete this step for the reader.

In the introduction to a piece of writing, Chinese writers often use a "clearing the terrain" approach, which involves discussing all of the ideas related to the main idea before exploring the main idea. Even once the main idea is introduced, Chinese writers have considerable freedom to digress and introduce related material. In legal writing, writers are expected to give a quick overview that may introduce the topic and set up the structure. Legal English readers want writers to get to the point quickly and answer their question, "What is this about?" Straying, even slightly, from the point puzzles and irritates legal English readers, who are likely to view writing with digressions as disorganized and unfocused.

In organizing a piece of writing, Chinese writers tend to use an inductive approach, moving from specific to general. As the writing unfolds, they tend to use centrifugal rather than linear organizational patterns, that is, they return to the main idea several times before moving on. Their readers expect this repetition of ideas, as well as the use and re-use of stock phrases. In contrast, legal English writers use a linear prose style that moves from general to specific. In English it is considered sophisticated writing to use a hierarchical approach with numerous levels of subordination to express ideas. Some repetition for effect and emphasis is tolerated, but on the whole it is considered a sign of the writer's intelligence and respect for his or her readers not to repeat points and to say a great deal in few words. Chinese writers favor additive conjunctions to connect ideas, but in English frequent use of coordination ("and") is considered a sign of an immature prose style.

To support their points, Chinese writers prefer elaborate metaphors and literary references. It is also common to use numerous references to historical events. Using the words of another without attribution is an accepted practice.

In contrast, English writers prefer facts, statistics, and other "hard data" to support their points. Metaphors and historical references are used occasionally but only briefly; literary references are rare. Legal English writers must cite to statutes, cases, and other legal authorities for support, and using the words of another without attribution is considered plagiarism, which is a serious transgression.

§ 1.5.6 Japanese Writers

Like Chinese, Japanese is a reader-responsible language. Readers have the primary responsibility for the communication between the reader and the writer. If there is misunderstanding between the two, it is the reader's fault for not understanding better what the writer is saying. Japanese readers do not expect sentences that can be automatically understood the first time they are read; instead, Japanese readers assume that the writer may have deliberately hidden some of the meaning. In writer-responsible languages like English, the responsibility for clear communication lies with the writer, who is consequently expected to write sentences that can be easily understood the first time they are read.

Unlike English writers, whose prose style usually moves from general to specific, Japanese writers move from specific to general. While English writers follow the introduction-body-conclusion organizational plan, Japanese writers use a *ki-shoo-ten-ketsu* formula for prose. *Ki*, which is comparable to the English introduction, does not, however, include the thesis. Using the *ki-shoo-ten-ketsu* organizational framework, Japanese writers abruptly shift the topic and look at it from a new angle when they are in the *ten* element. *Ketsu*, which is roughly comparable to an English conclusion, may state the thesis, but rather than just summarize the earlier ideas as an English writer would, the Japanese writer may introduce some new ideas at this point. In addition, *ketsu* need not have the closure expected in a conclusion in a legal English piece of writing; it may end with a question or otherwise express some lingering doubt. Japanese writers may even end an argument by taking a different position from the beginning position, whereas English writers are expected to state a position and stick to it.

The directness and explicitness prized in U.S. legal writing is equated with brashness in Japanese writing. Japanese writers strive to make their points indirectly; hinting at meaning is regarded as a sign of intelligence and sensitivity. Good Japanese writing implies or alludes to meaning rather than explicitly stating points. Even though a Japanese writer may continually return to a theme, the theme may not be stated explicitly.

A more subtle difference between the two cultures concerns how many qualifiers a writer tends to use. Japanese writers tend to be more tentative and use more qualifiers than writers in English, although U.S. legal writers use more qualifiers than other English writers, partly out of concern for accuracy but also as a form of self-protective understatement.

§ 1.5.7 Korean Writers

Like Chinese and Japanese writing, Korean expository writing tends to be organized from specific to general; consequently, Korean writers may find that the general to specific organizational pattern expected in English expository writing feels odd at first. Because arguing directly or explicitly is apt to have a negative effect on Korean readers, Korean writers may also be surprised that English legal writers use explicit description, explicit comparisons, and direct persuasion and that such directness and explicitness is well received by English readers.

The Korean cultural preference for indirectness in writing shows up in a number of other ways. For example, it is common to hide criticisms in metaphors. Rather than directly assert a controversial position, Korean writers may use a formulaic expression such as "some people say" as a way to introduce their view. Conclusions may also be indirect in that they may contain the writer's thesis, but it might not be explicitly stated.

In adapting to the expectations of English readers, Korean writers will notice that in the U.S. legal culture, writing is assumed to be the writer's own view or opinion. A stock phrase such as "some people say" would not be well received as an introduction to an argument; in fact, it would be interpreted as a weak and unsupported assertion. Readers in the United States expect writers to state a position and then defend it. Other people's writing is considered "fair game." That is, it is completely acceptable to openly challenge, disagree with, or criticize the writing of another, including an expert in the field or even a court, as long as the challenge, disagreement, or criticism is well supported and directed at the ideas and arguments and not at the individual. Attacking the arguments of one's opponents is expected, but once again the criticism should address the weaknesses in the arguments and not become personal.

While metaphors are not common in legal English, they are used occasionally to create a vivid or memorable analogy and not to hide or blunt a criticism. Legal English's penchant for directness continues throughout a document, all the way through the conclusion, so that when a reader finishes reading the document, he or she should have no doubt about the writer's thesis.

§ 1.5.8 French Writers

Writers of Romance languages, like French, pride themselves in using the language beautifully; consequently, they may be disappointed to find that legal English, while not averse to the well-turned phrase, does not place much emphasis on the writing being aesthetically pleasing. They quickly learn that there is a strong resistance to anything that may seem like a more "flowery" writing style or a writing style that is more "pretty" than functional.

French writers often use more of a meandering approach when organizing a piece of writing; it is common for them to touch on the topic initially and then circle back to it later in the writing. They have much more freedom than English writers to digress and introduce related material. They often conclude an essay by introducing a new but related topic, and they do not use topic sentences because they are deemed too obvious and condescending to readers. Similarly, they avoid a standard subject-verb-object order in sentences, preferring more complex sentence structures.

In transitioning to legal English, French writers may be surprised to find that they are expected to set out a clear-cut organizational structure and then stick to it without digressing. In legal English, new topics should be either woven into the overall structure of a piece of writing or omitted; they should not be tacked on to a conclusion. Topic sentences, particularly ones that go a step beyond being obvious introductions for the paragraphs that follow, will be well received by sophisticated readers of English, as will easy-to-read sentences that follow a subject-verb-object order.

§ 1.5.9 Spanish Writers

Like French writers, Spanish writers also pride themselves in using the language beautifully; consequently, they too may be disappointed to find that legal English emphasizes being clear and getting the job done over being aesthetically pleasing. When it comes to organizational preferences, the Spanish cultural tendency is to use a linear pattern but with tangential breaks. In fact, Spanish readers consider the exploration of side points as a sign that the writer is highly intelligent and well versed in the topic.

What is particularly noticeable about Spanish writing is the practice of using lengthy introductions that may take up to a third of the total pages of a document. Another noticeable characteristic of Spanish writing is the use of short paragraphs; it is common for Spanish writers to write numerous one- or two-sentence paragraphs. Finally, Spanish writers do not tend to use signposts or transitional words and phrases to guide readers through the text.

In transitioning to writing for U.S. legal readers, Spanish writers will need to (1) avoid straying from the central topic; (2) drastically shorten introductions; and (3) add signposts and transitions as guides for their U.S. legal English readers. Even though one- and two-sentence paragraphs are not strictly taboo in English writing, many readers of English consider short paragraphs the mark of underdeveloped ideas or superficial thinking. Consequently, Spanish writers transitioning to English will probably want to combine some of their shorter paragraphs into longer paragraphs. Most paragraphs in legal English should fall in the three- to six-sentence range.

§ 1.5.10 Slavic/Polish Writers

Polish writers tend to approach a topic from a variety of perspectives, some of which may appear to English readers as digressions. They then work toward the thesis, which usually does not appear until the end. This preferred Polish pattern, which is known as "circumvoluted discourse," is significantly different from the preferred "straight line" linear discourse style preferred in English.

Polish writers do not come from a tradition of respecting government officials or hierarchy; consequently, they are unlikely to quote statistics or government experts. Their preference is to compare and contrast ideas or restate an idea. In fact, constant restatement of the same idea is one of the most noticeable characteristics of Polish prose. English readers, on the other hand, will expect concrete support for ideas, including statistics or citations to experts, and they will be annoyed if the same ideas are repeated at length.

§ 1.5.11 Brazilian Writers

Writing in Portuguese, Brazilian writers have several noteworthy customs in their writing: a strong emphasis on details, less emphasis on focus, explicit references to the reader and writer ("you" and "I"), long sentences, emphasis on subordination, and repetition of key nouns.

While the emphasis on subordination and repetition of key nouns will be well received by legal English readers, those same readers will want the writer to be more selective about details and more tightly focused on the topic. Legal English readers will also expect the writer to avoid first- and second-person "I" and "you" references and instead use the third person (he," "she," occasionally "one," and especially "it"), and some will prefer shorter sentences or at least variety in sentence length.

§ 1.5.12 Arabic Writers

Arabic writers tend to place a strong emphasis on the form of language. They prefer richness in language, particularly in the form of metaphors and other figurative language, over conciseness. As they transition to writing for legal English readers, then, the challenge for Arabic writers is to adopt a more functional and less poetic prose style.

Introductions in Arabic writing tend to be broad statements about the general state of affairs. Once the main topic is introduced, Arabic writers pride themselves in making the same point in many different ways. A common rhetorical strategy is for the writer to restate his or her positions, often with warnings, rather than support them with examples. Arabic readers expect to "read between the lines" and draw appropriate conclusions on their own.

Readers of legal English tend to view broad generalizations about the world as unnecessary throat-clearing. Once a writer makes a point, readers of legal English do not expect the point to be repeated; they expect the point to be developed, particularly by analogizing factual situations with examples from precedential cases.

In general, the Arabic speaking culture does not particularly value hierarchy and subordination in ideas; coordination is preferred. Consequently, Arabic writers tend to join many of their ideas together with *wa*, the Arabic word for "and." Another key stylistic technique in Arabic writing is parallelism, which is a key ingredient for conveying a rich array of parallel ideas. Coordination and balance are signs of sophisticated Arabic prose.

While parallelism is also a key stylistic technique for writers in English, coordination ("and") is equated with less sophisticated prose, and hierarchy and subordination of ideas are viewed as signs of sophisticated writing.

§ 1.5.13 Russian Writers

The two-word phrase that best summarizes sophisticated Russian writing is "intentional complexity." Russian writers show their brilliance and the significance of their ideas by deliberately using complicated sentence structure, including a heavy use of subordination, parallelism, parenthetical asides, and technical terminology. They often do not define terms that would be unfamiliar to their readers. The signs of a sophisticated Russian writer are long sentences, long paragraphs, and sometimes even very long paragraphs that consist of a single sentence.

In contrast, the two-word phrase that best summarizes sophisticated English legal writing is "intentional simplicity." Legal English readers appreciate complex ideas being presented in a simple sentence structure. They are accustomed to, and indeed expect, frequent subordination and parallelism, but numerous parenthetical comments are not likely to be well-received. They will expect technical terms to be defined; if they are not, some busy English readers will simply skip over the terms without looking them up. Many will grow annoyed and impatient with numerous long sentences and paragraphs.

§ 1.5.14 Ugandan Writers

Ugandan judicial opinions reflect the fact that they are written to be read aloud in open court to the parties, many of whom speak English as a second or third language. To assure the parties that he or she has carefully considered the evidence and arguments, most magistrates and judges describe in detail the facts that were presented and the arguments that each side made, noting which testimony they found persuasive and which testimony they did not find persuasive.

The opinions use a script format (see Chapter 9): the decision is not announced until after the judge has finished reciting the facts, arguments, and reasoning. Instead of depersonalizing the decision-making process by using phrases like "the Court finds," judges tend to use personal pronouns. "I find the defendant guilty." In writing briefs, or submissions, to the courts, many Ugandan attorneys use language that U.S. judges would find overly formal or overly deferential. For example, reflecting Uganda's history as a British protectorate, attorneys use the phrases "My Lord" or "Your Worship" in addressing a judge.

In addition, while the organizational patterns that Ugandan attorneys use are very similar to the organizational patterns used by U.S. attorneys, the difficulty in obtaining copies of other Ugandan judicial opinions means that Ugandan attorneys rely more on factual arguments than on arguments based on analogous cases. Although there is limited access to Ugandan precedent, some opinions may rely on authority from other jurisdictions, such as other East African countries, Great Britain, and the United States, some of which are binding and some of which are not. In letters to clients, some Ugandan attorneys do what some U.S. attorneys do: try to establish their position through the use of legalese.

The most striking feature of well-written Ugandan opinions, briefs, and correspondence is, however, the vividness of the images that the writer creates and the passion that the writer imbeds in his or her prose. Another notable feature for U.S. legal readers is that Uganda English follows the British conventions for punctuation, spelling, and grammar.

§ 1.5.15 Indian Writers

Although Hindi is the official language of India, English was the official language for government business from 1950-1965, and it is now an "associate language," which can be used for official purposes. Because India was a British colony from the late 1700s until it became an independent country in 1947, the English that Indians speak and write has been heavily influenced by British English.

Indian lawyers typically use language that is more formal and indirect than U.S. lawyers. The preferred direct, "get it done" style of U.S. attorneys may require some adjustment for an Indian attorney who would find this style inappropriate in India. While an Indian lawyer may express a point in a way that makes it seem complex, a U.S. lawyer is likely to express the same point in a way that is as simple and easy as possible to understand. While both cultures value subtleties, there tends to be more of an effort to express subtlety in India than in the United States.

The preferred writing style of Indian English tends to be in the passive voice rather than the active voice preferred for U.S. legal English. Sophisticated Indian writers tend to use what U.S. readers would consider an overly flowery or verbose writing style. The most important adjustment Indian lawyers need to make when writing for U.S. legal readers, however, is to add citations to authority when writing briefs.

Understanding the United States Legal System

Just as everyone comes to law school with different writing experiences, everyone comes to law school with different amounts and kinds of information about the U.S. system of government and, in particular, the U.S. legal system. While students with undergraduate or graduate degrees in political science, American government, or U.S. history usually have a good understanding of U.S. history and the U.S. legal system, other students need a quick review of the basics.

§ 2.1 A Short History

Like most countries, the United States has a system of government that is a product of its history. From the early 1600s until the 1770s, the "United States" were not united. Instead, what is now the United States was a group of British colonies, each operating under its own charter and each having its own system of government. Although the colonies traded with each other, the connections among the colonies were no closer than the connections among the European countries prior to 1992 or the current connections among countries in Asia or Africa.

The colonies first came together in 1774 when, angered by Great Britian's decision to impose new taxes, twelve of the thirteen American colonies sent representatives to the First Continental Congress, which was held in Philadelphia, Pennsylvania. During this conference, the delegates established the Association of 1774, which urged colonists to boycott British goods and created committees to enforce that boycott. The British Parliament countered by enacting the New England Restraining Act, which banned trade between the New England colonies and any country other than Great Britain.

During the next year, relationships between the colonies and Great Britian deteriorated and, after battles between colonists and the British at Concord and Lexington, the same twelve colonies that had sent delegates to the First Continental Congress sent delegates to a Second Continental Congress. This Second Continental Congress, which was held in Philadelphia in May 1775, elected John Hancock as President of the Congress, established a Continental army, and named George Washington as commander in chief of the newly formed army. To pay for the newly formed army, the Congress issued bills of credit, and the twelve colonies promised to share in repaying those bills.

As tensions between the colonies and Great Britain escalated, the Second Continental Congress assumed more power, among other things creating a Navy, seeking aid from countries like France, and authorizing the colonies to draft new constitutions. On June 2, 1776, Richard Henry Lee made a motion urging the Continental Congress to declare independence. Three days later, the Continental Congress appointed a committee to draft the declaration, and that committee selected Thomas Jefferson to prepare the draft. Jefferson's draft was read to the Congress on June 28, 1776. On July 2, 1776, British ships entered New York Harbor, and on July 4, 1776, the members of the Continental Congress signed the Declaration of Independence.

Having declared independence, the Second Continental Congress began drafting and debating the Articles of Confederation, finally adopting them on November 15, 1777. In sending the Articles of Confederation to the newly formed states for ratification, the Continental Congress noted the difficulty of "combining in one general system the various sentiments and interests of a continent divided into so many sovereign and independent communities." Although South Carolina ratified the Articles of Confederation in February 1778, the last of the states, Maryland, did not ratify it until three years later.

The newly ratified Articles of Confederation, which went into effect on March 1, 1781, established a unicameral (one-house) Congress in which each state had one vote. Although the Articles gave the newly formed Congress some powers, for example, the power to declare war, it did not give it the tools that it needed to exercise those powers. For example, it did not give Congress the power to impose or collect taxes. Equally important, the Articles did not give Congress the power to regulate commerce either among the various states or between the various states and other countries. The only court established by the Articles was a maritime court.

A year later, in 1782, the American Revolution ended when representatives from the United States, Britain, and France met in Paris and drafted a peace treaty in which Great Britian recognized American independence, agreed to remove all of its troops from American soil, and ceded its rights to territory between the Mississippi River and the Allegheny Mountains. Congress ratified the Articles of Peace on April 15, 1883.

During the next months and years, Congress faced a number of problems: for example, the British government refused to enter into trade agreements because Congress could not force the states to comply with those agreements. Although members of Congress discussed revising the Articles of Confederation to give Congress more power, they did not believe that the states would agree to such changes and, thus, did not take action.

Eventually, though, the states recognized the need for change and, in 1778, every state except Rhode Island sent delegates to the Constitutional Convention, which was held in Philadelphia. During that convention, James Madison proposed what was, in the 1800s, an entirely new form of government, a government that had a legislative branch, an executive branch, and a judicial branch. Although initially some of the smaller states objected to Madison's plan on the grounds that the plan would put less-populated states at a disadvantage, this fear was allayed when the Convention agreed to two different bases for representation in Congress. While representation in the lower house (the House of Representatives) would be based on population, each state would have equal representation in the upper house (the Senate).

During the next year, the states debated whether to ratify the new Constitution, the "federalists" arguing for adoption and the "anti-federalists" opposing adoption. On June 21, 1778, New Hampshire became the ninth state to ratify the Constitution, and on July 2, 1778, Congress announced that the Constitution had been adopted. The transition from the government created by the Articles of Confederation to the government created by the Constitution occurred quickly. By September 1778, a congressional committee had set the dates for elections and for the first meeting of Congress, had selected New York City as the temporary capital, and had granted ten square miles of land to the new government for a federal town: Washington, D.C.

Although the new Constitution gave the federal government substantially more power, it also protected the rights of the states, allowing each to retain its own system of government. Thus, more than 200 years later, the U.S. system of government is really two systems, a federal system and fifty-state system, with the United States Constitution brokering the relationship between the federal and state systems.

§ 2.2 The Federal System

In drafting the United States Constitution, the delegates to the Constitutional Convention sought to balance the need for a stronger federal government against their fear that one individual or one group would assume too much power. Consequently, in addition to dividing the powers between three groups—the legislative branch, the executive branch, and the judicial branch—the delegates also created a system of checks and balances in which each branch was given the power to "check" or "limit" the powers of the other two branches.

§ 2.2.1 The Federal Legislative Branch

Article I of the United States Constitution creates the legislative branch and vests the powers of the legislative branch in Congress, which has two chambers, the House of Representatives and the Senate. The House of Representatives has 435 members, each of whom is elected by and represents the voters from a particular congressional district for a two-year term: states with larger populations have more congressional districts than states with smaller populations. In contrast, the Senate has 100 members, two from each of the fifty states. Senators are elected by their state's voters and serve six-year terms.

Among the powers granted to Congress are the power to lay and collect taxes, borrow money, regulate commerce with foreign nations and among the states, establish uniform naturalization and bankruptcy laws, promote the progress of science and the useful arts by creating copyright laws, and punish counterfeiting. In addition, Congress also has the power to check the powers of the executive and judicial branches. For example, the Constitution gives Congress the power to impeach and remove the President from office, and it can enact legislation that supersedes a common law or court-made rule.

For a description of the legislative process, see section 3.1.

§ 2.2.2 The Federal Executive Branch

Article II of the United States Constitution vests the powers of the executive branch in the President. In addition to serving as the commander in chief of the United States Armed Forces, the President has the power to appoint a cabinet and, through that cabinet, create and supervise the various departments and agencies of the federal government.

The Constitution also gives the executive branch the power to check the powers of the legislative and judicial branches. For example, the President can exercise control over the legislative branch by exercising his or her power to convene and adjourn the Congress and by approving or vetoing legislation. Similarly, the President can exercise control of the judicial branch through his or her judicial nominations or by directing the United States Attorney General to enforce or not enforce certain laws.

§ 2.2.3 The Federal Judicial Branch

Article III of the United States Constitution vests the judicial power of the federal government "in one supreme court and in such inferior courts as Congress may establish"—in other words, the judicial branch. To ensure that the federal judiciary remains independent, federal judges are appointed for life, and their compensation cannot be decreased while they are in office.

The federal court system is hierarchical: at the bottom of the pyramid are the United States District Courts, at the next level is the United States Courts of Appeals, and the highest level is the United States Supreme Court.

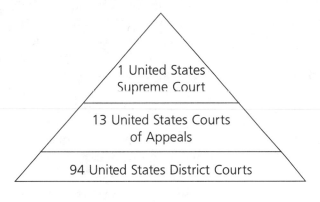

1 United States Supreme Court

13 United States Courts of Appeals

94 United States District Courts

There are currently ninety-four United States District Courts: while smaller states have only one United States District Court, a number of larger states have several. The United States District Courts are trial courts and hear cases brought under the United States Constitution and federal statutes (federal question jurisdiction) and cases involving state law that involve citizens from different states (diversity jurisdiction). Depending on the type of case and the decisions made by the parties, these trials can be jury trials or bench trials. In a jury trial, the judge decides questions of law, and the jury decides questions of fact. In contrast, in a bench trial, there is no jury, and the judge decides both questions of law and questions of fact.

If a party disagrees with the United States District Court decision, it can file an appeal with the United States Courts of Appeals for the circuit, or geographic region, in which the United States District Court is located. Currently, there are twelve circuits, plus a United States Court of Appeals for the Federal Circuit. The number of judges in a particular circuit depends on that circuit's case load. While most appeals are heard by a panel of three judges, in certain circumstances an appeal might be heard *en banc*, that is, by a larger group of judges. For example, in the Ninth Circuit, an appeal that is heard *en banc* is heard by the chief judge for the Ninth Circuit and fourteen other judges, who are randomly selected from the approximately fifty Ninth Circuit Court of Appeals judges. Because the United States Courts of Appeals are appellate courts, they do not conduct trials. Instead, they review the relevant clerk's papers (documents filed with the court), the relevant portions of the trial transcript (a written copy of the testimony presented at trial plus the arguments of counsel and statements by the trial court judge), and the relevant exhibits. Then, based on this record and the arguments of the parties, the United States Courts of Appeals decide (1) whether a federal statute is or is not constitutional, (2) whether the trial court applied the right law correctly, (3) whether the trial court judge abused his or her discretion in granting or denying a motion or granting or denying an objection, and/or (4) whether there is sufficient evidence to support the trial court judge's findings of fact or the jury's verdict.

At the top level is the United States Supreme Court. The number of Justices who sit on the Supreme Court is determined by Congress: since 1869 there has been one Chief Justice and eight Associate Justices. Each year, the United States Supreme Court receives more than 7,000 requests for review (*writs of certiorari*). Of the approximately 100 cases that the United States Supreme Court hears, the overwhelming majority are appeals from the federal courts. Although many people believe that the Supreme Court is all-powerful, it is not. While the United States Supreme Court has the power to decide issues involving the United States Constitution and federal statutes, it does not have the power to hear cases that involve only questions of state law. Thus, while the United States Supreme Court has the power to determine whether a state's marriage dissolution statute violates the United States Constitution, it does not have the power to decide whether, under a state statute, it would be in the best interests of a child for a father to be granted custody or whether child support should be set at $300 rather than $400 per month.

In addition to the courts just described, there are a number of specialized courts. For example, there is a Bankruptcy Court, a Tax Court, a Court of Federal Claims, and a Court of International Trade.

|  | For more information on the federal courts, see the United States Judiciary's website, http://www.uscourts.gov. |

§ 2.3 The State Systems

Because each state is a "state" or sovereign entity, each has its own state constitution. While the details vary from state to state, each of these state constitutions divides the powers reserved to that state between three branches of government—a state legislative branch, a state executive branch, and a state judicial branch.

§ 2.3.1 The State Legislative Branch

The state constitutions vest the power of the legislative branch in a state legislature or state assembly. Except for Nebraska, these state legislatures and assemblies have two chambers and have the power to enact legislation for that state. In most states, the legislative branch can check the power of the state executive and judicial branches by approving or denying the state executive's proposed annual budget and by enacting legislation that supplants common or court-made law.

§ 2.3.2 The State Executive Branch

Each state also has an executive branch in which the power is vested in a governor, who has the power to establish state departments and agencies. Generally, a governor can check the power of the state legislative branch by vetoing legislation enacted by the state legislature or state assembly and can check the power of the judicial branch by nominating judges and granting pardons.

§ 2.3.3 The State Judicial Branch

Each state has its own court system, which has the power to hear cases brought under that state's constitution, state statutes, and state common law. Just as the federal court system is hierarchical, so are the state systems. At the bottom of the pyramid are courts of limited jurisdiction. These courts can hear only certain types of cases or cases involving only limited amounts of money. Municipal or city courts are courts of limited jurisdiction, as are county or district courts and small claims courts.

At the next level are courts of general jurisdiction. In some instances, these courts act as appellate courts, reviewing decisions by courts of limited jurisdiction. Most often, though, they act as trial courts, hearing both criminal and civil cases.

About three-quarters of the states now have an intermediate court of appeals, which reviews decisions by state courts of general jurisdiction. Because of the size of their workload, many of these intermediate courts of appeals have several divisions or districts. Just as the United States Court of Appeals does not conduct trials, these intermediate courts of appeals do not conduct trials. Instead, they review the record from the trial court to determine, for example, (1) whether a statute is constitutional, (2) whether the trial court applied the applicable rule, (3) whether the trial court judge abused his or her discretion in granting or denying a motion or granting or denying an objection, and (4) whether there is sufficient evidence to support the trial court judge's findings of fact or the jury's verdict.

Every state has a state "supreme" court. These courts review the decisions of the state trial courts and courts of appeals and are the final arbiters of questions of state constitutional, statutory, and common law.

PRACTICE POINTER

Not all states call their highest court the "supreme court." For example, as those who watch any of the "Law and Order" television shows know, the highest court in New York is called the Court of Appeals, and the trial courts are called the supreme court.

An example illustrates the role each state court plays. In *State v. Strong*, a criminal case, the defendant was charged with violating a state statute that prohibited possession of a controlled substance. At the trial court level, both the state and the defendant presented witnesses and physical evidence. On the basis of this evidence, the trial court decided the case on its merits, the trial judge deciding the questions of law (for example, whether certain evidence should be suppressed), and the jury deciding the questions of fact (for example, whether the state had proved beyond a reasonable doubt that the substance was a controlled substance). Both issues were decided against the defendant: the trial court judge ruled that the evidence was admissible, and the jury found that the state had met its burden of proof.

Disagreeing with both determinations, the defendant filed an appeal with the state's intermediate court of appeals, alleging (1) that the trial court judge erred when she denied the defendant's motion to suppress and (2) that there was not sufficient evidence to support the jury's verdict. Because the first issue raised a question of law, the appellate court could review that issue *de novo*. It did not need to defer to the judgment of the trial court judge. Instead, it could exercise its own independent judgment to decide the issue on its merits. The appellate court had much less latitude with respect to the second issue. Because the second issue raised a question of fact and not law, the appellate court could not substitute its judgment for that of the jury. It could only review the jury's findings to make sure that they were supported by the evidence. When the question is one of fact, the appellate court can decide only whether there is sufficient evidence to support the jury's verdict. It cannot substitute its judgment for the judgment of the jury. Regardless of the type of issue (law or fact), the appellate court must base its decision on the written trial court record and exhibits and the attorneys' arguments. Consequently, in *Strong*, the intermediate court of appeals did not see or hear any of the witnesses.

If Strong lost his first appeal, he could petition the state's highest appellate court, asking it to review the intermediate court of appeals' decision. If the state's highest appellate court granted the petition, its review, like that of the intermediate court of appeals, would be limited. Although the supreme court would review the issue of law *de novo*, it would have to defer to the jury's decision on the questions of fact.

§ 2.4 Other Court Systems

There are also several other court systems. As sovereign entities, many Native American tribes have their own judicial systems, and the U.S. military has its own judicial system.

§ 2.5 The Relationship Between the Federal and State Systems

Unfortunately, understanding the federal and state systems is not enough. You also need to understand the relationship between those two systems. In particular, you need to understand the relationship between the laws enacted by Congress and the state legislatures, the relationships between the federal and state courts, and the relationships between the federal and state prosecutors.

§ 2.5.1 The Relationship Between Laws Enacted by Congress and Those Enacted by the State Legislatures

As citizens of the United States, we are subject to two sets of laws: federal law and the law of the state in which we are citizens (or in which we act). Most of the time, there is no conflict between these two sets of laws: federal law governs some conduct; state law, other conduct. For example, federal law governs bankruptcy proceedings and state law governs divorce.

Occasionally, however, both Congress and a state legislature enact laws governing the same conduct. Sometimes these laws can coexist. For example, both Congress and the states have enacted drug laws. Acting under the powers granted to it under the Commerce Clause (see United States Constitution, Article I, Section 8, Clause 3) Congress has made it illegal to import controlled substances or to transport them across state lines; the states, acting consistently with the powers reserved to them, have made the possession or sale of controlled substances within their respective states illegal. In such instances, citizens are subject to both laws. A defendant can be charged under federal law with transporting a drug across state lines and under state law with possession.

There are times, however, when an act is legal under federal law but illegal under state law or vice versa. In such instances, federal law supersedes state law, provided that the federal law is constitutional. As provided in the Supremacy Clause (see United States Constitution, Article VI, Paragraph 2), laws enacted by Congress under the powers granted to it under the Constitution are the "supreme Law of the Land; and the Judges in every State shall be bound thereby . . . ."

The answer is different when the conflicting laws are from different states. Although there are more and more uniform laws (the Uniform Child Custody Act, the Uniform Commercial Code), an activity that is legal in one state may be illegal in another state. For instance, although prostitution is legal in Nevada as a local option, it is illegal in other states.

§ 2.5.2 The Relationship Between Federal and State Courts

The relationship between the federal and state court systems is complex. Although each system is autonomous, in certain circumstances the state courts can hear cases brought under federal law and the federal courts can hear cases brought under state law.

For example, although the majority of cases heard in state courts are brought under state law, state courts also have jurisdiction when a case is brought under a provision of the United States Constitution, a treaty, or certain federal statutes. Similarly, although the majority of cases heard in the federal courts involve questions of federal law, the federal courts have jurisdiction over cases involving questions of state law when the parties are from different states (diversity jurisdiction).

The appellate jurisdiction of the courts is somewhat simpler. In the state system, a state's supreme, or highest, court is usually the court of last resort. The United States Supreme Court can review a state court decision only when the case involves a federal question and when there has been a final decision by the state's supreme, or highest, court. If a state has an intermediate court of appeals, that court has the power to review the decisions of the lower courts within its geographic jurisdiction. In the federal system, the United States Supreme Court is the court of last resort, having the power to review the decisions of the lower federal courts. The United States Courts of Appeals have appellate jurisdiction to review the decisions of the United States District Courts and certain administrative agencies.

§ 2.5.3 The Relationship Among Federal, State, and Local Prosecutors

The power to prosecute cases arising under the United States Constitution and federal statutes is vested in the Department of Justice, which is headed by the Attorney General of the United States, a Presidential appointee. Assisting the United States Attorney General are the United States Attorneys for each federal judicial district. The individual United States Attorneys' offices have two divisions: a civil division and a criminal division. The civil division handles civil cases arising under federal law, and the criminal division handles cases involving alleged violations of federal criminal statutes.

At the state level, the system is slightly different. In most states, the attorney for the state is the state attorney general, usually an elected official. Working for the state attorney general are a number of assistant attorney generals. However, unlike the United States Attorneys, most state attorney generals do not handle criminal cases. Instead, their clients are the various state agencies. For example, an assistant attorney general may be assigned to the department of social and health services, the department of licensing, the consumer protection bureau, or the department of worker's compensation, providing advice to the agency and representing the agency in civil litigation.

In most states, criminal prosecutions are handled by county and city prosecutors. Each county has its own prosecutor's office, which has both a civil and a criminal division. Attorneys working for the civil division play much the same role as state assistant attorney generals; they represent the county and its agencies, providing both advice and representation. In contrast, the attorneys assigned to the criminal division are responsible for prosecutions under the state's criminal code. The county prosecutor's office decides whom to charge and then tries the cases.

Like the counties, larger cities have their own city attorney's offices, which may have civil and criminal divisions. Attorneys working in the civil division advise city departments and agencies and represent the city in civil litigation; attorneys in the criminal division prosecute criminal cases brought under city ordinances. State, county, and city prosecutors do not represent federal departments or agencies, nor do they handle cases brought under federal law.

§ 2.6 Types of Law

As the preceding sections illustrate, the U.S. system of government, and its system of law, is complicated. Not only is there a federal constitution, federal statutes and regulations, and federal cases, but there are also fifty state constitutions, fifty sets of state statutes and regulations, and fifty different sets of state cases. In addition, each county, or parish, and each city has its own charter and its own ordinances.

In talking about this system of law, U.S. judges and lawyers use a number of different terms. Some of the most frequently used terms are set out below.

Case Law:

Judges and attorneys use the phrase "case law" to refer both to court decisions setting out and/or applying a common law rule and to court decisions applying enacted law.

> Case Law = Cases establishing and applying common law
>
> and
>
> Cases applying enacted law

Common Law:

The colonies and then the states adopted England's common law system. Under this system, the law is established by the judicial branch through court decisions rather than by the legislative branch through statutes. Through a series of cases, the courts create legal doctrines and rules that the courts then apply in subsequent cases. Adverse possession is a common law doctrine.

Enacted Law:

Enacted law is law that is enacted by the legislative branch. Federal statutes, state statutes, and county and city ordinances are enacted law.

Mandatory Authority:

Judges and attorneys use the phrase "mandatory authority" to refer to law that the court must apply in a particular case. For example, a case is mandatory authority if the court must apply the rules set out in that case. See section 2.7 below for a description of the process that is used in determining whether a particular authority is mandatory authority.

Persuasive Authority:

Judges and attorneys use the phrase "persuasive authority" to refer to law that the court can look to for guidance but that the court does not have to apply. For example, although the California Supreme Court does not have to apply the rules set out by the Florida Supreme Court, the California Supreme Court can look to the Florida cases for guidance.

§ 2.7 Mandatory and Persuasive Authority

Determining which statutes or cases govern is a two-step process. First, determine which jurisdiction's law applies. Is the issue governed by federal law or state law? If it is governed by state law, which state's law? Second, determine which of that jurisdiction's statutes and cases are mandatory authority.

§ 2.7.1 Determine Which Jurisdiction's Law Applies

Sometimes determining which jurisdiction's law applies is relatively easy. For example, experience suggests that federal law probably applies in the granting of visas and immigration. Similarly, common sense suggests that a contract for the sale of a car from one Texas resident to another Texas resident would be governed by Texas state law. At other times, though, the determination is much more difficult. Even experienced attorneys might not know which jurisdiction's law governs a real estate contract between a resident of New York and a resident of Pennsylvania for a piece of property located in Virginia.

Although the rules governing the determination of which jurisdiction's law applies are beyond the scope of this book (they are covered in courses and books that discuss civil procedure, federal courts, and conflicts of laws), keep two things in mind.

First, remember that in the U.S. legal system, federal law almost always "preempts" or takes precedence over state law. Consequently, if there is both a federal and a state statute on the same topic, the federal statute will preempt the state statute to the extent that the two are inconsistent. For example, if a federal statute makes it illegal to discriminate in the renting of an apartment on the basis of familial status but under a state statute such discrimination is lawful, the federal statute governs—it is illegal to discriminate on the basis of familial status. There are a few instances, however, when a state constitutional provision or a state statute will govern: if the state constitution gives a criminal defendant more rights than does the federal constitution, the state constitution applies. While states can grant an individual more protection, they cannot take away or restrict rights granted by the United States Constitution or a federal statute.

Second, although legal scholars still debate whether there is a federal common law, in the federal system there is not the same body of common law as there is in the states. Unlike the state systems, in the federal system, there are no common law rules governing adverse possession or intentional torts such as assault and battery, false imprisonment, or the intentional infliction of emotional distress. Thus, if the cause of action is based on a common law doctrine, the case is probably governed by state and not federal law.

§ 2.7.2 Determine What "Law" Is Binding

Within each jurisdiction, the authorities are ranked. The United States Constitution is the highest authority, binding both state and federal courts. Under the Constitution are the federal statutes and regulations, and under the federal statutes and regulations are the cases interpreting and applying them. In the state system, the ranking is similar. The highest authority is the state constitution, followed by (1) state statutes and regulations and the cases interpreting and applying those statutes and regulations and (2) the state's common law.

In addition, the cases themselves are ranked. In both the federal and state systems, decisions of the United States Supreme Court carry the most weight: When deciding a case involving the same law and similar facts, both the courts of appeals and the trial courts are bound by the decisions of the supreme, or highest, state courts. Decisions of intermediate courts of appeals come next; the trial courts under the jurisdiction of the intermediate court of appeals are bound by the court of appeals' decisions. At the bottom are the trial courts. Trial court decisions are binding only on the parties involved in the particular case.

Statutes and cases are also ranked by date. More recent statutes supersede earlier versions, and more recent common law rules supersede earlier rules by the same-level court. Courts are bound by the highest court's most recent decision. For example, if there is a 1967 state intermediate court of appeals decision that makes an activity legal and a 1986 state supreme court decision that makes it illegal, in the absence of a statute, the 1986 supreme court decision governs. The 1986 decision would be mandatory authority, and all of the courts within that jurisdiction would be bound by that decision.

§ 2.8 Exercise

The following exercise tests your ability to determine whether a particular case or statute is mandatory or persuasive authority.

1. In 1930, in Case A, the Supreme Court of your state set out a common law rule. In 1956, in Case B, the Supreme Court of your state changed that rule. In your state, which case would be binding on a trial court: Case A or Case B?

2. Same facts as in Question 1 except that in 1981, in Case C, the Supreme Court of your state modified the rule set out in Case B, adding a requirement. In your state, which rule would a trial court use: the rule set out in Case A, the rule set out in Case B, or the rule set out in Case C?

Case A	State Supreme Court	1930
Case B	State Supreme Court	1956
Case C	State Supreme Court	1981

3. Same facts as in Question 2 except that in 1983 your state legislature enacted a statute that completely changed the common law rule. What is now binding on the trial court: the cases or the statute?

Case A	State Supreme Court	1930
Case B	State Supreme Court	1956
Case C	State Supreme Court	1981
State Statute		1983

4. Same facts as in Question 3 except that in 1985, in Case D, a case involving the application of the 1983 statute, the Court of Appeals of your state gave one of the words in the statute a broad interpretation. (The word was not defined in the statute.) In applying the statute, which courts are bound by the Court of Appeals' decision in Case D: a trial court within the Court of Appeals' geographic jurisdiction? A trial court outside the Court of Appeals' geographic jurisdiction? The division of the Court of Appeals that decided Case D? A division of the Court of Appeals other than the division that decided Case D? Your state's Supreme Court?

State Statute	1983
Case D	1985

5. In 1995, in Case E, a different division of the Court of Appeals applied the 1983 statute. In reaching its decision, the court declined to follow the decision in Case D. Instead of interpreting the word broadly, the court interpreted it narrowly. The losing party disagreed with this decision and filed an appeal with your state's Supreme Court. In deciding the appeal, is the Supreme

Court bound by the Court of Appeals' decision in Case D? The Court of Appeals' decision in Case E?

State Statute		1983
Case D	Court of Appeals	1985
Case E	Court of Appeals	1995

6. Same facts as in Question 5 except that in 2000 the state legislature amended the statute in question, explicitly defining the word that was the subject of debate in Cases D and E. The legislature elected to give the word a very narrow meaning. In Case F, which is brought before a state trial court in 2005, what would be controlling: The 1983 version of the statute? The 1985 decision in Case D? The 1995 decision in Case E?

Note: In Case E, the Supreme Court reversed the Court of Appeals and interpreted the term broadly.

State Statute		1983
Case D	Court of Appeals	1985
Case E	Court of Appeals	1995
Case E	Supreme Court	1996
Amended State Statute		2000

CHAPTER 3

Understanding Statutes

The last fifty to eighty years have seen a fundamental change in American law. In this time we have gone from a legal system dominated by the common law, divined by courts, to one in which statutes, enacted by legislatures, have become the primary source of law. The consequences of the "orgy of statute making," in Grant Gilmore's felicitous phrase, are just beginning to be recognized. The change itself and its effect on our whole legal-political system have not been systemically treated.

Guido Calabresi,
A Common Law for the Age of Statutes

The "orgy of statute making" Guido Calabresi described has created a legal system dominated by statutes. Although no one knows for sure how many statutes there are, one fact is certain: the ability to read and analyze statutes is a skill that every attorney needs.

§ 3.1 How Statutes Are Enacted

Because attorneys are often called upon to make arguments based on a statute's legislative history, we begin this chapter by briefly describing the processes through which federal and state statutes are enacted. If you are already familiar with this process, you can skip to section 3.2. If, however, you are not familiar with the process, or if all you remember is the song from the "Schoolhouse Rock" video, *I'm Just a Bill,* then read the following two subsections, noting both how complex the process is and the names of the documents that are created at each stage.

§ 3.1.1 Federal Statutes

In the United States, federal statutes are enacted by Congress, which is made up of two houses, the House of Representatives and the Senate. See section 2.2.1. All federal statutes begin as a bill, which is the name used to refer to proposed statutes. Although a bill may be drafted by anyone, only a member of Congress can introduce, or present, a bill to Congress. The member of Congress who introduces the bill becomes the bill's sponsor and usually works to get the bill passed into law.

For the purpose of this example, presume that the bill's sponsor is a member of the United States House of Representatives. To introduce the bill, the sponsor places a copy of the bill in the "hopper," which is a box located on the platform where the Speaker of the House of Representatives sits. After the bill is placed in the hopper, the Clerk of the House assigns the bill a number that begins with "H.R.," which stands for House of Representatives, and the bill is sent to one of the House of Representatives' twenty standing committees, for example, the Committee on Agriculture, the Committee on Homeland Security, or the Committee on International Relations.

The standing committee reviews the bill, debates its merits and, if it chooses, makes changes to it. If, after debating the bill, a majority of the members of the standing committee believe that the bill is unnecessary or unwise, the standing committee can vote to table the bill or can let the bill "die in committee." If, however, the standing committee decides that the bill has merit, the committee will usually refer it to a subcommittee for further study and debate. The subcommittee may conduct hearings, during which experts, supporters, and opponents may testify or speak about the need for the bill and its effect. After these hearings and debate, the members of the subcommittee can vote to table the bill, let the bill die, or vote to send the bill back to the standing committee for further action. If the subcommittee sends the bill back to the standing committee, the standing committee can vote to table the bill, let it die, or release the bill and send it, along with a committee report that explains the bill, back to the full House of Representatives.

When the House of Representatives receives a bill from a standing committee, the Clerk of the House places the bill on the House of Representatives' calendar, scheduling it for consideration by the membership of the House of Representatives. During these public debates, members of the House of Representatives can offer amendments, which will be voted on by all of the members of the House of Representatives. At the close of the debates, the bill is placed before the membership for a vote. If a majority of the House of Representatives approves the bill, the engrossed bill, which is the version of the bill passed by the House of Representatives, is sent to the Senate for its consideration.

When the Senate receives a bill, or act, from the House of Representatives, it refers it to one of the Senate's sixteen standing committees. This standing committee will consider the bill and do one or more of the following: (1) approve the bill as it was passed by the House of Representatives and send it back to the full Senate for a vote; (2) send the bill to a Senate subcommittee for further consideration, including additional hearings; (3) send the bill to a joint subcommittee made up of members of the House of Representatives and the Senate, which will attempt to draft a compromise bill that is acceptable to both the members of the House of Representatives and the Senate; or (4) let the bill die. If the Senate standing committee recommends passage of the bill as it was passed by the House of Representatives, it will release the bill and send it to the full Senate for its consideration and its vote. If, however, the Senate subcommittee sends the bill to a joint committee, any compromise bills that are drafted must be approved by the membership of both the House of Representatives and the Senate.

Once a bill has been approved by both the House of Representatives and the Senate, the enrolled bill, which is a bill that has been passed by both houses, is sent to the President. If the President signs the bill, the bill is assigned a public law number (beginning with "P.L."). If, however, the President vetoes the bill, the bill does not become law unless both the House of Representatives and the Senate override that veto by a two-thirds vote. Chart 3.1 summarizes the process and lists the documents that are created at each stage in the process.

Chart 3.1	How a Bill Introduced in the United States House of Representatives Becomes a Law	
Step		**Document**
1. A member of the House of Representatives introduces the bill.		• Bill
2. The bill is referred to a committee. The committee may then refer the bill to a subcommittee. (Most bills die in committee.)		• Transcripts from Committee Hearings • Committee Print
3. If the bill does not die in committee, the committee submits its report on the bill to the House.		• Committee Report
4. The bill is presented to the House for debate, amendments, and a vote.		• Engrossed Bill
5. If bill is approved, it is sent to the Senate. The Senate repeats steps 1-4.		• Engrossed Bill

(continues)

Continued	
Step	**Document**
6. If the Senate passes the bill, it returns the bill, with any amendments, to the House. The House then approves the amendments, determines that the amendments are unacceptable, or creates a Conference Committee to create a compromise bill	• Conference Committee Report • Enrolled Bill
7. If both House and Senate pass the same version of the bill, the bill is sent to the President for signature. If the President signs the bill, it becomes law.	• Presidential Statement • Public Law

The process is the same if a bill is introduced in the Senate. The only difference is that when a Senator introduces a bill, the bill is assigned a number that begins with an "S." and if the majority of the Senate approves the bill, it is then sent to the House of Representatives for consideration.

Once a bill has been signed into law, it is assigned a public law number, and the law is codified, or placed into the appropriate section or sections of the *United States Code* (U.S.C.).

PRACTICE POINTER

For a more detailed explanation of how federal statutes are enacted, see http://thomas.loc.gov/home/lawsmade.toc.html or http://thomas.loc.gov/home/enactment/enactlawtoc.html.

§ 3.1.2 State Statutes

In the forty-nine states that have a bicameral legislature—a legislature with two houses or chambers—the process is similar. A member of one of the state's two houses will introduce a bill, the bill will be read and referred to a committee, and the committee will debate the bill and either let it die or send it back to the house in which the bill originated. If that chamber approves the bill, the bill will be sent to the other chamber for its consideration. If the other chamber approves the bill, the bill will be sent to the governor, who can either sign the bill, making it law, or veto the bill. If the governor vetoes the bill, the state legislature can overturn that veto by a two-thirds vote. The exception is Nebraska: the Nebraska legislature has only one house.

§ 3.2 How Regulations Are Promulgated

In enacting statutes, the legislative branch can give the executive branch the power to promulgate regulations implementing the provisions set out in the statute. If the executive branch does not exceed the powers granted to it by the legislative branch, these regulations have the force of law. For example, in enacting the Clean Air Act, a federal statute, Congress gave the Environmental Protection Agency, an agency created by the President, the power to promulgate regulations implementing the Clean Air Act.

The process of promulgating a federal regulation is relatively straightforward. The federal agency that has been given the power to promulgate regulations publishes proposed regulations in the *Federal Register* and invites comments from the public. After the comment period ends, the agency considers the comments and prepares the final version of the regulations. The final versions of federal regulations are published in the *Federal Register* and then in the *Code of Federal Regulations* (C.F.R.), which is republished each year.

At the state level, the process is similar. The state agency that has been given the power to promulgate regulations publishes proposed regulations in some type of state register, and invites public comment. When the comment period ends, the state agency considers the comments and then publishes the final version of the regulations in its state administrative code.

§ 3.3 The Relationship Among Statutes, Regulations, and Cases

The relationships among statutes, regulations, and cases are both simple and complex. They are simple in the sense that there is a hierarchy: statutes, which set out the law, are at the top; regulations, which implement the law, are in the middle; and cases, which apply the statutes and regulations, are at the bottom.

Statute
↓
Regulations Implementing Statutes
↓
Cases Applying the Statute and Regulations

The relationships are, however, also complex in that they involve both the federal government and the state governments and, within each of those governments, the system of checks and balances that the drafters of our Constitution created. See section 2.2.

Federal Statutes	State Statutes
Statutes (Legislative Branch)	Statutes (Legislative Branch)
Regulations (Executive Branch)	Regulations (Executive Branch)
Cases (Judicial Branch)	Cases (Judicial Branch)

We start with two simple examples and then move to some of the more complex situations that you may encounter.

§ 3.3.1 Federal Statute Governs

Presume for a moment that you have been asked to research an immigration issue. Historically, there was no common law governing immigration and, under the United States Constitution, only the federal government has the power to regulate immigration. Thus, immigration issues are governed by federal statutes, federal regulations, and federal cases that have applied those statutes and regulations.

Because the statutes are the "highest authority," you will want to start your research, and your analysis, with these statutes. You will, however, also need to look for federal regulations. While the federal statutes will set out the general principles and rules, the federal regulations will provide more specific information, for example, definitions, standards, and procedures. If the statute and/or regulations are ambiguous, you will also want to look for cases that have applied the statutes and regulations. In looking for cases, look first for mandatory authority: a United States Supreme Court decision or, if there are no United States Supreme Court decisions, for a decision from the court of appeals for the circuit that will hear the case. If there are no court of appeals decisions from the circuit that will hear the case, look for decisions from other circuits and for district court decisions. For more on mandatory and persuasive authority, see sections 2.6 and 2.7.

Immigration Issue

Federal Statutes Governing Immigration
Title 8 of the *United States Code*
See, for example, 8 U.S.C. § 1551 (2006)

↓

Federal Regulations Governing Immigration
Title 8 of the *Code of Federal Regulations*
See, for example, 8 C.F.R. § 2.1 (2006)

↓

United States Supreme Court Cases

↓

United States Court of Appeals Cases

↓

United States District Court Cases

In reading federal statutes, regulations, and cases, keep the following "checks and balances" in mind. First, in promulgating regulations, a federal agency cannot exceed the authority granted to it by Congress. Therefore, a federal agency cannot promulgate regulations unless Congress has authorized it to do so, and the regulations that it promulgates cannot contradict the statute. Second, while the federal courts have the power to hold that a federal statute is unconstitutional, if the statute is constitutional, the courts must interpret and apply the statute in a way that is consistent with the statutory language and Congress's intent.

§ 3.3.2 State Statute Governs

Now presume that you have been asked to work on a landlord-tenant case involving a house located in California. Because the United States Constitution does not give the federal government the power to regulate relationships between landlords and tenants in California, the case will be governed by California law. Although historically, most state law was common law, today much of that common law has been replaced by enacted law, that is, by statutes. Consequently, you would begin researching a California landlord-tenant issue by looking for California statutes.

While in some instances state legislatures give state agencies the power to promulgate regulations implementing a state statute, the California legislature has not authorized a state agency to promulgate regulations relating to landlord-tenant issues. Therefore, your issue will be governed by the California statutes and by the California cases that have applied those statutes. Although a California court might, in some circumstances, look to court decisions from other states, those decisions will never be more than persuasive authority. For more on mandatory and persuasive authority, see sections 2.6 and 2.7.

Landlord–Tenant Issues in California

California Landlord-Tenant Statutes

↓

California Supreme Court Cases

↓

California Court of Appeals Cases

§ 3.3.3 Both Federal and State Statutes Govern

Sometimes an issue will be governed by both federal and state law. For example, a company operating in New York will have to comply both with federal statutes governing employment and with New York laws governing employment.

In general, federal laws establish the minimum standards. For example, there is a federal statute that establishes the federal minimum wage, a federal statute that establishes minimum safety standards, and a federal statute that guarantees family leave benefits to some classes of employees. While a state cannot enact a statute that reduces these benefits, it can enact a statute that gives employees additional benefits. For example, a state can enact a statute that provides for a higher minimum wage than that provided for by the federal statute, a state can enact a statute that imposes additional safety standards, and a state can enact a statute that provides additional classes of employees with family leave benefits.

When there is both a federal and a state statute that govern, you will need to look not only for the federal statute, federal regulations implementing that federal statute, and federal cases interpreting and applying that statute but also for the state statute, any applicable state regulations, and state cases interpreting and applying the state statute and state regulations.

Federal Statute Sets Minimum	State Statute Provides Additional Benefits
Federal Statutes	State Statute
↓	↓
Federal Regulations	State Regulations
↓	↓
Federal Cases	State Cases

In working on cases that are governed by both federal and state law, keep the following in mind.

1. In general, federal law preempts, or takes precedence over, state law. (See United States Constitution, Article VI, Clause 2, which states that laws enacted by Congress under the powers granted to it under the Constitution are the "supreme Law of the Land; and the Judges in every State shall be bound thereby . . . .")

   Thus, if the state statute provides fewer benefits or protections, it will not be enforced. In some instances, however, a state can provide its citizens with additional benefits.
2. Federal regulations implement federal statutes, and state regulations implement state statutes.
3. In most instances, it is the federal courts that interpret and apply federal statutes and the state courts that interpret and apply state statutes.

§ 3.3.4 Party Argues that a Statute Is Unconstitutional

Occasionally, a party will argue that a statute is unconstitutional either because the legislative body that enacted the statute did not have the authority to enact the statute or because the statute is unconstitutionally vague and/or overbroad.

When the statute at issue is a federal statute, it is the federal courts that must decide whether the statute is, or is not, unconstitutional. While most of these cases are first heard in a United States District Court, a party who loses at the District Court level can file an appeal, asking the appropriate

United States Court of Appeals to review the District Court's decision. In addition, the party losing at the United States Court of Appeals level can file a petition for a *writ of certiorari* with the United States Supreme Court, asking the United States Supreme Court to review the United States Court of Appeals' decision.

When the statute is a state statute, the issue is a bit more complicated. If the party challenging the statute alleges that the statute violates the state's constitution, then the challenge will be decided by the state's courts. While initially the issue will be decided by a state trial court, the party that loses at the trial court level can appeal to the state's intermediate court of appeals, if the state has such a court, or to the state's highest appellate court. If, however, the party challenging the statute alleges that the statute violates the federal constitution, the party can raise the issue in either a state court or a federal court. In such instances, the final arbiter is not the state's highest court but the United States Supreme Court.

§ 3.3.5 Party Argues that Agency Exceeded Its Authority in Promulgating a Particular Regulation

Some cases involving federal regulations are first heard, not in the federal courts, but by an administrative law judge who is employed by the executive branch of the federal government. For instance, an individual who believes that the Social Security Administration has incorrectly denied his or her claim for disability benefits can appeal the agency's decision, asking a federal administrative law judge to review that decision. In these cases, claims that a regulation is invalid because the agency that promulgated it exceeded the authority granted to it by Congress will be decided by the administrative law judge. The losing party can, however, appeal the administrative law judge's decision. These appeals are heard initially by a United States District Court. However, the party losing at the District Court level can ask the United States Court of Appeals to review the District Court's decision, and the party losing at the United States Court of Appeals level can ask the United States Supreme Court to review the United State Court of Appeals' decision.

In other cases, for example, cases in which an individual or a company has been charged in a United States District Court with violating a federal statute and regulation, the individual or company can, as part of its defense, argue that the regulation is invalid. In this situation, the United States District Court will make the initial decision about whether the regulation is invalid, and the losing party can appeal the decision to the United States Court of Appeals, and the party that loses at the United States Court of Appeals can file a petition for a *writ of certiorari*, asking the United States Supreme Court to review the United States Court of Appeals' decision.

Likewise, some cases involving state regulations are heard first by state administrative law judges who are employed by the executive branch of the state government. For example, an individual who believes that the state has improperly denied his or her claim for state worker's compensation benefits can ask a state administrative law judge to review the agency's decision. In these situations, an individual's claim that a state regulation is invalid will be decided by the state administrative law judge, subject to review by the state's courts. In contrast, in cases in which an individual has been charged in a state court with violating a state statute and regulation, the state courts will decide whether or not the regulation is invalid. The only time that a federal court will review a state regulation is when a party claims that the state regulation violates the United States Constitution.

PRACTICE POINTER

Given the relationships between federal and state statutes and regulations and the relationships among the various branches, the statements set out in the left-hand column are incorrect.

The state statute **preempts** federal statute	If there is a conflict between a state statute and federal statute, the federal statute governs unless the state statute provides additional protections.
The court **overruled** the statute	Although courts can hold that a statute is unconstitutional, they cannot overrule a statute. If a statute is constitutional, the court must apply that statute.
The regulations **supersede** the statute	Although the regulations are promulgated after the statute is enacted, the regulations do not supersede the statute. In promulgating regulations, administrative agencies can only exercise the authority granted to them by the legislative branch. Regulations implement, but do not add to, subtract from, or change the statute itself.

§ 3.4 Reading and Analyzing Statutes

Statutes can be difficult to read. Sometimes, a statute is difficult to read because the person or group that drafted the original bill did not do a good job drafting the bill; more often, however, a statute is hard to read because statutes are the product of a system that requires compromise to get a bill enacted into law. Although the initial bill may have been well written, during the legislative process the bill was amended one or more times to get the votes needed to get the bill out of committee, to get the votes needed to have the first house or chamber approve the bill, to get the votes needed to have the second house or chamber approve the bill, and/or to ensure that the President or governor will sign and not veto the bill.

Although reading and analyzing statutes is time consuming, it is time well-spent. When an issue is governed by a state statute, that statute is the "highest" authority: the regulations must be consistent with the statute and, unless the courts decide that the statute is unconstitutional, they must apply the statute as it is written and not as they wish it had been written.

The following sections walk you through the process of finding, reading, and analyzing a statute,

§ 3.4.1 Finding Statutes Using the Citation

If you have been given the citation to the applicable statute, finding the statute is easy. Simply locate the statute in the book version of the applicable code, on a free website, or on a fee-based service (e.g., LexisNexis, Loislaw, VersusLaw, or Westlaw).

PRACTICE POINTER   You can find federal statutes on the following free websites:

- http://www.gpoaccess.gov/uscode
- http://uscode.house.gov
- http://www.law.cornell.edu/uscode
- http://www.findlaw.com/casecode/uscodes

You can find state statutes on the following free websites:

- http://www.law.cornell.edu/states/listing.html
- http://www.llsdc.org/sourcebook/state-leg.htm
- http://www.findlaw.com/casecode/#statelaw
- Each state's official website

Although the citation formats vary from jurisdiction to jurisdiction, most citations to statutes contain three types of information: (1) an abbreviation that identifies the name of the code in which the statute can be found, (2) the title and section number, and (3) the year of the code. Look at the following citation, which is a citation to a federal statute.

42 U.S.C. § 12101 (2006)

In this citation, the letters "U.S.C." identify the code: "U.S.C." stands for *United States Code*, which is the official code for federal statutes. The number before "U.S.C." is the title number; the cited statute is in Title 42 of the *United States Code*. The number following "U.S.C" is the section number: the cited statute is section 12101 of Title 42 of the *United States Code*. The final number, which is in parentheses, is the year of the code. To find the cited statute, you need to look at the 2006 version of the *United States Code*.

42	U.S.C.	§ 12101	(2006)
Title	Name of Code	Section	Year of Code

Now look at the following citation, which is the citation to the Florida statute governing service of process.

Fla. Stat. § 48.031 (2006)

In this citation, "Fla. Stat." is the abbreviation for the Florida's official code, which is called the *Florida Statutes*. The number that follows that abbreviation is the title and section number; the number before the period, the "48," is the title, and the number following the period, "031," is the section number. The last number, the number in parentheses, is the year of the code.

Fla. Stat.	§ 48.031	(2006)
Name of Code	Title and Section Number	Year of Code

PRACTICE POINTER   To find the name of each state's code or codes and the abbreviations that are used for the codes, see Appendix 1 in *The ALWD Citation Manual, Third Edition,* or Table 1 in *The Bluebook, A Uniform System of Citation, Eighteenth Edition*.

If you have not been given the citation to the statute, finding the applicable statutory section or sections can be more difficult. If you are using books, the easiest way to find a statute is to use the index that comes with the book version of the code. (This index is usually set out in a separate volume at the end of the code.) If you are using a fee-based service, such as LexisNexis or Westlaw, the easiest way is to use either the table of contents option or the index option. If you are using a free source, use the table of contents or index option if the source offers that option. Otherwise, locate the applicable sections by doing a Boolean or terms and connectors search.

For more information on finding state statutes and regulations, see Chapter 4 in *Just Research*, and for more information on finding federal statutes and regulations, see Chapter 5 in *Just Research*. For more information on finding county and city ordinances, see Chapter 6 in *Just Research*.

§ 3.4.2 Distinguishing Between the Text of the Statute and Other Material Provided by the Publisher

What you find when you look up a statute will depend on the source that you use. If you use a free website, more likely than not, you will find only the text of the statute, credits, and historical notes. If, however, you use a fee-based service or the book form of an annotated code, you will find not only the text of the statute, credits, and historical notes but also other material provided by the publisher, for example, cross-references to other sources and notes of decisions that you can use to locate cases that have applied the statute. Chart 3.2 sets out excerpts from the Westlaw version of Fla. Stat. § 48.031 (2006).

Chart 3.2	Florida Statute § 48.031 (2006) as on Westlaw

West's F.S.A. § 48.031 <u>Next Section</u> ▶

48.031. Service of process generally; service of witness subpoenas
Effective: July 01, 2004 <u>Prior</u>
Approx. 21 pages West's Florida Statutes Annotated
<u>Currentness</u>

Title VI. Civil Practice and Procedure (Chapters 45-89) (<u>Refs & Annos</u>)

Chapter 48. Process and Service of Process (<u>Refs & Annos</u>)

➡**48.031. Service of process generally; service of witness subpoenas**

(1)(a) Service of original process is made by delivering a copy of it to the person to be served with a copy of the complaint, petition, or other initial pleading or paper or by leaving the copies at his or her usual place of abode with any person residing therein who is 15 years of age or older and informing the person of their contents. Minors who are or have been married shall be served as provided in this section.

* * *

CREDIT(S)

Act Nov. 23, 1828, § 5; Rev.St.1892, § 1015; Gen.St.1906, § 1402; Rev.Gen.St.1920, § 2599; Comp.Gen.Laws 1927, § 4246; Laws 1955, c. 29737, § 6; <u>Fla.St.1965, § 47.13</u>; Laws 1967, c. 67-254, § 4; Laws 1975, c. 75-34, § 1; Laws 1979, c. 79-396, § 3; Laws 1982, c. 82-118, § 3; Laws 1984, c. 84- 339, § 1; Laws 1985, c. 85-80, § 7; <u>Laws 1987, c. 87-405, § 2; Laws 1993, c. 93-208, § 6</u>. Amended by <u>Laws 1995, c. 95-147, § 269, eff. July 10, 1995</u>; <u>Laws 1995, c. 95-172, § 1, eff. Oct. 1, 1995</u>; <u>Laws 1998, c. 98-410, § 1, eff. Oct. 1, 1998</u>; <u>Laws 2004, c. 2004-273, § 1, eff. July 1, 2004</u>.

- The Westlaw citation for the statute.
- Links to the statute's history and information about when the statute was last undated.

- The title for the section.

- The text of the statute.

- List showing date that the statute was enacted and amendments.

(continues)

Continued

HISTORICAL AND STATUTORY NOTES

Amendment Notes:

Former § 47.13 was amended in 1955 to replace the
following earlier text: "Service of the original writ or
summons shall be effected by reading the writ or summons to the person to be served, or by delivering him a
copy thereof, or by leaving such copy at his usual place of
abode with some person of the family above fifteen years
of age, and informing such person of the contents
thereof."

* * *

- Additional
  information
  about amend-
  ments.

CROSS REFERENCES

Constructive service of process, see § 49.011 et seq.
Labor organizations, service of process on, see § 447.11.
Leaving copy of complaint for defendant, see Civil Proce-
dure Rule 1.070.
Optional methods of service on certain parties, see
§ 48.22.
Process and service,
County court, see § 34.07.
Criminal courts, see § 900.03.
Juvenile courts, see § 985.219.
Witness testifying pursuant to a subpoena, termination of
employment prohibited, see § 92.57.

- Links to other
  statutes that
  may be relevant.

LAW REVIEW AND JOURNAL COMMENTARIES

Citation and notice in probate and guardianship proceedings. Judge Frank B. Dowling, 42 Fla.B.J. 28 (January
1968).

Citation and notice; guardianship proceedings. Judge
Frank B. Dowling, 42 Fla.B.J. 28 (1968).

Process: immunity of nonresident from service while in
attendance at litigation. 5 U.Fla.L.Rev. 210 (Summer
1952).

Service of process on nonresidents. 4 U.Fla.L.Rev. 385 (Fall
1951).

- Citations to
  secondary
  sources that may
  be relevant.

LIBRARY REFERENCES

2006 Main Volume

Process ⟸ 57, 61, 64, 76.
Witnesses ⟸ 13.

- Links to other
  publications
  available on
  Westlaw that
  may be relevant.

(continues)

Continued

Westlaw Topic Nos. 313, 410.
C.J.S. Process §§ 38 to 40, 42, 50, 52 to 55, 73.
C.J.S. Witnesses §§ 2, 20 to 22, 25 to 29.

RESEARCH REFERENCES

ALR Library32 ALR 3rd 112, Construction of Phrase "Usual Place of Abode," or Similar Terms Referring to Abode, Residence, or Domicile, as Used in Statutes Relating to Service of Process.

87 ALR 2nd 1163, Place or Manner of Delivering or Depositing Papers, Under Statutes Permitting Service of Process by Leaving Copy at Usual Place of Abode or Residence.

* * *

NOTES OF DECISIONS

Abode 9
Acceptance of service 5-7
Acceptance of service - In general 5
Acceptance of service - Avoidance of acceptance of service 6
Acceptance of service - Servants accepting service 7
Agents 23
Associations, service on 22
Avoidance of acceptance of service 6
Burden of proof 32

* * *

Substituted service 14-18
Substituted service - In general 14
Substituted service - Family member 15
Substituted service - House guest 18

* * *

1. Validity

This section providing for substituted service of process is a valid method of acquiring jurisdiction over defendant. Barnett Bank of Clearwater, N.A. v. Folsom, App. 2 Dist., 306 So.2d 186 (1975). Process ⚷ 70

* * *

9. Abode

The requirement that substituted service of process be at a defendant's "usual place of abode" means the place

- "Table of Contents" for the Notes of Decisions. The number is the number for the subsection dealing with the topic. To get to that subsection, either click on the link or scroll down.

- Notes of decision.

- Notes of decision are written by an attorney working for the publishing company and provide a

(continues)

Continued

where the defendant is actually living at the time of service. Thompson v. State, Dept. of Revenue, App. 1 Dist., 867 So.2d 603 (2004). Process ⚷ 78

Word "abode" means one's fixed place of residence for the time being when service is made as that word is used in statute providing that service of original process is made by delivering a copy of it to the person to be served with a copy of the complaint or by leaving the copies at his or her usual place of abode with any person residing therein who is 15 years of age or older and informing the person of their contents. Torres v. Arnco Const., Inc., App. 5 Dist., 867 So.2d 583 (2004). Process ⚷ 78

* * *.

15. — Family member, substituted service

Substituted service was not made on prospective home-owner at his usual place of abode when construction company served homeowner's mother in Florida with substitute service on homeowner in connection with construction company's claim against homeowner for breach of contract arising out of agreement for construction of house; affidavit of homeowner specifically denied that his place of abode was in Florida and specifically averred that his place of abode was in New York where company, which was apparently aware of this, tried unsuccessfully to serve him, and affidavit of New York process server supported homeowner's position. Torres v. Arnco Const., Inc., App. 5 Dist., 867 So.2d 583 (2004). Process ⚷ 78; Process ⚷ 149

Substituted service of support petition on mother of the child's father at mother's residence was effective in Department of Revenue's (DOR) support action on behalf of mother; father failed to prove by convincing evidence that mother's address was not his usual place of abode at time of service. Department of Revenue ex rel. Williams v. Wright, App. 2 Dist., 813 So.2d 989 (2002), rehearing denied. Child Support ⚷ 180

* * *

West's F. S. A. § 48.031, FL ST § 48.031
Current with Chapter in effect from the 2006 Second Regular Session of the

one-sentence summary of a point of law set out in a case. If the case sets out more than one point of law that relates to the statute, the case will be listed more than once, under the same topic headings or under different topic headings.

• To see the text of the opinion, click on the link to the case or use the citation to locate the case in the book form of the reporter or on a free Internet site.

• Note that the citation form is West's citation form and that the citations may not, therefore, comply with the rules set out in the *ALWD Citation Manual* or *The Bluebook.*

• Information showing the

(continues)

§ 3.4.3 Making Sure You Have the Right Version of the Statute

Before spending time reading and analyzing a statute, make sure that you are reading the right version of the statute. If the issue that you have been asked to research involves an event that happened in the past, you will need to find the version of the statute that was in effect at the time that event occurred. In contrast, if the client has asked you to determine what he or she can do next month, you need to find the version of the statute that will be in effect next month.

To determine whether the version of the statute that you have found is the right version, use the credits and historical notes that are set out after the text of the statute. See Chart 3.2, page 53. If the statute has been amended since your cause of action arose, use the version of the statute that was in effect on the applicable date. If you are advising a client about what it can or cannot do in the future, use an online source to see if there is pending legislation.

§ 3.4.4 Identifying the Elements or Requirements

While some disciplines and cultures focus on the "whole," in law, at least as it is practiced in the United States, the focus is on the "parts." Thus, in reading a statute, most United States attorneys are looking for the elements, that is, for the requirements set out in the statute. For example, in reading the following Florida statute dealing with substituted service of process, an attorney would try to identify the elements, or requirements, for substituted service of process.

Fla. Stat. § 48.031. Service of process generally; service of witness subpoenas

(1)(a) Service of original process is made by delivering a copy of it to the person to be served with a copy of the complaint, petition, or other initial pleading or paper or by leaving the copies at his or her usual place of abode with any person residing therein who is 15 years of age or older and informing the person of their contents. . . .

While sometimes Congress or the state legislature sets out the elements in a list, most of the time the elements are embedded in the text of the statute. In these situations, you will need to read and re-read the statute, determining, as best you can, what the elements are. One of the easiest, and most reliable ways of doing this type of analysis is to do a form of sentence diagramming. Begin by identifying each clause and phrase. For example, in analyzing Fla. Stat. § 48.031(a)(1) (2006), you find the following clauses and phrases.

Fla. Stat. § 48.031(a)(1) (2006)

Service of original process is made

by delivering a copy of it
to the person to be served
with a copy of the complaint, petition, or other initial pleading
   or paper
or by leaving the copies at his or her usual place of abode
with any person residing therein
who is 15 years of age or older
and informing the person of their contents.

Once you have listed the clauses and phrases, look at the words that the legislature used to connect those clauses and phrases and the words in those clauses and phrases. In particular, note whether the clauses, phrases, and words are connected with "and" or with "or." In addition, try to determine what modifies what.

In our example, the statute begins with a subject, "service of original process," and a verb, "is made." This subject and verb are followed by two phrases that begin with the word "by": "by delivering" or "by leaving." Thus, it appears that service of process can be made either (1) by delivering a copy of the process to the person to be served or (2) by leaving a copy at his or her usual place of abode. A close reading of the language used to describe the second option suggests that there are four sub-elements or requirements: (a) the process must be left at the person's usual place of abode, (b) the process must be left with a person residing therein, (c) the person with whom the process is left must be fifteen years or older, and (d) the person serving the process must inform the person served about "their contents." By reformatting your first list of phrases and clauses, you can see the two options and the requirements for each option.

Service of original process is made

(1) **by delivering** a copy of it to the person to be served with a copy of the complaint, petition, or other initial pleading or paper

or

(2) **by leaving** the copies at
    (a) his or her usual place of abode
    (b) with any person residing therein
    (c) who is 15 years of age or older

and

    (d) informing the person of their contents.

The next step is to look for other statutory sections that are on point. Begin by looking for statutory definitions. Are the terms in the subsection that you just read defined in a different subsection of the same statute or in a different section of the same chapter or act? If there are statutory definitions, you need to use those definitions. If the statutory language is ambiguous, also look for a findings and purpose section that explains why the statute was enacted and what drafters hoped to accomplish. Finally, if your statute contains cross references to other statutes, look up and read those cross references.

A second way is identify the elements is to create a flow chart for your statute. Look, for example, at the Chart 3.3, which a first-year student created to analyze a section of the Americans with Disabilities Act.

Chart 3.3   Flow Chart

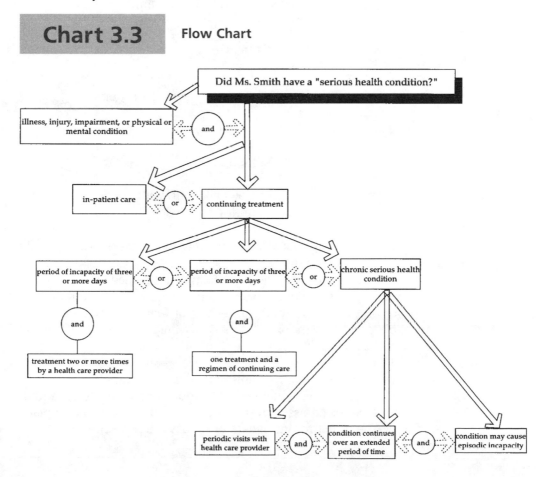

If you use a flow chart, remember to look for statutory sections that define terms used in the statute that you are analyzing, and for a findings and purpose section that sets out Congress's or the state legislature's intent in enacting the statute. Finally, remember to look up and read any cross references.

PRACTICE POINTER Once you have done your own analysis of the statute, check your analysis against the analysis that others have done. For example, have the courts, in interpreting and applying the statute, listed the elements and does their list match yours? In cases in which a jury would decide whether the statute has or has not been violated, are there any pattern jury instructions, and how are the elements listed in those jury instructions? Is the statute discussed in a practice manual, a treatise, a law review article, or other secondary source and, if it has, how has the source listed the elements? If your list matches the list set out in the cases, the jury instructions, and secondary sources, you can be confident that you have read the statute correctly. If your list does not match those lists, you will usually want to go with the list set out in a case that is mandatory authority or in the pattern jury instructions unless that reading of the statute does not favor your client and you can make a good faith argument that the courts or the authors of the pattern jury instructions have misread the statute.

---

§ 3.5 Exercise

Read the following statute and then answer the questions.

Text of statute:

Wash. Rev. Code § 9A.46.110 (2006):

(1) A person commits the crime of stalking if, without lawful authority and under circumstances not amounting to a felony attempt of another crime:

    (a) He or she intentionally and repeatedly harasses or repeatedly follows another person; and

    (b) The person being harassed or followed is placed in fear that the stalker intends to injure the person, another person, or property of the person or of another person. The feeling of fear must be one that a reasonable person in the same situation would experience under all the circumstances; and

    (c) The stalker either:

        (i) Intends to frighten, intimidate, or harass the person; or

        (ii) Knows or reasonably should know that the person is afraid, intimidated, or harassed even if the stalker did not intend to place the person in fear or intimidate or harass the person.

(2) (a) It is not a defense to the crime of stalking under subsection (1)(c)(i) of this section that the stalker was not given actual notice that the person did not want the stalker to contact or follow the person; and

(b) It is not a defense to the crime of stalking under subsection (1)(c)(ii) of this section that the stalker did not intend to frighten, intimidate, or harass the person.

(3) It shall be a defense to the crime of stalking that the defendant is a licensed private investigator acting within the capacity of his or her license as provided by chapter 18.165 RCW.

(4) Attempts to contact or follow the person after being given actual notice that the person does not want to be contacted or followed constitutes prima facie evidence that the stalker intends to intimidate or harass the person. . . .

. . .

(6) As used in this section:

(a) "Follows" means deliberately maintaining visual or physical proximity to a specific person over a period of time. A finding that the alleged stalker repeatedly and deliberately appears at the person's home, school, place of employment, business, or any other location to maintain visual or physical proximity to the person is sufficient to find that the alleged stalker follows the person. It is not necessary to establish that the alleged stalker follows the person while in transit from one location to another.

(b) "Harasses" means unlawful harassment as defined in RCW 10.14.020.

. . .

(d) "Repeatedly" means on two or more separate occasions.

Questions:

1. How would you determine whether the statute above governs acts that occurred in April 2007?
2. To convict an individual of stalking, what does the State have to prove? List the elements.
3. What is and is not a defense to the crime of stalking?
4. What other types of statutory sections would you want to look for?
5. What other statutory sections would you want to read and analyze?

CHAPTER

4

Understanding Judicial Opinions

Although sometimes a statute will answer the question that you have been asked to research, more often than not you will also need to look at judicial decisions, which are also called judicial opinions or, more simply, cases. If the issue is governed by common law, you will be looking at the cases to find the common law rule and examples of how that common law rule has been applied in analogous cases. In contrast, if the issue is governed by a statute, you will be looking at the cases to determine how the courts have applied the statute, or a particular part of the statute, in cases that are analogous, or similar to, your client's case.

§ 4.1 Which Cases Are Binding on Which Courts

The image created by most casebooks, TV shows, and news articles is that all cases are created equal. Nothing could be further from the truth. Even though a criminal law casebook may set out cases from United States District Court for the Northern District of California, from the United States Court of Appeals for the Third Circuit, and from the Mississippi Supreme Court, in practice your search for cases will be more focused. While casebooks are designed to illustrate the historical development of a rule or the ways in which different jurisdictions have approached the same issue, as a practicing attorney you will look first for cases that are mandatory authority, that is, cases that are binding on the court that will be deciding your case. You will look at persuasive authority, for example cases from outside your jurisdiction, only when there is no mandatory authority or when you are asking a court to overrule, or invalidate, one of its decisions.

Three examples illustrate when cases from a particular court are mandatory authority. In the first example, the issue is governed by a state statute and the cases that have interpreted and applied that statute. In the second example, the issue is governed by federal statutes and regulations and the cases that have interpreted and applied those statutes and regulations. The third example involves an issue governed by common law.

§ 4.1.1 Issue Governed by State Statute and Cases that Have Interpreted and Applied that Statute

Presume for a moment that the State of Oregon has charged Martin Obote with assault under an Oregon statute. Because Mr. Obote has been charged under an Oregon statute, the case will be heard by the Oregon courts and, in deciding whether Mr. Obote is guilty, the Oregon courts will apply the Oregon statute and Oregon cases that have interpreted and applied that statute.

Initially, the case will be heard by one of Oregon's circuit courts, which are trial courts that have jurisdiction to hear cases in which the defendant is charged under an Oregon statute with a misdemeanor, gross misdemeanor, or a felony. Mr. Obote can choose to have a bench trial or a jury trial. If Mr. Obote chooses to have a bench trial, there will not be a jury, and the trial court judge will decide both issues of fact and issues of law. If, however, Mr. Obote chooses a jury trial, the judge will decide issues of law, and the jury will decide issues of fact. Under both options, the State has the burden of proof and must prove each element of the crime beyond a reasonable doubt.

At the trial court level, the Oregon statute, Oregon Supreme Court cases, and Oregon Court of Appeals cases are mandatory authority. Thus, in deciding issues of law, the trial court must apply the Oregon statute in a manner that is consistent with the ways in which the Oregon Supreme Court and Oregon Court of Appeals have applied that statute in other analogous cases. The only exception is for issues that involve a right guaranteed by the United States Constitution, for example, an individual's Fourth Amendment right to be free from unreasonable searches and seizures. When the issue involves a right guaranteed under the United States Constitution, United States Supreme Court decisions are mandatory authority.

If, after hearing the witnesses and viewing the exhibits, the judge or jury finds that Mr. Obote is guilty, Mr. Obote can file an appeal, which in most instances will be heard by the Oregon Court of Appeals, which is Oregon's intermediate court of appeals. The Oregon Court of Appeals does not conduct trials. Instead, it reviews the written record from the trial conducted before the circuit court and any exhibits that were admitted at trial. With only a few exceptions, the Oregon Court of Appeals can hear and decide only four types of issues: (1) whether a statute is constitutional, (2) whether the trial court applied the right law and properly instructed the jury, (3) whether the trial court judge abused his or her discretion in granting or denying a motion or granting or denying an objection, and (4) whether there is sufficient evidence to support the trial court judge's findings of fact or the jury's verdict.

In deciding these issues, the Oregon Court of Appeals must apply mandatory authority. Consequently, if the issue is an issue of state law, the Oregon Court of Appeals must apply the rules set out in decisions by the Oregon Supreme Court. In contrast, if the issue involves a right guaranteed under the United States Constitution, the Oregon Court of Appeals must apply the rules set out by the United States Supreme Court. While most of the time the Oregon Court of Appeals will follow its own prior decisions, it is not required to do so.

If the Oregon Court of Appeals affirms Mr. Obote's conviction, Mr. Obote can file a petition for discretionary review, asking the Oregon Supreme Court, which is Oregon's highest court, to hear his case. If the Oregon Supreme Court grants Mr. Obote's petition, it will review his conviction; if it denies his petition, it will not review the conviction, and the Oregon Court of Appeals' decision is the final decision.

Like the Oregon Court of Appeals, the Oregon Supreme Court does not conduct trials. Instead, like the Oregon Court of Appeals, it reviews the written record from the trial court and reviews exhibits introduced at trial. In addition, like the Oregon Court of Appeals, it can decide only certain types of issues. With just a few exceptions, it can determine only (1) whether the statute is constitutional; (2) whether the trial court applied the right law and correctly instructed the jury; (3) whether the trial court judge abused his or her discretion in granting or denying a motion or granting or denying an objection; and (4) whether there is sufficient evidence to support the trial court judge's findings of fact or the jury's verdict.

Just as the Oregon Court of Appeals is not bound by its earlier decisions, the Oregon Supreme Court is not bound by its earlier decisions. Thus, in cases heard by the Oregon Supreme Court, the only mandatory authority are United States Supreme Court decisions, and those decisions are only mandatory authority insofar as they involve rights guaranteed by the United States Constitution.

Although the names of the courts will vary from state to state, for example, in New York the trial court is called the "Supreme Court," the roles that trial courts, intermediate courts of appeal, and the highest court play are the same in each state. Chart 4.1, summarizes the role that each court plays and lists the authorities that are mandatory authority.

Chart 4.1	Role Each State Court Plays and List of Authorities that Are Mandatory Authority	
Court	**Role**	**Mandatory Authority**
State trial courts	• Conducts trial • In a bench trial, the judge decides questions of law and questions of fact and enters findings of fact and conclusions of law. • In a jury trial, the judge decides questions of law, and the jury decides questions of fact and enters a verdict.	• If the issue is governed by a state statute, the state statute and decisions of the state's highest court and, if it has one, intermediate court of appeals are mandatory authority. • If the issue is governed by the United States Constitution, United States Supreme Court decisions are mandatory authority.
State intermediate courts of appeals Note: Some of the smaller states (e.g., Nevada) do not have an intermediate court of appeals.	• Does not conduct trials, hear testimony, or accept new evidence. • Reviews trial court record to determine whether (1) the statute is constitutional, (2) the trial court applied the right law and correctly instructed the jury, (3) the trial court judge abused his or her discretion in granting or denying a motion or granting or denying an objection, and (4) there is sufficient evidence to support the trial court judge's or the jury's findings of fact.	• If the issue is governed by a state statute, the state statute and decisions of the state's highest court are mandatory authority. • If the issue is governed by the United States Constitution, United States Supreme Court decisions are mandatory authority. • Although a state's intermediate court of appeals will usually follow its own prior decisions, those decisions are not mandatory authority.
State's highest court or court of last resort Note: In many states this court is called the Supreme Court.	• Does not conduct trials, hear testimony, or accept new evidence. • Reviews trial court record to determine (1) whether the statute is constitutional; (2) whether the trial	• If constitutional, the state statutes are mandatory authority. • For issues governed by United States Constitution, United States Supreme Court decisions are mandatory authority.

(continues)

Continued

Court	Role	Mandatory Authority
	court applied the right law correctly; (3) whether the trial court judge abused his or her discretion in granting or denying a motion or granting or denying an objection; and (4) whether there is sufficient evidence to support the trial court judge's findings of fact or the jury's verdict.	• Although the state's highest court will usually follow its own prior decisions, those decisions are not mandatory authority.

§ 4.1.2 Issue Governed by Federal Statute and Regulations and Cases that Have Interpreted that Federal Statute and the Federal Regulations

In our second example, Sanjee Singh wants to sue her employer under the Family and Medical Leave Act (FMLA) on the grounds that her employer illegally fired her after she took three weeks off from work to care for her dying mother. Because the FMLA is a federal statute, the issue is governed by the FMLA, the regulations that implement the FMLA, and the federal cases that have applied the FMLA.

If Ms. Singh does sue her employer, her case would be heard by a United States District Court. As in the state system, Ms. Singh can ask for a bench trial, in which the trial court judge will decide both issues of fact and issues of law, or a jury trial, in which the judge would decide issues of law, and the jury would decide issues of fact. As the plaintiff, Ms. Singh would have the burden of proof. At the District Court, or trial court level, the FMLA, the applicable federal regulations, United States Supreme Court decisions, and United States Court of Appeals decisions from the same circuit as the circuit in which the District Court is located are mandatory authority.

If Ms. Singh loses at the district court level, she can appeal that decision to the United States Court of Appeals for the circuit in which the District Court that heard the case is located. Similarly, if Ms. Singh wins, her employer can file an appeal. Like state intermediate courts of appeals, the United States Court of Appeals does not conduct trials, hear witnesses, or admit new exhibits. Instead, it just reviews the written record from the trial court and the exhibits admitted at trial. In addition, just as the state intermediate court of appeals can decide only certain types of issues, the United States Court of Appeals can decide only certain types of issues: (1) whether the statute is constitutional, (2) whether the regulations are valid, (3) whether the district court judge applied the right law and correctly instructed the jury, (4) whether the district court judge abused his or her discretion in granting or denying a motion or granting or denying an objection, and (5) whether there is sufficient evidence to support the trial court judge's findings of fact or the jury's verdict. When a case is heard by a United States Court of Appeals, the statute, the regulations, and United States Supreme Court decisions are mandatory authority.

Although the United States Supreme Court hears relatively few cases each year, the party that loses at the Court of Appeals level has the right to file a petition for a *writ of certiorari* asking the United States Supreme Court to review the United States Court of Appeals' decision. If the United States Supreme Court accepts review, it would review the trial court record and determine (1) whether the statute is constitutional, (2) whether the regulations are valid, (3) whether the district court judge applied the right law correctly and correctly instructed the jury, (4) whether the trial court judge abused his or her discretion in granting or denying a motion or granting or denying an objection, and (5) whether there is sufficient evidence to support the district court judge's findings of fact or the jury's verdict. The only mandatory authority would be statutes and regulations, and those statutes and regulations are only mandatory authority if the statute is constitutional and the regulations are valid.

Chart 4.2 summarizes the role each federal court plays, and it identifies the authorities that are mandatory authority.

Chart 4.2	Role Each Federal Court Plays and List of Authorities that Are Mandatory Authority	
Court	**Role**	**Mandatory Authority**
United States District Court (trial court)	• Conducts trial. • In a bench trial, judge decides questions of law and questions of fact and enters findings of fact and conclusions of law. • In a jury trial, judge decides questions of law, and the jury hears questions of fact and enters verdict.	• Federal statutes.* • Federal regulations.** • United States Supreme Court decisions. • United States Court of Appeals decisions from same circuit in which District Court is located.
United States Court of Appeals	• Does not conduct trials, hear testimony, or accept new evidence. • Reviews trial court record to determine	• Federal statutes.* • Federal regulations.** • United States Supreme Court

(continues)

Continued

Court	Role	Mandatory Authority
	whether (1) the statute is constitutional, (2) the regulations are valid, (3) the district court judge applied the right law and correctly instructed the jury, (4) the district court judge abused his or her discretion in granting or denying a motion or granting or denying an objection, and (5) whether there is sufficient evidence to support the district court judge's or the jury's findings of fact.	decisions. • Although the United States Courts of Appeals will usually follow their own prior decisions, those decisions are not mandatory authority.
United States Supreme Court	• Does not conduct trials, hear testimony, or accept new evidence. • Reviews trial court record to determine (1) whether the statute is constitutional, (2) whether regulations are valid, (3) whether the trial court applied the applicable law correctly, (4) whether the trial court judge abused his or her discretion in granting or denying a motion or granting or denying an objection, and (5) whether there is sufficient evidence to support the trial court judge's findings of fact or the jury's verdict.	• Federal statutes.* • Federal regulations.** • Although the United States Supreme Court will usually follow its own decisions, those decisions are not mandatory authority.

* If constitutional
** If valid

§ 4.1.3 Issue Governed by Common Law

For this last example, presume that you represent Mr. Garcia, who is concerned that a group that runs a summer camp has obtained, through adverse possession, title to land that he owns in Washington. Because adverse possession is a common law doctrine, the only statute that is on point is a Washington statute that sets out the statutory period for adverse possession.

Because the land is located in Washington, the case would be heard by one of Washington's trial courts, the Superior Court. In hearing the case, the Superior Court would apply the common law rules set out in Washington cases and the statutory time periods set out in Washington statutes. Because Washington has an intermediate court of appeals, the decisions of that court, the decisions of the Washington Supreme Court, and Washington statutes are mandatory authority.

The party that loses at trial can file an appeal with the Washington Court of Appeals. At the Washington Court of Appeals, the only mandatory authorities are decisions by the Washington Court and the Washington statutes that set out the length of time a person must possess the property to establish title through adverse possession. Although in most situations the Washington Court of Appeals would follow its own earlier decisions, those decisions are not mandatory authority. The party that loses at the Court of Appeals level can ask the Washington Supreme Court to review the Washington Court of Appeals' decision. If the Washington Supreme Court accepts review, the only authority that is mandatory authority is the statute that sets out the time limits.

§ 4.2 How Attorneys Use Cases

Attorneys use cases in two ways: (1) as authority for a common law rule or for a rule that the courts have created in interpreting and applying a statute or regulation and (2) to illustrate how the courts have applied a common law rule or a statute or regulation in analogous cases.

PRACTICE POINTER   Sometimes an attorney will use one case as authority for a rule and another case to illustrate how that rule has been applied. At other times, an attorney will use the same case both as authority for a rule and as an analogous case to illustrate how that rule has been applied.

§ 4.2.1 Case as Authority for Rule

When an issue is governed by a common law rule, you will cite to one or more cases as authority for that common law rule. For instance, in the adverse possession case described in section 4.1.3, you would need to cite to a case or cases for both the general rules, that is, for the test the courts apply in determining whether an individual has gained title to land through adverse possession, and for the specific rules, that is, for the tests that the courts apply in determining whether a particular element is or is not met.

EXAMPLE 1   **Author Cites Cases as Authority for the Common Law Rule**

To establish title through adverse possession, the claimant must prove that its possession was (1) exclusive, (2) actual and uninterrupted, (3) open and notorious, and (4) hostile for the statutory period. *ITT Rayonier, Inc. v. Bell*, 112 Wn.2d 754, 757, 774 P.2d 6 (1989); *Chaplin v. Sanders*, 100 Wn.2d 853, 857, 676 P.2d 431 (1984).[1]

When the issue is governed by a statute, you will cite to the statute for the rules set out in the statute but to the cases for the rules that the courts have created in applying that statute. For example, if the courts have defined a word that is used in the statute, you will set out that definition and then cite a case as authority. Likewise, if the courts have set out rules or tests for determining whether a particular element is met, you will set out those rules or tests and cite a case or cases as authority.

EXAMPLE 2   **Author Sets Out Definition Developed by Florida Courts in Interpreting and Applying Florida's Service of Process Statute**

The Florida courts have defined "usual place of abode" as "the fixed place of residence for the time being when the service is made." *Shurman v. A. Mortg. & Inv. Corp.*, 795 So. 2d 952, 953-54 (Fla. 2001). "If a person has more than one residence, a summons must be served at the residence at which the defendant is actually living at the time of service." *Id.* at 954.

If there are only one or two cases that have set out a common law, or court-made rule, cite those one or two cases as authority. If, however, there are a number of cases that have set out the same rules, do not cite all of the cases. Instead, select the one, two, or three "best" cases. Begin by identifying the cases that are mandatory authority. From this group, you will usually want to select cases from higher courts over cases from lower courts and more recent cases over older cases. The exception is when all of the decisions from the higher courts are quite old. In this situation, you will usually want to cite one of the older higher court cases to show that the rule

---

[1] Because the issue would be decided by a Washington court, the author has used the Washington Style Sheet. See Appendix 2 in the *ALWD Citation Manual, 3d ed.*

was established by the jurisdiction's highest court and then cite to one of the newer lower court decisions to show that the rule is still good law.

Selecting Cases to Cite as Authority for a Common Law or Court-Made Rule

1. Select cases that are mandatory authority over cases that are persuasive authority.
2. Of those cases that are mandatory authority, select cases that are from higher courts over cases from lower courts.
3. Of those cases that are from higher courts, select more recent cases over older cases.

Exception:

If all of the cases from higher courts are old, also cite to a more recent lower court decision to show that the rule is still being applied by the courts.

For more on setting out the general and specific rules, see Chapters 9, 10, and 11.

§ 4.2.2 Using Analogous Cases to Illustrate How Courts Have Applied a Statute or Common Law Rule

In addition to citing cases as authority for a common law, or court-made, rule, attorneys also use cases to illustrate how the courts have applied a particular rule. For example, attorneys will use cases to illustrate the types of situations in which the courts have held that a particular element of a statute or common law rule was met or not met. In selecting these analogous cases, most attorneys try to select cases that illustrate the types of situations in which the courts have held that the element was met and cases that illustrate the types of situations in which the courts have held that the element was not met. The attorneys then place those cases and their client's case along a continuum, arguing either that their client's case is more like the cases in which the element was met or more like the cases in which the element was not met.

Element Met	Client's Case	Element Not Met

The criteria for selecting analogous cases are a bit different from the criteria for selecting cases to cite as authority for a rule. Although you want to select cases that are mandatory authority over cases that are only persuasive authority, you will not always choose cases from higher courts over cases from lower courts or more recent cases over older cases. Instead, the cases that will be the "best" cases will be those that are most factually analogous to your case. Thus, you might select an intermediate court of appeals decision over a case from the jurisdiction's highest appellate court if the facts in the intermediate court of appeals decision are more similar to the facts in your case. Similarly, you might select an older case over a more recent one if the facts in the older case are more analogous to the facts in your case.

Selecting Analogous Cases

1. Select cases that are mandatory authority over cases that are persuasive authority.
2. Select cases that are more factually analogous over cases that are less factually analogous.
3. When possible, select representative cases in which the element was met and representative cases in which the element was not met.

§ 4.3 Reading and Analyzing Cases

Just as some statutes are hard to read and analyze, so too are some cases. Sometimes, a case is difficult to read and analyze because it has a complicated set of facts and a complicated procedural history. In these cases, just figuring out who the parties are and who did what may take effort. At other times, the case is difficult to read and analyze because it involves a complicated area of law and a complicated issue or set of issues. Unless you already understand the area of law, you will have a difficult time understanding the court's opinion. At still other times, the judge simply did a bad job writing the opinion: the opinion is poorly organized, the sentences are hard to read, or the writing is wordy or imprecise.

In the end, though, it does not matter whether a case is easy or difficult to read and analyze or why that might be the case. To do your job, you need to figure out what the case says and does not say and how the case might be applied.

§ 4.3.1 Finding Cases Using the Citation

Just as you can use the citation to a statute to find a copy of the statute (see section 3.4.1), you can use the case citation to find a copy of the case in the book form of a reporter, which is the name that is given to the sets of books that contain copies of judicial opinions. For more on state reporters, see section 4.2.4 in *Just Research*; for more on federal reporters, see section 5.2.3 in *Just Research*. You can also use the citation to find copies of cases on fee-based services—for example, on LexisNexis, Loislaw, VersusLaw, or Westlaw—or on free websites.

Most case citations contain three parts: the name of the case; references to the reporter or reporters in which the case can be found; and a parenthetical that includes, at a minimum, the year in which the opinion was issued. A case citation may also include a subsequent history section that provides information about what happened after the court issued its opinion and a parenthetical that provides the reader with additional information about the case. The following citation is a typical case citation.

***Thompson v. State, Dept. of Revenue*, 867 So. 2d 603 (Fla. App. 1 Dist., 2004).**

In this citation, the first piece of information is the name of the case: *Thompson v. State, Dept. of Revenue*. The second piece of information is the name of the reporter in which the case is published. The first number, "867," is the volume number; the letters "So. 2d" are the abbreviation for the reporter; and the second number, "603," is the page on which the case begins. Thus, you can find a copy of *Thompson v. State, Dept. of Revenue* in volume 867 of the *Southern Reporter, Second Series,* beginning on page 603. The parenthetical gives you the information you need to determine whether the case is mandatory or persuasive authority: the name of the court that decided the case and the year of the decision.

***Thompson v. State, Dept. of Revenue*, 867 So. 2d   603   (Fla. App. 1 Dist., 2004).**

Case Name   Vol. Reporter Page   Court   Year

|  | For more on case citations, see Rule 12 in *ALWD Citation Manual, Third Edition*; Rule 10 in *The Bluebook, Eighteenth Edition*; or your jurisdiction's citation rules. |

To find a copy of a case in the book form of a reporter, locate the appropriate set of reporters in the library, locate the correct volume, and then turn to the correct page. To find a copy of a case on a fee-based or free website, type in the citation in the "find by citation" search box.

|  | The following websites are free websites that contain the text of court opinions. |

A. Federal Cases

1. United States Supreme Court

http://www.supremecourtus.gov/opinions/opinions.html
http://www.gpoaccess.gov/judicial.html

(continues)

Continued

http://supct.law.cornell.edu/supct/
http://www.findlaw.com/casecode/supreme.html
http://www.lexisone.com/lx1/caselaw/freecaselaw

2. United States Courts of Appeal, United States District Courts, and
Specialized Courts

http://www.uscourts.gov/links.html
http://www.gpoaccess.gov/judicial.html
http://www.law.cornell.edu/federal/opinions.html
http://www.law.emory.edu/FEDCTS/
http://www.findlaw.com/10fedgov/judicial/appeals_courts.html
http://www.hg.org/judges.html
http://www.lexisone.com/lx1/caselaw/freecaselaw

B. State Cases

http://www.law.cornell.edu/opinions.html
http://www.lexisone.com/lx1/caselaw/freecaselaw
state court websites

§ 4.3.2 Distinguishing Between Text of an Opinion and Material Added by Publisher

What you see when you locate a copy of a case depends on the source in which you have looked up that case. If you have found a copy of the case on a free website, more likely than not all that you will see is the text of the court's opinion. If, however, you have looked up the case in the book form of a reporter or on a fee-based website such as LexisNexis or Westlaw, you will find not only the text of the court's opinion but also editorial enhancements, for example, a syllabus and headnotes. Although these editorial enhancements are not part of the court's opinion and cannot, therefore, be cited as authority, they are useful tools for obtaining an overview of the opinion and for locating those parts of the opinion that are most relevant to the issue you have been asked to research.

Chart 4.3 walks you through the Westlaw version of *Thompson v. State, Dept. of Revenue.*

Chart 4.3

Thompson v. State, Dept. of Revenue, **as It Appears on Westlaw**

Thompson v. State, Dept. of Revenue
867 So.2d 603
Fla.App. 1 Dist.,2004.
March 05, 2004 (Approx. 3 pages)

Caption as set out by Westlaw:

- Case name.
- Citation.
- Name of court, year of decision, and approximate length.

West Reporter Image (PDF)

Link to the PDF version of case: the PDF version shows case as it appears in the book form of *Southern Reporter, Second Series.*

867 So.2d 603, 29 Fla. L. Weekly D566

Cites to the reporters in which you can find a copy of the case.

Briefs and Other Related Documents

Links to the briefs filed by the parties and other documents.

District Court of Appeal of Florida,
First District.
Calvin THOMPSON, Appellant,
v.
STATE of Florida, DEPARTMENT OF REVENUE, Appellee.
No. 1D03-2975.
March 5, 2004.

The caption as provided by the court.

Docket number. Date of decision.

Background: Department of Revenue filed action against father to establish and enforce child support for daughter. The Circuit Court, Duval County, E. McRae Mathis, J., denied father's motion to quash service of process. Father appealed.

Holding: The District Court of Appeal, Van Nortwick, J., held that father made prima facie showing that

This section and the following section are written by the court staff as an aid to attorneys. Thus, they are not part

(continues)

Continued

Department's petition was not served on him at his usual place of abode.

Reversed and remanded.

West Headnotes

[1] KeyCite Notes 🔲

🔑76E Child Support
   🔑76EV Proceedings
      🔑76EV(A) In General
         🔑 76Ek180 k. Process. Most Cited Cases

Father's affidavit stating that he was separated from wife and had not resided with her for over three years was sufficient to make a prima facie showing that Department of Revenue's petition to establish and enforce child support, which was left with wife at her residence, was not served on father at his usual place of abode, for purposes of Department's attempt to establish valid substituted service. West's F.S.A. § 48.031.

[2] KeyCite Notes 🔲

🔑313 Process
   🔑313II Service
      🔑313II(B) Substituted Service
         🔑313k76 Mode and Sufficiency of Service
            🔑313k78 k. Leaving Copy at Residence or Other Place. Most Cited Cases

The requirement that substituted service of process be at a defendant's "usual place of abode" means the place where the defendant is actually living at the time of service. West's F.S.A. § 48.031.

[3] KeyCite Notes 🔲

🔑313 Process
   🔑313II Service
      🔑313II(A) Personal Service in General
         🔑313k48 k. Nature and Necessity in General. Most Cited Cases

of the opinion and cannot be cited.

West headnotes are written by attorneys employed by Thomson Publishing Company, the company that owns Westlaw. The attorney who is assigned the case reads the case and, for each rule of law set out by the court, prepares a one-sentence statement. These statements are then placed at the beginning of the case as headnotes, in West's digests, and, if the case involves a statute, in the notes of decision following the statute in the West version of the code.

To find the place in the court's opinion from which the attorney drew the statement, click on

(continues)

Continued

⟸313 Process KeyCite Notes 🔳
 ⟸313II Service
  ⟸313II(E) Return and Proof of Service
   ⟸313k144 Evidence as to Service
    ⟸313k145 k. Presumptions and Burden of Proof.
Most Cited Cases

The burden of proof to sustain the validity of service of process is upon the person who seeks to invoke the jurisdiction of the court and, without proper service of process, the court lacks personal jurisdiction over the defendant. West's F.S.A. § 48.031.

[4] KeyCite Notes 🔳

⟸313 Process
 ⟸313II Service
  ⟸313II(E) Return and Proof of Service
   ⟸313k144 Evidence as to Service
    ⟸313k145 k. Presumptions and Burden of Proof.
Most Cited Cases

⟸313 Process KeyCite Notes 🔳
 ⟸313II Service
  ⟸313II(E) Return and Proof of Service
   ⟸313k144 Evidence as to Service
    ⟸313k149 k. Weight and Sufficiency. Most Cited
Cases

A process server's return of service on a defendant which is regular on its face is presumed to be valid absent clear and convincing evidence presented to the contrary.

[5] KeyCite Notes 🔳

⟸313 Process
 ⟸313II Service
  ⟸313II(E) Return and Proof of Service
   ⟸313k144 Evidence as to Service
    ⟸313k148 k. Evidence to Impeach or Contradict
Return, Certificate, or Affidavit of Service. Most Cited
Cases

A simple denial of having received service is not sufficient to contradict a process server's return of service that is regular on its face.

the bracketed number that is next to the head-note or scroll through the opinion until you find the bracketed number. For example, to find the place where the attorney drew the rule set out in headnote 3, click on the [3].

To find other cases that deal with the same issue, click on the key number link or on the link to "Most Cited Cases."

(continues)

Continued

*604 Esther A. Zaretsky, West Palm Beach, for Appellant. Charles J. Crist, Jr., Attorney General and Toni C. Bernstein and William H. Branch, Assistant Attorneys General, Tallahassee, for Appellee.

The "*604" indicates a page break. If you looked up the case in the book form of the *Southern Reporter, Second Series,* this is the material that would be at the top of page 604. The names are the names of the parties' attorneys on appeal.

VAN NORTWICK, J.

Last name of the judge who authored the opinion. The "J." stands for "Judge" or "Justice."

Calvin Thompson appeals a non-final order denying his motion to quash service of process in this support-administrative paternity action filed by the Department of Revenue. We reverse and remand for an evidentiary hearing pursuant to *Venetian Salami Co. v. Parthenais,* 554 So.2d 499, 502-03 (Fla.1989). Pursuant to section 409.2564, Florida Statutes (2002), the Department filed an action to establish and enforce child support for Thompson's four year-old daughter. The petition was served at 625 F Covenant Drive, Belle Glade, Florida 33430, and accepted by Thompson's wife. Thompson filed a motion to dismiss/ quash for lack of service of process stating that he was not present at the Belle Glade address and was not personally served. In his attached affidavit, Thompson stated that he has been separated from his wife, that he has not resided at that address for over three years, and that he did not authorize anyone to accept service of process on his behalf.

This is the beginning of the court's opinion. Thus, this is the material that can be cited as authority.

The trial court entered an order ruling that any jurisdictional defect could be cured by mailing a copy of the petition and accompanying documents to Thompson's attorney, "who has made a general appearance." The

(continues)

Continued

Department correctly concedes that the jurisdictional defect cannot *605 be cured in the manner suggested by the trial court and that Thompson's argument that the trial court lacked personal jurisdiction was not waived because Thompson neither took affirmative action nor sought affirmative relief prior to raising the alleged defect. *See Coto-Ojeda v. Samuel*, 642 So.2d 587, 588 (Fla. 3d DCA 1994)(Cope, J., specially concurring).

[1] KC [2] KC [3] KC Turning to the merits, "[s]ection 48.031 expressly requires that substituted service be at the person's usual place of abode." *Shurman v. A. Mortg. & Investment Corp.*, 795 So.2d 952, 954 (Fla.2001). The requirement "usual place of abode" means "the place where the defendant is actually living at the time of service." *Id., citing State ex rel. Merritt v. Heffernan*, 142 Fla. 496, 195 So. 145, 147 (1940). The burden of proof to sustain the validity of service of process is upon the person who seeks to invoke the jurisdiction of the court and, without proper service of process, the court lacks personal jurisdiction over the defendant. *M.J.W. v. Department of Children and Families*, 825 So.2d 1038, 1041 (Fla. 1st DCA 2002).

[4] KC [5] KC "[A] process server's return of service on a defendant which is regular on its face is presumed to be valid absent clear and convincing evidence presented to the contrary." *Telf Corp. v. Gomez*, 671 So.2d 818 (Fla. 3d DCA 1996). Although simple denial of service is not sufficient, *id.* at 819, Thompson's motion and affidavit are based on the fact that the service did not comply with section 48.031 and was therefore legally deficient. *National Safety Associates, Inc. v. Allstate Insurance Co.*, 799 So.2d 316, 317 (Fla. 2d DCA 2001). Thompson's affidavit makes a *prima facie* showing that he was not served at his usual place of abode by valid substituted service. *See, e.g., S.H. v. Department of Children and Families*, 837 So.2d 1117, 1118 (Fla. 4th DCA 2003)(invalidating substituted service on father at mother's address, where mother's residence was not father's "usual place of abode" at the time of service); *Gonzalez v. Totalbank*, 472 So.2d 861 (Fla. 3d DCA 1985)(invalidating substituted service when wife was separated from husband and not living at

The "*605" indicates a page break. The material before the "*605" was on page 604 and the material after the "*605" is on page 605.

The bracketed numbers tell you that this is the portion of the opinion from which the attorney who drafted the headnotes drew the material for headnotes 1, 2, and 3. If you click on the "KC" logo, you can KeyCite that particular headnote to locate other cases that have cited *Thompson* for the point of law set out in that headnote. For more on KeyCiting, see section 11.3 in *Just Research*.

(continues)

Continued

address where service was attempted). Having raised the issue of personal jurisdiction, Thompson's motion and accompanying affidavit placed the burden on the Department to establish the validity of service of process. *M.J.W.*, 825 So.2d at 1041. Accordingly, the cause is reversed and remanded for an evidentiary hearing to determine whether the attempted service of Thompson pursuant to section 48.031, Florida Statutes (2003), was valid. *See Venetian Salami*, 554 So.2d at 502-03; *Mowrey Elevator of Florida, Inc. v. Automated Integration*, 745 So.2d 1046, 1047-48 (Fla. 1st DCA 1999).

REVERSED and REMANDED.

This line tells you how the court "disposed" of the case. In this instance, the court reversed the trial court's decision and remanded the case to the trial court for further action consistent with the court's opinion.

KAHN and BENTON, JJ., concur.

The names of the judges who concurred in the decision. If there had been a concurring opinion and/or a dissent, those opinions would appear here.

Reprinted with permission of West, a Thomson business.

§ 4.3.3 Reading the Opinion

If the opinion is relatively short, for example, only two or three pages long, you will usually want to begin by reading quickly through the entire case. If, however, the case is longer, you will want to make sure that the case is on point or relevant to the issue you have been asked to research before you invest too much time reading and analyzing it. Therefore, if the case is more than a few pages long, begin by reading any introductory material, for example, the background section or the syllabus and the headnotes. If the introductory material or headnotes indicate that the case deals with the statute, common law doctrine, or issue that you have been asked to research, use the headnote numbers to locate those portions of the opinion from which the headnotes were drawn, and read those portions of the opinion. If those portions of the opinion appear to be on point, go back and read the entire opinion.

While the time saved by reading just the headnotes may seem to outweigh the cost of taking the time to read the entire case, you cannot cite headnotes. Because the headnotes are written by an attorney working for a publishing company and not by the court, they are not authority.

When you read the full opinion, look for specific types of information. First, identify the issue. If the opinion is a trial court opinion, was the issue a procedural issue, for example, whether the plaintiff was entitled to summary judgment, or did the court decide the case on its merits? In contrast, if the opinion is from an appellate court, was the issue (1) whether the statute is constitutional, (2) whether the regulations are valid, (3) whether the trial court set out the law correctly or correctly instructed the jury, (4) whether the trial court judge abused his or her discretion in granting or denying a motion or granting or denying an objection, or (5) whether there is sufficient evidence to support the trial court judge's or the jury's findings of fact?

Second, if the opinion is from an appellate court, determine what standard of review the appellate court applied. If the issue involves an issue of law, the standard of review is usually *de novo*. Under this standard of review, the appellate court does not defer to the trial court. Instead, it makes its own independent determination of what law applies or what the law is. In contrast, if the issue involves an issue of fact or an exercise of judgment, the standard of review is usually more deferential. For example, in reviewing most factual determinations, the standard of review is a sufficiency of the evidence standard. The appellate court looks to see only if there is sufficient evidence to support the trial court's findings of fact or the jury's verdict. Similarly, in reviewing a trial court's decision to admit evidence, the appellate courts usually defer to the trial court, reversing the trial court only when the appellate court determines that the trial court judge abused his or her discretion.

Third, determine what rule or test the court applied in deciding the issue. Begin by determining whether the parties agreed about what the rule was. If the parties agreed on the rule, the issue is not what the rule is but how that rule should be applied in a particular fact situation. If the parties did not agree about what the rule was, what rule did the plaintiff ask the court to apply? What rule did the defendant ask the court to apply? What rule did the court choose?

Fourth, evaluate the court's reasoning. If the parties agreed about what the rule was, what facts did the court consider in applying that rule to the facts of the case? If the parties disagreed about what the rule was, why did the court pick one rule over another? For example, in deciding how to interpret a statute, did the court rely on the plain language of the statute, on the canons of statutory construction, or on the statute's legislative history?

Fifth, look carefully at the court's disposition of the case. Did the court affirm the trial court? Reverse the trial court? Remand the case back to the trial court for further action?

Last, think about how you might be able to the use the case. Can you use the case as authority for a rule? To illustrate how the courts have applied a particular rule? Similarly, think about how the other side might use the case, about how a trial court might use the case, and how the appellate court might use the case.

As the preceding paragraphs indicate, in reading and analyzing a case, your role is anything but that of a passive reader. Instead, you are reading the case as a lawyer, looking not only for the rules and how those rules have been applied, but also for how you and any other parties might be able to use the case.

Chart 4.4 demonstrates how an attorney would approach the reading of an opinion on Westlaw. In this "think aloud," the attorney who is reading the case represents Ms. Olsen, a woman who wants to overturn a decision terminating her parental rights on the grounds that she was not properly served. At the time of service, Ms. Olsen was spending four nights each week at a halfway house for recovering addicts and three nights each week at her sister's house. The summons was left with her sister at her sister's house on a day on which Ms. Olsen was not at her sister's house. The text of the opinion is in the left-hand column and what the defense attorney thought as she read the opinion is in the right-hand column. Because the case is short, the attorney read the entire case.

Chart 4.4	Defense Attorney's Thoughts While Reading *Thompson v. State, Dept. of Revenue*

Text of Opinion	What Attorney Thought as She Read Opinion
Thompson v. State, Dept. of Revenue 867 So.2d 603 Fla.App. 1 Dist.,2004. March 05, 2004 (Approx. 3 pages) West Reporter Image (PDF) 867 So.2d 603, 29 Fla. L. Weekly D566	Okay, this case is mandatory authority. In addition, it is pretty recent. I need to remember to cite-check it to make sure that it is still good law.

(continues)

Continued

Briefs and Other Related Documents

District Court of Appeal of Florida,
First District.
Calvin THOMPSON, Appellant,
v.
STATE of Florida, DEPARTMENT OF REVENUE,
Appellee.
No. 1D03-2975.
March 5, 2004.

Background: Department of Revenue filed action against father to establish and enforce child support for daughter. The Circuit Court, Duval County, E. McRae Mathis, J., denied father's motion to quash service of process. Father appealed.

Holding: The District Court of Appeal, Van Nortwick, J., held that father made prima facie showing that Department's petition was not served on him at his usual place of abode.

Reversed and remanded.

West Headnotes

[1] KeyCite Notes 🔲

⚷ 76E Child Support
  ⚷ 76EV Proceedings
    ⚷ 76EV(A) In General
      ⚷ 76Ek180 k. Process. Most Cited Cases

Father's affidavit stating that he was separated from wife and had not resided with her for over three years was sufficient to make a prima facie showing that Department of Revenue's petition to establish and enforce child support, which was left with wife at her residence, was not served on father at his usual place of abode, for purposes of Department's attempt to establish valid substituted service. West's F.S.A. § 48.031.

[2] KeyCite Notes 🔲

⚷ 313 Process
  ⚷ 313II Service
    ⚷ 313II(B) Substituted Service

If it turns out that this case is on point, I should look at the briefs to see what the parties argued and which of those arguments the court found persuasive.

The father wanted the same thing that I want: to quash service.

Good. The issue in this case seems to be the same as the issue in my case. I want to establish that the sister's house was not my client's usual place of abode.

The facts in this case seem to be pretty different from the facts in my case. My client was staying with her sister a couple of nights a week. I may not be able to use this case as an analogous case.

(continues)

Continued

⟸313k76 Mode and Sufficiency of Service
⟸313k78 k. Leaving Copy at Residence or Other
Place. Most Cited Cases

The requirement that substituted service of process be at a defendant's "usual place of abode" means the place where the defendant is actually living at the time of service. West's F.S.A. § 48.031.

This looks like the rule. It also looks like a rule that I can use to support our argument. I need to look at this part of the opinion.

[3] KeyCite Notes 📖

⟸313 Process
  ⟸313II Service
    ⟸313II(A) Personal Service in General
      ⟸313k48 k. Nature and Necessity in General. Most
Cited Cases

⟸313 Process KeyCite Notes 📖
  ⟸313II Service
    ⟸313II(E) Return and Proof of Service
      ⟸313k144 Evidence as to Service
        ⟸313k145 k. Presumptions and Burden of Proof.
Most Cited Cases

The burden of proof to sustain the validity of service of process is upon the person who seeks to invoke the jurisdiction of the court and, without proper service of process, the court lacks personal jurisdiction over the defendant. West's F.S.A. § 48.031.

Good. Here is the rule about burden of proof. It looks like the state has the burden. I need to look at this part of the opinion.

[4] KeyCite Notes 📖

⟸313 Process
  ⟸313II Service
    ⟸313II(E) Return and Proof of Service
      ⟸313k144 Evidence as to Service
        ⟸313k145 k. Presumptions and Burden of Proof.
Most Cited Cases

⟸313 Process KeyCite Notes 📖
  ⟸313II Service
    ⟸313II(E) Return and Proof of Service
      ⟸313k144 Evidence as to Service
        ⟸313k149 k. Weight and Sufficiency. Most Cited
Cases

(continues)

Continued

A process server's return of service on a defendant which is regular on its face is presumed to be valid absent clear and convincing evidence presented to the contrary.

[5] KeyCite Notes [KC]

⌐313 Process
  ⌐313II Service
    ⌐313II(E) Return and Proof of Service
      ⌐313k144 Evidence as to Service
        ⌐313k148 k. Evidence to Impeach or Contradict Return, Certificate, or Affidavit of Service. Most Cited Cases

A simple denial of having received service is not sufficient to contradict a process server's return of service that is regular on its face.

*604 Esther A. Zaretsky, West Palm Beach, for Appellant. Charles J. Crist, Jr., Attorney General and Toni C. Bernstein and William H. Branch, Assistant Attorneys General, Tallahassee, for Appellee.

VAN NORTWICK, J.

Calvin Thompson appeals a non-final order denying his motion to quash service of process in this support-administrative paternity action filed by the Department of Revenue. We reverse and remand for an evidentiary hearing pursuant to *Venetian Salami Co. v. Parthenais*, 554 So.2d 499, 502-03 (Fla.1989).

Pursuant to section 409.2564, Florida Statutes (2002), the Department filed an action to establish and enforce child support for Thompson's four year-old daughter. The petition was served at 625 F Covenant Drive, Belle Glade, Florida 33430, and accepted by Thompson's wife. Thompson filed a motion to dismiss/quash for lack of service of process stating that he was not present at the Belle Glade address and was not personally served. In his attached affidavit, Thompson stated that he has been separated from his wife, that he has not resided at that address for over three years, and that he did not author-ize anyone to accept service of process on his behalf. The trial court entered an order ruling that any jurisdictional defect could be cured by mailing a copy of the petition and accompanying documents to Thompson's attorney, "who has made a general appearance." The Department correctly concedes that the jurisdictional defect cannot

---

This rule may hurt us. If the phrase "return of service" means what I think it does, then there will be a presumption that the service is valid, and we will have to present clear and convincing evidence. I need to read this part of the opinion, make sure that I know what return of service means, and check the file to see if in our case the return of service was regular.

This is just the procedural history. This was a paternity action. Thompson, who seems to be the father, moved to quash service.

Okay, the court is setting out the facts.

The petition was served at his wife's house, and his wife accepted service.

Thompson filed an affidavit stating that

(continues)

Continued

*605 be cured in the manner suggested by the trial court and that Thompson's argument that the trial court lacked personal jurisdiction was not waived because Thompson neither took affirmative action nor sought affirmative relief prior to raising the alleged defect. *See Coto-Ojeda v. Samuel*, 642 So.2d 587, 588 (Fla. 3d DCA 1994)(Cope, J., specially concurring).

he had been separated from his wife and had not resided at her house for three years.

Given our facts, most of this does not seem relevant.

[1] 🔲 [2] 🔲 [3] 🔲 Turning to the merits, "[s]ection 48.031 expressly requires that substituted service be at the person's usual place of abode." *Shurman v. A. Mortg. & Investment Corp.*, 795 So.2d 952, 954 *(Fla.2001)*. The requirement "usual place of abode" means "the place where the defendant is actually living at the time of service." *Id., citing State ex rel. Merritt v. Heffernan*, 142 Fla. 496, 195 So. 145, 147 (1940).

Although the court does not set out the issue on appeal, the issue seems to be whether the service was at the defendant's usual place of abode.

Good. Here is a definition of usual place of abode. Court cites an old Florida Supreme Court decision as authority.

The burden of proof to sustain the validity of service of process is upon the person who seeks to invoke the jurisdiction of the court and, without proper service of process, the court lacks personal jurisdiction over the defendant. *M.J.W. v. Department of Children and Families*, 825 So.2d 1038, 1041 (Fla. 1st DCA 2002).

Here are the rules about the burden of proof.

[4] 🔲 [5] 🔲 "[A] process server's return of service on a defendant which is regular on its face is presumed to be valid absent clear and convincing evidence presented to the contrary." *Telf Corp. v. Gomez*, 671 So.2d 818 (Fla. 3d DCA 1996). Although simple denial of service is not sufficient, *id.* at 819, Thompson's motion and affidavit are based on the fact that the service did not comply with section 48.031 and was therefore legally deficient. *National Safety Associates, Inc. v. Allstate Insurance Co.*, 799 So.2d 316, 317 (Fla. 2d DCA 2001). Thompson's affidavit makes a *prima facie* showing that he was not served at his usual place of abode by valid substituted

Okay, we are going to have to do more than just allege that the sister's house is not our client's usual place of abode. We are going to have to submit an affidavit establishing that her residence was somewhere else.

(continues)

Continued

service. *See, e.g., S.H. v. Department of Children and Families*, 837 So.2d 1117, 1118 (Fla. 4th DCA 2003)(invalidating substituted service on father at mother's address, where mother's residence was not father's "usual place of abode" at the time of service); *Gonzalez v. Totalbank*, 472 So.2d 861 (Fla. 3d DCA 1985)(invalidating substituted service when wife was separated from husband and not living at address where service was attempted). Having raised the issue of personal jurisdiction, Thompson's motion and accompanying affidavit placed the burden on the Department to establish the validity of service of process. *M.J.W.*, 825 So.2d at 1041. Accordingly, the cause is reversed and remanded for an evidentiary hearing to determine whether the attempted service of Thompson pursuant to section 48.031, Florida Statutes (2003), was valid. *See Venetian Salami*, 554 So.2d at 502-03; *Mowrey Elevator of Florida, Inc. v. Automated Integration*, 745 So.2d 1046, 1047-48 (Fla. 1st DCA 1999).
REVERSED and REMANDED.

KAHN and BENTON, JJ., concur.

These cases look like they are on point. I need to look at them once I finish reading this case.

I don't know whether Mr. Thompson won. However, the affidavit was enough to get the case back to the trial court for an evidentiary hearing.

We can use this case for the rules relating to what is and is not a person's usual place of abode and for the rules relating to the burden of proof. The State is going to say that our case is much weaker than this case. While Ms. Olson was staying with her sister three nights a week, Mr. Thompson hadn't (or says he hadn't) lived with his wife for three years. We are going to have to focus on the language—"actually living at the time of service" to argue that at the time of service Ms. Olsen was not actually living with her sister.

§ 4.4 Exercise

As you read the following case, write in the right-hand margin what you are thinking as you read. After you have finished doing your own "think aloud," compare what you wrote to what one of your classmates wrote.

Text of Opinion	What You Thought as You Read the Opinion
Shurman v. Atlantic Mortg. & Inv. Corp. 795 So.2d 952 Fla., 2001. September 06, 2001 (Approx. 5 pages)	

Supreme Court of Florida.
Gerald R. SHURMAN, Petitioner,
v.
ATLANTIC MORTGAGE & INVESTMENT
CORPORATION, Respondent.
No. SC96918.
Sept. 6, 2001.

Mortgage brought mortgage foreclosure action against inmate. The Circuit Court, Lake County, Don F. Briggs, J., entered final judgment against inmate based on default. Inmate appealed. The District Court of Appeal, 740 So.2d 1221, affirmed. Inmate sought discretionary review. The Supreme Court held that inmate's "usual place of abode" for service of process was prison, not home where inmate had lived with his wife.
Quashed and remanded.
Wells, C.J., concurred in result only and filed opinion, in which Harding, J., joined.

West Headnotes

[1] KeyCite Notes

313 Process
  313II Service
    313II(A) Personal Service in General
      313k48 k. Nature and Necessity in General. Most Cited Cases

The fundamental purpose of service of process is to give proper notice to the defendant in the case that he is answerable to the claim of plaintiff and, therefore, to vest jurisdiction in the court entertaining the controversy. West's F.S.A. § 48.031.

[2] KeyCite Notes [KC]

🔑313 Process
  🔑313II Service
    🔑313II(A) Personal Service in General
      🔑313k49 k. Statutory Provisions. Most Cited Cases

🔑313 Process KeyCite Notes [KC]
  🔑313II Service
    🔑313II(A) Personal Service in General
      🔑313k64 k. Mode and Sufficiency of Service. Most Cited Cases

Because of the importance of litigants receiving notice of actions against them, statutes governing service of process are to be strictly construed and enforced. West's F.S.A. § 48.031.

[3] KeyCite Notes [KC]

🔑266 Mortgage
  🔑266X Foreclosure by Action
    🔑266X(E) Parties and Process
      🔑266k440 k. Process in General. Most Cited Cases

Inmate's "usual place of abode" for service of process in foreclosure action was prison, not house where prisoner formerly lived with his wife, where inmate actually lived in prison. West's F.S.A. § 48.031.

*952 Gerald R. Shurman, pro se, Orlando, FL, for Petitioner. Anne S. Mason and Jennifer S. Ebanks of Mason & Associates, P.A., Clearwater, FL, for Respondent.

PER CURIAM.
We have for review *Shurman v. Atlantic Mortgage & Investment, 740 So.2d 1221 (Fla. 5th DCA 1999)*, which expressly and directly conflicts with *953 *State ex rel. Merritt v. Heffernan, 142 Fla. 496, 195 So. 145 (1940)*. We have jurisdiction. *See* art. V, § 3(b)(3), Fla. Const. For the reasons set forth below, we quash the decision of the district court.

FACTS

The record reflects that Gerald Shurman was criminally prosecuted, convicted, and incarcerated in state prison in May of 1997. Subsequently, Shurman was named as a defendant in a mortgage foreclosure action commenced in March of 1998 by Atlantic Mortgage & Investment Corporation (Atlantic). Service of process was effected on Shurman by substituted service on his wife, Emily, at their home where they had resided together before Shurman's incarceration. At the time of service of process Shurman was incarcerated in state prison. Because no responsive pleadings were filed by Shurman a default was entered against him in May of 1998. Thereafter, the trial court granted Atlantic's motion for final summary judgment of foreclosure and the property was sold at a foreclosure sale on June 25, 1998, to the second mortgagee.

On January 11, 1999, Shurman filed a motion to set aside the judgment alleging that he was not properly served process in the action and, therefore, the judgment as to his interest in the property was void. Following an evidentiary hearing on Shurman's motion, the trial court concluded that Shurman's "usual place of abode" for purposes of serving process under section 48.031, Florida Statutes (1997), was the residence where he lived with his wife prior to his incarceration and where his wife continued to reside afterward. As such, the trial court found that service was perfected when a copy of the process and complaint was left with Shurman's wife at their marital residence. In light of its finding that service was valid and that Shurman had not demonstrated any meritorious defense to the foreclosure action, the trial court denied Shurman's motion to set aside the judgment.

On appeal, the Fifth District affirmed the trial court's denial of Shurman's motion to set aside the judgment. *See Shurman v. Atlantic Mortgage & Inv.*, 740 So.2d 1221 (Fla. 5th DCA 1999). Relying on *Bull v. Kistner*, 257 Iowa 968, 135 N.W.2d 545 (1965), and *Montes v. Seda*, 157 Misc.2d 895, 599 N.Y.S.2d 401, 403 (Sup.Ct.1993), *aff'd*, 208 A.D.2d 388, 626 N.Y.S.2d 61 (1994), the district court agreed with the trial court's conclusion that service was made at Shurman's "usual place of abode." *Shurman*, 740 So.2d at 1222. The district court noted that Shurman and his wife had resided at the subject property for years prior to his incarceration and his family continued to reside there afterward. *See id.* at 1223. Accordingly, the court held that service was valid. *See id.* Shurman subsequently sought discretionary review in this Court.

ANALYSIS

The issue presented in this case is whether Shurman was properly served at his "usual place of abode" as required under section 48.031, Florida Statutes (1997). Shurman argues that since he was incarcerated at the time of service his "usual place of abode" was prison and, as such, he should have been served there in order to be afforded due process. By contrast, Atlantic asserts that an incarcerated party's "usual place of abode" is where the party resided prior to incarceration if the party's family continues to reside there.

[1] It is well settled that the fundamental purpose of service is "to give proper notice to the defendant in the case that he is answerable to the claim of plaintiff and, therefore, to vest jurisdiction in the court entertaining the controversy." *State ex rel. Merritt v. Heffernan*, 142 Fla. 496, 195 So. 145, 147 (1940); *see also* *954 *Klosenski v. Flaherty*, 116 So.2d 767, 768 (Fla.1959) (quoting *Heffernan*); *Clark v. Clark*, 158 Fla. 731, 30 So.2d 170, 171 (1947) ("The purpose of constructive or substituted service is to bring knowledge of the pending litigation to the defendant in order that he may appear and guard his interests."); *Gribbel v. Henderson,* 151 Fla. 712, 10 So.2d 734, 739 (1942); *Arcadia Citrus Growers Ass'n v. Hollingsworth*, 135 Fla. 322, 185 So. 431, 434 (1938). In other words, the purpose of this jurisdictional scheme is to give the person affected notice of the proceedings and an opportunity to defend his rights.

[2] Section 48.031, Florida Statutes (1997), provides in pertinent part:

> (1)(a) Service of original process is made by delivering a copy of it to the person to be served with a copy of the complaint, petition, or other initial pleading or paper or by leaving the copies at his or her usual place of abode with any person residing therein who is 15 years of age or older and informing the person of their contents.

§ 48.031(1)(a), Fla. Stat. (1997). Section 48.031 expressly requires that substituted service be at the person's "usual place of abode." *Id.* Further, because of the importance of litigants receiving notice of actions against them, statutes governing service of process are to be strictly construed and enforced. *See Schupak v. Sutton Hill Assocs.*, 710 So.2d 707, 708 (Fla. 4th DCA 1998); *Aero Costa Rica, Inc. v. Dispatch Servs., Inc.*, 710 So.2d 218, 219 (Fla. 3d DCA 1998); *Hauser v. Schiff*, 341 So.2d 531, 531 (Fla. 3d DCA 1977).

In *Heffernan*, this Court defined the term "usual place of abode" as meaning the place where the defendant is actually living at the time of service. *See Heffernan*, 195 So. at 147. In so doing, we quoted favorably from *Eckman v. Grear*, 14 N.J. Misc. 807, 187 A. 556 (Com.Pl.1936), and *Mygatt v. Coe*, 63 N.J.L. 510, 44 A. 198 (Sup.Ct.1899):

We quote further from the case of *Eckman v. Grear*, 187 A. 556, 558, 14 N.J.Misc. 807:

"Going one step further, 'usual place of abode' is the place where the defendant is actually living at the time of the service. The word abode means one's fixed place of residence for the time being when the service is made. Thus, if a person have several residences, he must be served at the residence in which he is actually living at the time service is made."

And in *Mygatt v. Coe*, 63 N.J.L. 510, 512, 44 A. 198, 199, the following pertinent statement appears:

"The statute does not direct service to be made at the 'residence' of the defendant, but at his 'dwelling house' or 'usual place of abode,' which is a much more restricted term. As was said in *Stout v. Leonard*, 37 N.J.L. 492, many persons have several residences, which they permanently maintain, occupying one at one period of the year and another at another period. Where such conditions exist, a summons must be served at the dwelling house in which the defendant is living at the time when the service is made."

Heffernan, 195 So. at 147. *See also Milanes v. Colonial Penn Ins. Co.*, 507 So.2d 777, 778 (Fla. 3d DCA 1987); *Panter v. Werbel-Roth Securities, Inc.*, 406 So.2d 1267, 1268 (Fla. 4th DCA 1981); *Hauser*, 341 So.2d at 532.

Not surprisingly, in applying the definition of the term "usual place of abode" set forth in *Heffernan*, courts have frequently invalidated substituted service of process in cases where the defendant was not actually living at the place where service was made. *See, e.g.,* *955 *Alvarez v. State Farm Mutual Auto Ins. Co.*, 635 So.2d 131, 132 (Fla. 3d DCA 1994) (invalidating substituted service on defendant's cousin where affidavits and supporting documentation, including a telephone bill and marriage license, established defendant was not living at that address on the date of service); *Milanes*, 507 So.2d at 778 (noting that service of process on the residence of defendant's ex-wife did not satisfy section 48.031); *Stern v. Gad*, 505 So.2d 531, 532 (Fla. 3d DCA 1987) (holding mere ownership of a condominium and service upon the wife of an owner will not suffice to establish "usual place of abode," when defendant submitted affidavit that he was not in the jurisdiction on the date of purported service and did not reside in the United States); *Gonzalez v. Totalbank*, 472 So.2d 861, 864 (Fla. 3d DCA 1985) (invalidating substituted service where wife was separated from husband and no longer living at address where service was attempted); *Panter*, 406 So.2d at 1268 (finding substituted service at home of appellant's father invalid where uncontradicted affidavits stated appellant was living in Michigan when service was made). Notably, several of these cases involved familial relationships where presumably the defendant would be more likely to receive notice, yet the courts still invalidated the service of process because the defendant was not actually living at the place where service was made. *See Alvarez*, 635 So.2d at 132 (substituted service on defendant's cousin); *Stern*, 505 So.2d at 532 (substituted service on wife); *Panter*, 406 So.2d at 1268 (substituted service on appellant's father).

[3] In this case it is uncontradicted that Shurman had been incarcerated in prison in May of 1997 and had not been living with his wife for at least nine months prior to the time substituted service was effected. Although Atlantic argues that Shurman's "usual place of abode" was where he lived with his family before being incarcerated, Shurman was "actually living" in prison at the time of service. Thus, under our obligation to strictly construe the statutory notice provisions and our analysis in *Heffernan,* it is apparent that Shurman's "usual place of abode" was prison, not his prior residence. *See Heffernan*, 195 So. at 147.

We find additional support for our decision in *Heffernan* and our conclusion that prison was Shurman's "usual place of abode" in *Fidelity & Deposit Co. v. Abagnale*, 97 N.J.Super. 132, 234 A.2d 511 (1967), and *Saienni v. Oveide*, 355 A.2d 707 (Del.Super.Ct.1976).[FN1] In *Abagnale,* the court rejected the defendant's argument that he could be reached by substituted service in New Jersey while he was incarcerated out-of-state. The court explained:

    FN1. We recognize that the majority of jurisdictions have reached a different conclusion. *See Blue Cross & Blue Shield v. Chang*, 109 F.R.D. 669 (E.D.Mich.1986); *Bohland v Smith*, 7 F.R.D. 364 (F.D.Ill.1947); *Grant v. Dalliber*, 11 Conn. 234 (1836); *Bull v. Kistner*, 257 Iowa 968, 135 N.W.2d 545 (1965); *Fidelity & Deposit Co. v. Boundy*, 236 Mo.App. 656, 158 S.W.2d 243 (1942); *Walker v. Stevens*, 52 Neb. 653, 72 N.W. 1038 (1897); *Montes v. Seda*, 157 Misc.2d 895, 599 N.Y.S.2d 401 (Sup.Ct.1993), *aff'd,*208 A.D.2d 388, 626 N.Y.S.2d 61 (1994); *Smith v. Hooton*, 3 Pa.D. 250 (1894). *See generally* Allen E. Korpela, Annotation, *Construction of Phrase "Usual Place of Abode," or Similar Terms Referring to Abode, Residence, or Domicil, as Used in Statutes Relating to Service of Process,* 32 A.L.R.3d 112, § 16 (1970). However, we believe that the better view is that one's "usual place of abode" is where the person is actually living at the time of service, even in cases involving prisoners.

The law in this State has developed in somewhat rigid conformity to the principle that provisions for substituted service, being in derogation of the common law, must be strictly construed. Hence, the rule has been consistently applied *956 that one's "dwelling house or usual place of abode" is limited in its meaning to the place where one is "actually living" at the time when service is made. The expectation that a defendant will normally receive notice of process served through a competent member of his household living at the same place of abode as he, does not, it seems to me, prevail in the setting of familial disorganization frequently ensuing where the head of the household is committed to prison. *Abagnale*, 234 A.2d at 519 (citations omitted). While the court recognized some jurisdictions had concluded that an incarcerated party's usual place of abode continues to be where his family resides, it distinguished those cases on the basis that they were "largely influenced, if not governed, by a hybrid of residence and domicile." *Id.* The Delaware court in *Saienni* followed *Abagnale* and held that the defendant, who was incarcerated in Pennsylvania, was not properly served at his usual place of abode by substituted service on his wife in Delaware. The court noted that in Delaware a person's usual place of abode is not the equivalent of his domicile. *See Saienni, 355 A.2d at 708.* Rather, for purposes of substituted service, a defendant must be served at the place where he is actually living at the time service is made. *See id.* (citing *Whetsel v. Gosnell*, 181 A.2d 91 (Del.1962)). Relying on *Abagnale* and *Whetsel,* the court concluded that the defendant's usual place of abode was the Pennsylvania State Correctional Institution since that was where the defendant was physically living at the time of service. *See id.* We find the reasoning of the courts in *Abagnale* and *Saienni* persuasive in this case. As stated previously, the object of all process is to impart to the person affected notice of the proceeding and an opportunity to defend his rights. *See Klosenski*, 116 So.2d at 768; *Clark*, 30 So.2d at 171; *Gribbel*, 10 So.2d at 739; *Heffernan*, 195 So. at 147; *Arcadia Citrus Growers Ass'n*, 185 So. at 434. By applying the definition of "usual place of abode" set forth in *Heffernan* to the facts in this case, we are adhering to this underlying principle. Further, it is clear that the Legislature contemplated that people in prison would be sued and served with process. Section 48.051, Florida Statutes (1997), provides that "[p]rocess against a state prisoner shall be served on the prisoner." *Id. Cf. State ex rel. Page v. Hollingsworth*, 117 Fla. 288, 157 So. 887 (1934). Had the Legislature intended the term "usual place of abode" to apply differently to prisoners, it could have so stated. Hence, we see no need to depart from *Heffernan* in cases involving prisoners. In sum, we adhere to *Heffernan* and reaffirm that for purposes of substituted service one's "usual place of abode" is where the person is actually living at the time of service. In this case, it is uncontroverted that Shurman was actually living in prison at the time substituted service was made on his wife at their marital residence. Thus, Shurman was not properly served at his usual place of abode as required under section 48.031(1)(a), Florida Statutes (1997). Accordingly, we quash the decision of the district court of appeal and remand for further proceedings consistent herewith.

It is so ordered.

SHAW, HARDING, ANSTEAD, PARIENTE, LEWIS, and QUINCE, JJ., concur.

WELLS, C.J., concurs with an opinion, in which HARDING, J., concurs.

WELLS, C.J., concurring.

I concur in result only in this case. I conclude that this decision should be controlled by the plain meaning of *957 section 48.051, Florida Statutes, which states: "Process against a state prisoner shall be served on the prisoner." I would read this to mean that process should be served on the prisoner at the prison. I do not believe reliance on section 48.031(1)(a), Florida Statutes, is appropriate.

HARDING, J., concurs.

Reprinted with permission.

Reading Statutes and Cases

Until a few years ago, most law professors and experienced attorneys assumed that law students and new attorneys read statutes and cases in the same way that they read them. While some individuals come to law school reading as experienced attorneys read, most do not. As a consequence, during their first year of law school, many law students have to "unlearn" the reading strategies that they used as undergraduates or in their home countries and learn a new way of reading. For example, many first-year law students have to change their focus from passively reading for information to a much more engaged and critical form of reading.

This chapter tries to speed up the process of learning how to read as lawyers read by identifying both the characteristics of good legal readers and the strategies that good legal readers use. Although you may be tempted to skip this chapter, don't. While the research on legal reading is limited, the research that does exist suggests that there is a strong correlation between reading like a lawyer and doing well on law school exams.

§ 5.1 Good Lawyers Are Good Readers

Good lawyers are good readers. When they read a document, statute, or case, they read exactly what is on the page. They do not skip words, read in words, or misread words. In addition, they have good vocabularies. They recognize and understand most of the words that they read, and the ones that they do not recognize or understand they look up either in a book or an online dictionary.

There are a number of good, free online dictionaries. For example, *Merriam-Webster's Online Dictionary* is at http://www.m-w.com; the *Cambridge Dictionaries Online* is at http://dictionary.cambridge.org; *JURIST's Legal Dictionaries* are at http://jurist.law.pitt.edu/dictionary.htm; and *FindLaw's Legal Dictionary* is at http://dictionary.lp.findlaw.com.

Poor reading skills can significantly affect your ability to understand what you are reading. For instance, in the following example, which is taken from the transcript of a law student reading a case aloud, Jackie, a first-year student, mispronounced and apparently did not recognize the word "palatial."[1]

EXAMPLE   **Transcript of Jackie's Think Aloud**

Some months prior to the alleged imprisonment, the plaintiff, while in Jaffa, announced her intention to leave the sect. The defendant, with the help of the plaintiff's husband, persuaded the plaintiff to return to the United States aboard the sect's [platial] yacht, the Kingdom.

James, another student who read the same case, misread the following sentence. The first example shows how the sentence appears in the casebook. The second sentence shows how James read it when he read the sentence aloud.

EXAMPLE   **Sentence as It Appears in the Casebook**

According to the uncontradicted evidence, at no time did any one physically restrain the plaintiff except for the defendant's refusal, once the plaintiff announced her decision to quit the yacht, to let the plaintiff use a small boat to take herself, her children, and belongings ashore.

---

[1] The examples in this section come from Laurel Currie Oates, *Beating the Odds, Reading Strategies of Law Students Admitted Through Special Admissions Programs*, 83 Iowa L. Rev. 139 (1997). See also Laurel Currie Oates, *Leveling the Playing Field: Helping Students Succeed by Helping Them Learn to Read as Expert Lawyers*, 80 St. John's L. Rev. 227 (2006).

EXAMPLE   **Sentence as James Read It**

According to the uncontradicted evidence, at no time did any one physically restrain the plaintiff except for the defendant's (pause) defendant's refusal once (pause) defendant's refusal once (pause) the plaintiff announced her decision to quit the yacht to let the plaintiff use a small boat to take herself, her children, and belongings ashore.

When questioned about what the court was saying in this sentence, James stated that the defendant had, on one occasion, refused to let the plaintiff take the boat. In fact, the court says that the refusal came once the defendant announced her decision to quit the yacht.

Although at first these errors may seem insignificant, in each instance they resulted in the student misunderstanding the case and, thus, the rules and the court's reasoning. In addition, in both instances, the errors were a harbinger of things to come. Both students ended up doing poorly on their exams. At the end of the first year, Jackie was in the bottom 20 percent of her class, and James had flunked out.

To determine whether you may be misreading cases, make two copies of one of the cases in your casebook. Keep one copy for yourself, and give the other to a trusted classmate or teaching assistant. Then read aloud from your copy while your partner follows along on his or her copy, highlighting any words or phrases that you misread and any words that you mispronounce or do not appear to understand. After you have finished your reading of the case, compare your understanding of the case with your partner's. Did you both read the case in essentially the same way? If your partner noted more than one or two problems or if your understanding of the case is substantially different from your partner's, try the following. First, try reading more slowly. You may be trying to read the material too quickly. Second, take the time to look up any words that you are not sure that you understand. Third, if the problems appear to be serious, ask your school's learning center if it can provide you with a more thorough evaluation of your reading skills.

§ 5.2 Good Legal Readers Read and Reread Material Until They Are Sure They Understand It

While in some types of reading you can skip sections that you do not completely understand, such a strategy does not work when you are doing legal reading. If the document, statute, or case is one that is relevant to your problem, you need to read and reread it until you are sure that you understand it.

The following example shows how a first-year student, William, read and reread a case until he was sure that he understood it. The material in the regular typeface is the text of the case. The material in italics is what William said after he had read that section of the text.

EXAMPLE   ### Excerpt from William's Think Aloud

Whittaker v. Sanford
110 Me. 77, 88 S. 399 (1912)

Savage, J. Action for false imprisonment. The plaintiff recovered a verdict for $1100. The case comes up on defendant's exceptions and a motion for a new trial.

So the defendant is the appellant and is appealing the verdict of $1100.

The plaintiff had been a member of a religious sect, which had colonies in Maine and in Jaffa, Syria, and of which the defendant was a leader. Some months prior to the alleged imprisonment, the plaintiff, while in Jaffa, announced her intention to leave the sect.

I need to reread this again [rereads sentence]. So just prior to the alleged imprisonment the plaintiff was in Jaffa and expressed an intention to leave the sect. At this point, I am a bit confused about who the parties are. I need to reread this to make sure that I have the facts straight, [rereads from the beginning.] OK. This is an action for false imprisonment. The plaintiff recovered a verdict for $1100. The case came up on the defendant's exceptions. The plaintiff is a member of the sect and the defendant is the head of the sect so Whittaker is the member of the sect and Sanford is its leader.

Although it took William more time to read the case than it took some of the other students, the payoff was substantial. Although his undergraduate GPA and LSAT placed William in the bottom 10 percent of his entering law school class, at the end of his first year, his law school GPA placed him in the top 10 percent.

There are several things you can do to make sure that you understand the cases that you are reading. First, see if you can diagram the action. At the trial court level, who sued whom and what was the cause of action? Who "won" at trial, who filed the appeal, and what is the issue on appeal?

PRACTICE POINTER   In some instances, you may be able to compare your chart showing the case's prior and subsequent history with the chart that is on KeyCite under Direct History, Graphical View.

Second, do not underestimate the value of preparing your own case briefs. While it may be faster and easier to highlight sections of a statute or case, highlighting does not ensure that you understand the material you are reading. In fact, there is some evidence that students who highlight remember less than students who do not highlight: (In highlighting a section, some students focus their attention on the process of highlighting and not on the material that they are highlighting. As a result, when they are asked to recall what it is that they just highlighted, they are unable to do so.)

Finally, after reading a statute or case, test yourself to make sure you understand what you just read. After reading a statute, diagram that statute. See section 3.4.4. After reading a case, answer the following questions: (1) What issue was before the court? (2) What was the standard of review? (3) What rule did the court apply? (4) In applying the rule, what facts did the court consider? (5) What did the court decide, and why did it decide the case that way? (6) What was the disposition: did the appellate court affirm, reverse, or remand? See section 3.4.4. If you cannot diagram the statute or answer these questions about the case, keep reading until you can.

§ 5.3 Good Legal Readers Synthesize the Statutes and Cases They Read

In addition to reading accurately and until they understand the statutes and cases, good legal readers synthesize the statutes and cases that they read.

Synthesis is the process of putting the pieces together. You take each of the statutory sections and cases you have read and try to make sense of them. Are they consistent? What are the steps in the analysis? How do they fit into your existing conceptual frameworks?

The following example shows the type of synthesis that a law professor did in reading a restatement section and a case. The text is set out in regular type and the professor's comments in italics.

EXAMPLE   **Excerpt from Law Professor's Think Aloud**

There was evidence that the plaintiff had been ashore a number of times, had been on numerous outings and had been treated as a guest during her stay aboard the yacht. According to the uncontradicted evidence, at no time did anyone physically restrain the plaintiff except for the defendant's refusal, once the plaintiff announced her decision to quit the yacht, to let the plaintiff use a small boat to take herself, her children, and her belongings ashore.

I'm sort of getting a visual image of the boat that she was in and out of . . . uhm . . . the plaintiff had been ashore. I'm thinking about the elements that I just read [a reference to the *Restatement* section that had been set out immediately before the case] *and I'm trying to see how, I guess, frankly how I would decide the case on a certain level before I even want to know what Judge Savage thought.* [pause] *I need to look at the Restatement section* [looks back at the *Restatement* section]. *Is the defendant acting to or with intent to confine the plaintiff? She got off the boat. That kind of bothers me. That results directly or indirectly in confinement. Maybe that's relevant here. The other is conscious of the confinement or is harmed by it. Given the facts, that bothers me too.*

Doing synthesis is time consuming and hard work. You are no longer reading just for information. Instead, as you are reading, you are either

placing new information into existing conceptual frameworks or constructing completely new frameworks.

If you are like most law students, at some point you will argue that law
school would be a lot easier if your professors put the pieces together for
you, if they just gave you their conceptual frameworks. If you had come to
law school just to learn the law, you would be right. It would be easier for
both you and your professors if they just gave you the law. However, there
is a lot more to law school than just learning the law. Although you will
learn some law while you are in law school, the real reason that you came
to law school was to learn to think like a lawyer. Thus, the primary skills you
will need to teach yourself while you are in law school are how to do legal
analysis and synthesis. You need to be able to look at a statute and a group
of cases and determine what the law is and how it might be applied in a
particular situation.

§ 5.4 Good Legal Readers Place Statutes and Cases into Their Historical, Social, Economic, Political, and Legal Contexts

Good legal readers understand that statutes are usually enacted to solve a
problem or to promote certain interests and that judicial decisions reflect,
at least in part, the time and place in which they were written. As a consequence, in reading statutes and cases, good legal readers place those statutes and cases in their historical, social, economic, political, and legal
contexts. They note the date that the statute was enacted and amended (if
applicable) and the year in which the case was decided. They think about
the social and economic conditions during those periods and about the
political issues that were in the headlines when the statute was enacted or
amended or the case was decided. Finally, they place the case in its larger
legal context. They determine how the particular issue fits into the broader
area of law, they note whether the decision is from an intermediate court
of appeals or from the highest court in the jurisdiction, and they read the
court's decision in light of the standard of review that the court applied.
Was the court deciding the issue *de novo,* or was it simply looking to see
whether there was sufficient evidence to support the jury's verdict?

PRACTICE POINTER   If you do not know what the phrase *de novo*
means, look it up in a print or online dictionary.
When you use the online link on FindLaw, you
retrieve the following information:

[de̱-'no̱-vo̱, da̱-]
Medieval Latin, literally, from (the) new
: over again: as if for the first time: as

(continues)

Continued

> a: allowing independent appellate determination of issues (as of fact or law)
> Example: a de novo review
> b: allowing complete retrial upon new evidence
> (compare abuse of discretion clearly erroneous)
>
> Note: A *de novo* review is an in-depth review. Decisions of federal administrative agencies are generally subject to *de novo* review in the United States District Courts, and some lower state court decisions are subject to *de novo* review at the next level.

Reprinted with permission.

In reading the case that is set out in the examples in this chapter, the professor placed the case in its historical, social, and political context. First, she noted that the case was an old one. It was decided by the Maine Supreme Judicial Court in 1912. Second, she noted that in 1912, $1,100 would have been a substantial amount of money. Third, she considered the social climate in 1912: the role of women and their rights and the public's attitudes about "religious cults." She knew that in 1912 women had far fewer rights than they do today. For instance, it was often the husband who determined where the couple lived and what religion they practiced. What she did not know was how religious cults were viewed. In 1912 did people view religious cults in the same way that most people view them today? Were cults seen as a problem? How did these factors influence the court's decision and the way it wrote its opinion?

You need to think about the cases that you read in similar ways. When you are reading cases, pay close attention to the dates of the decisions and the courts that issued them. If you read the cases in chronological order, can you discern a trend? Over the last five, twenty-five, or fifty years have the rules or the way the courts apply those rules changed? If the answer is yes, what social, economic, or political events might account for those changes? In contrast, if you arrange the decisions by jurisdiction, does a pattern appear? For example, do industrial states tend to take one approach and more rural states another? Are some jurisdictions more conservative while others more liberal? If you read between the lines, what do you think motivated the judges and persuaded them to decide the case in one way rather than another?

§ 5.5 Good Legal Readers "Judge" the Statutes and Cases They Read

As a beginning law student, you may be tempted to "accept" everything you read. You may be thinking, who am I to judge the soundness of a Supreme Court Justice's analysis or Congress's choice of a particular word or phrase? Do not give in to this temptation. If you are going to be a good legal reader, you need to question and evaluate everything you read.

In judging the cases that you read, make sure you do more than evaluate the facts. Although in the following example William engages in some evaluation, it is the evaluation of a non-lawyer. He evaluates the witness's testimony but not the court's choice of rule, application of the rules to the facts, or reasoning. Once again, the text of the case is set out using a regular typeface and William's thoughts are in italics.

EXAMPLE   **Excerpt from William's Think Aloud**

There was evidence that the plaintiff had been ashore a number of times, had been on numerous outings and had been treated as a guest during her stay aboard the yacht.

So at this point I'm getting a picture of what happened . . . I'm not sure though. There is evidence that the plaintiff had been ashore so at this point I'm thinking was she really held against her will. So I have doubts . . . doubts about the plaintiff's story at this point.

According to the uncontradicted evidence, at no time did anyone physically restrain the plaintiff except for the defendant's refusal, once the plaintiff announced her decision to quit the yacht, to let the plaintiff use a small boat to take herself, her children, and her belongings ashore.

Well . . . the defendant by this point isn't really stopping the plaintiff from leaving.

Throughout the entire episode the plaintiff's husband was with her and repeatedly tried to persuade her to change her mind and remain with the sect.

At this point, mentally, I think . . . I don't think the plaintiff's story holds water . . . that's what I am thinking. Because her husband was there so maybe you, there's in my mind that her story doesn't hold water. So I am thinking at this point that the court might end up reversing her position.

In contrast, the professor evaluated the court's conclusion and reasoning. After she finished reading the case, the professor made the following comments. (Note how the professor talks about the elements of the tort and how she poses a hypothetical.)

EXAMPLE   **Excerpt from Professor's Think Aloud**

I'm not sure that the plaintiff proved all of the elements of false imprisonment. For example, I'm not sure that the plaintiff proved that the defendant intended to confine the plaintiff. If I remember correctly, [pause] on a number of occasions he allowed her to go ashore. He just wouldn't let her use the small boat to take her children and their things ashore. It would have been interesting to know what would have happened if a boat had come to get the plaintiff. Would the defendant have let her go? If he would have, there wouldn't have been false imprisonment [pause]. The facts may, however, support a finding that the defendant's actions resulted in confinement. In those days, the plaintiff may not have had a way to contact anyone on shore to ask them to come get her. Although the court may have reached the right result, I wish Judge Savage had done more analysis [pause]. I get the feeling that he had made up is mind, maybe he didn't like cults, and then just tried to justify his conclusion.

§ 5.6 Good Legal Readers Read for a Specific Purpose

The reading you do for your law school classes is very different from the reading you will do in practice. In law school, you read so you will be prepared for class. Consider the following comment made by James.

> When I read cases, I usually read them not for briefing cases per se, but more out of fear of being called on in class. I don't want to look like a fool so I just want to know the basic principles.

In contrast, in practice, you will read for a specific purpose. For example, you will read to keep up to date in an area of law, to find the answer to a question a client has posed, to find statutes or cases to support your client's position, or to find holes in your opponent's arguments.

In reading the statutes and cases for your legal writing assignments, read not as a student, but as a lawyer. Initially, read to find out what the law is. Analyze the statutes and cases that you have found, and then put the pieces together. Then read the cases as the parties and the court would read them. Begin by putting yourself in your client's position. How can your client use the statutes and cases to support its position? Put yourself in the other side's shoes. How could the other side use the same statutes and cases to support its position? Finally, put yourself in the court's position. If you were the judge, how would you read the statutes and cases?

§ 5.7 Good Legal Readers Understand that Statutes and Cases Can Be Read in More than One Way

Different people have different beliefs about text. While some people believe that there is a right way to read each statute or case, others believe that most statutes and cases can be read in more than one way. For those in the first group, the meaning of a particular text is fixed. For those in the second group, the meaning of a particular text is "constructed" by juries and judges and the attorneys who practice before them.

As a general rule, the students who seem to have the easiest time in their first year of law school are those students who believe that statutes and cases can be read in more than one way, that the meaning of a particular text is socially constructed. These students have an easier time seeing how each side might interpret a particular statute and in stating a rule so it favors their client's position. When they talk about a court's holding, they refer to it as "a holding" and not "the holding."

If you are a student who believes that meaning is fixed, be aware of how your belief system is affecting the way you read statutes and cases and the way you make arguments. In reading cases, can you see how both the plaintiff and the defendant might be able to use the same case to support its argument? In making arguments, are you able to see what the other side might argue and how you might be able to respond to those arguments? Are you spending too much time looking for the correct answer and not enough time creating that answer? In contrast, if you are a student who believes that meaning is socially constructed, be careful that you do not become cynical or only a hired gun. Although there may be many ways of reading a particular statute or case, not all of those readings will lead to a "just" result.

In closing, keep in mind that learning to read, think, and write like a lawyer takes time. There are no crash courses, shortcuts, or magic wands. Instead, you will learn to read and think like a lawyer through trial and error and by observing how real lawyers—not T.V. lawyers—read and think about statutes and cases.

§ 5.8 Exercise

Using the think aloud that you did as an exercise at the end of Chapter 4 (see section 4.4), diagnose your own strengths and weaknesses as a legal reader.

1. Did you read what was on the page? Did you skip words, read in words, or misread words? Did you look up words that you did not know?
2. If you did not understand the opinion, or a part of it, did you read and reread until you did?
3. Did you engage in synthesis? For example, did you compare the court's decision in *Shurman* (the case set out in section 4.4) with the court's decision in *Thompson* (the case set out Chart 4.3)? Did both cases involve the same issue? Are the decisions consistent? Did both courts rely on the same authorities? Did both courts employ the same reasoning?
4. Did you put *Shurman* in its historical, political, social, economic, and legal context? Is *Shurman* a relatively old or a relatively new case? Was there anything going on at the time that *Shurman* was decided that might have influenced the court? Have political, social, or economic conditions changed since *Shurman* was decided? How are the issues that were raised in *Shurman* related to other legal issues?
5. Did you evaluate the court's decision? Did the majority apply the rule or rules that it set out? Is the majority's reasoning

sound? Is the approach that is set out in the concurring opinion better or worse than the approach set out in the majority opinion? Is the result "just"?

6. In reading the opinion, what role did you assume? Did you think about how you might use the case if you were representing a client who wanted to challenge service of process? If you were representing a client who wanted to argue that service was proper? If you were a trial court judge?

7. Is there more than one way to read the court's opinion? What would be a narrow reading of the court's holding? A broad reading of the court's holding?

PART

II

Objective
Memoranda

6

Drafting
Memos

So how difficult can it be to write a memo? Unfortunately, if the memo is a legal memo, it can be very difficult. To write a good memo, you need to know how to do legal research; how to analyze and synthesize statutes, regulations, and cases; how to construct arguments; how to evaluate the relative merits of different arguments; and how to write about complex issues clearly and concisely. In other words, you need to be able to think and write like a lawyer.

While this chapter and the other chapters in this part give you the information that you need to draft a memo, it will take time—and several dozen memos—to become proficient. Just as it takes years for doctors to develop the expertise to diagnose an illness or perform surgery, it takes years for lawyers to develop the expertise required to do sophisticated analysis, to construct winning arguments, and to predict with confidence how a court might rule on a particular issue.

There is, however, good news. Although it may take you years to become an expert, you can write a good memo if you keep in mind who you your audience is, what your purpose is, and the conventional formats for memos.

§ 6.1 Audience

For an objective memo, or office memo, your primary audience is other attorneys in your office. In most instances, a more experienced attorney asks a law student or newer attorney to research an issue and write a memo setting out not only the law but also how that law applies to a particular situation, for example, how the law might apply in a particular client's case. While sometimes a copy of the memo will be sent to the client, memos are attorney work product and, therefore, are not discoverable. Thus, neither an opposing party nor the courts have a right to see these memos.

§ 6.2 Purpose

Your primary purpose in writing an office memo is to give the attorneys in your law office the information they need to evaluate a case, advise a client, or draft another document, for example, a complaint, brief, or contract. Thus, your memo needs to be objective. In drafting the statement of facts, include both the facts that favor your client and the facts that favor the other side. In addition, in setting out the issue and the rules, be neutral. Do not slant your statement of the issue or your statement of the rules so that they favor your client. Most importantly, in setting out the arguments, give appropriate weight to each side's arguments and, in setting out your conclusions, be critical and candid.

§ 6.3 Conventions

Because objective memos are in-house documents, there are no rules governing their format. As a result, the format used for a memo varies from office to office and even from lawyer to lawyer. Consequently, before writing a memo, ask the attorney who is assigning the project what format he or she prefers and for an example of a well-written memo.

While this book shows you how to write a formal memo, there will be times when the attorney you are working for wants something different. For example, there may be times when the only thing that the attorney wants is a summary of the law: he or she does not want you to apply that law to the facts of the client's case, set out each side's arguments, or predict how a court might decide the issue. (For an example of such a memo, see the memo set out in section 6.4.1.) At other times, the attorney will want you to use a format that is different from the ones used in this book. For instance, the attorney may want you to set out the issues before the facts, or the attorney may not want a brief answer. (For an example of memo written using a different format, see the memo set out in section 6.4.3.) Finally, while some attorneys may want you to organize your discussion of the issues using a script format, others may want you to use a more integrated format. (Compare the discussion section of the memo set out in section 6.4.2 with the discussion section of the memo set out in section 6.4.3.) The bottom line is that you should give the attorney what he or she wants. Take what you learn in this book and modify it so it meets the needs, and preferences, of your particular audience.

§ 6.4 Sample Memos

The examples set out below illustrate some of the types of memos you may be asked to write. The first example (see section 6.4.1) is a relatively informal memo in which the writer sets out the law but does not apply it. The second, third, and fourth memos (sections 6.4.2 through 6.4.4) are more formal memos. While both the second and the third examples involve a single issue that requires an elements analysis, the examples differ in two ways. In the second example, the writer sets out the facts before the issue statement and brief answer and organizes the discussion section using a script format. In contrast, in the third example, the writer sets out the issue statement first, does not include a brief answer, and organizes the discussion section using an integrated format. (For more on organizing the discussion section using a script format, see Chapter 9. For more on organizing the discussion section using an integrated format, see Chapter 10.) The fourth example is a formal memo that discusses three issues, the last of which involves an issue of first impression. (For more on organizing the discussion section for a memo involving an issue of first impression, see Chapter 11.) The last example is a bench memo.

§ 6.4.1 Informal Memo in Which the Writer
Sets Out but Does Not Apply the Law

TO: Supervising Attorney
FROM: Legal Intern
DATE: October 18, 2006
RE: Washington's recreational use statutes

You have asked me to provide you with a brief summary of Washington's recreational use statutes and the cases that have applied those statutes.

The Washington State Legislature enacted Washington's recreational use statutes to encourage property owners to open their property to the public for recreational purposes by providing property owners with immunity from liability. RCW 4.24.200.[1] Subsection (1) of RCW 4.24.210 reads as follows:

---

[1] Because this memo was written for a Washington attorney, the author used the Washington citation rules. See Appendix 2 in the *ALWD Citation Manual, 3d ed.*

(1) Except as otherwise provided in subsection (3) or (4) of this section, any public or private landowners or others in lawful possession and control of any lands whether designated resource, rural, or urban, or water areas or channels and lands adjacent to such areas or channels, who allow members of the public to use them for the purposes of outdoor recreation, which term includes, but is not limited to, the cutting, gathering, and removing of firewood by private persons for their personal use without purchasing the firewood from the landowner, hunting, fishing, camping, picnicking, swimming, hiking, bicycling, skateboarding or other nonmotorized wheel-based activities, hang gliding, paragliding, rock climbing, the riding of horses or other animals, clam digging, pleasure driving of off-road vehicles, snowmobiles, and other vehicles, boating, nature study, winter or water sports, viewing or enjoying historical, archaeological, scenic, or scientific sites, without charging a fee of any kind therefor, shall not be liable for unintentional injuries to such users . . . .

Thus, under this subsection, landowners who open their land to the public for recreational purposes are not liable for unintentional injuries. RCW 4.24.210(4) does, however, set out an exception.

(4) Nothing in this section shall prevent the liability of a landowner or others in lawful possession and control for injuries sustained to users by reason of a known dangerous artificial latent condition for which warning signs have not been conspicuously posted. A fixed anchor used in rock climbing and put in place by someone other than a landowner is not a known dangerous artificial latent condition and a landowner under subsection (1) of this section shall not be liable for unintentional injuries resulting from the condition or use of such an anchor. Nothing in RCW 4.24.200 and 4.24.210 limits or expands in any way the doctrine of attractive nuisance. Usage by members of the public, volunteer groups, or other users is permissive and does not support any claim of adverse possession.

In applying this subsection, the courts have stated that the terms "known," "dangerous," "artificial," and "latent" modify the term "condition," rather than each other. *Davis v. State*, 144 Wn.2d 612, 616, 30 P.3d 462 (2001). Therefore, under this exception a landowner is liable if the condition that caused the injury was known, dangerous, artificial, and latent.

Condition

In identifying the "condition" that caused the injury, the courts look both at the specific object that caused the injury and at the larger picture:

For purposes of RCW 4.24.210(3) the "condition" is "the injury-causing instrumentality itself and its relatedness to the external circumstances in which the instrumentality is situated, or operates."

Van Dinter, 121 Wn.2d at 43, 846 P.2d 522. To view the instrumentality alone "as having been the injury-causing condition would be to artificially isolate some particular aspect of the total condition that caused [plaintiff's] injury." *Van Dinter*, 121 Wn.2d at 44, 846 P.2d 522. "Identifying the condition that caused [the] injury is a factual determination." *Van Dinter*, 121 Wn.2d at 44, 846 P.2d 522.

Cultee v. City of Tacoma, 95 Wn. App. 505, 515, 977 P.2d 15 (1999). In particular, the courts look at whether external circumstances transformed the object that caused the injury. *See e.g. Davis v. State*, 144 Wn.2d 612, 616, 30 P.3d 462 (2001); *Ravenscroft v. Wash. Water Power Co.*, 136 Wn.2d 911, 922, 969 P.2d 75 (1998). For example, in *Davis*, a case in which the plaintiff followed tire tracks over a steep sand dune, the court held that the "condition" did not include the tire tracks that led to the drop-off because the tire tracks had not transformed the sand dune. *Id.* at 616. In contrast, in *Ravenscroft*, a case in which the plaintiff hit a submerged tree stump while boating, the court held that the "condition" was the relationship between the tree stump (the object that caused the injury) and the tree stump's location in a water channel where the water level had been raised (the external circumstances). *Id.* at 922. According to the court, by flooding the area, the Power Company had transformed the stump. *Id.*

1. Known

To prove that the injury-causing condition was "known," the plaintiff must prove that the landowner had actual knowledge of the injury-causing condition or must present facts from which the trier of fact can infer that the landowner had actual knowledge. *Nauroth v. Spokane County*, 121 Wn. App. 389, 393, 88 P.3d 996 (2004). In *Tabak v. State*, 73 Wn. App. 691, 695, 870 P.2d 1014 (1994), the court held that there was an issue of fact about whether the landowner knew about the condition when the landowner testified that he had repaired the condition and had no knowledge that further repairs were required. In contrast, in *Nauroth*, the court held that there was no issue of fact when the plaintiff did not present any evidence that the landowner knew that the stairs were dangerous when there was no evidence that others had been injured on the stairs and when the landowner's maintenance workers used the stairs infrequently. *Id.* at 393.

2. Dangerous

A "dangerous" condition is a condition that poses an unreasonable risk of harm. *Cultee*, 95 Wn. App. at 518. In *Cultee*, the court held that the road was dangerous because "[w]ater moving in and over the property, combined with uneven, eroding roads, made it nearly impossible to move safely about the property." *Id.* at 519. In the other cases, the defendants conceded that the condition was dangerous. *Davis v. State*, 144 Wn.2d at 616 (case involved a sand dune); *Ravenscroft v. Wash. Water Power Co.*, 136 Wn.2d at 916 (case involved a submerged tree stump).

3. Artificial

In deciding whether a condition is "artificial," the courts have applied a dictionary definition: an artificial condition is a condition that is "contrived through human art or effort and not by natural causes detached from human agency: relating to human direction or effect in contrast to nature: a. formed or established by man's efforts, not by nature." *Davis*, 144 Wn.2d at 617 (citing *Webster's Third New International Dictionary* 124 (1986)).

For example, in *Ravenscroft*, a divided court held that the injury-causing condition was artificial because it was "contrived through human effort." *Id.* at 923. In that case, the defendant cut down trees and raised the water level of a reservoir so as to cover the tree stumps. *Id.* The court reasoned that the defendant had artificially changed the natural condition of the water channel by enlarging the water channel. *Id.* The configuration of the tree stump in relation to the raised water level, which constituted the injury-causing condition, was created by man, not nature. *Id.* at 924. Thus, the court concluded that the injury-causing condition was artificial. *Id.*

Conversely, in *Davis*, a unanimous court held that the injury-causing condition was not artificial because the external circumstances did not transform the natural state of the specific object that caused the plaintiff's injuries to an artificial state. *Id.* at 618. While the plaintiff argued that the injury-causing condition was artificial because tire tracks leading to the drop off created an artificial condition, the court disagreed. *Id.* According to the court, the tire tracks modified only the flat surface of the sand dunes and not the drop off itself. *Id.* at 619. Thus, the court concluded that the injury-causing condition was not artificial. *Id.*

4. Latent

Under RCW 4.24.210(4), a "latent" condition is a condition that is not readily apparent to the general class of recreational users, rather than a specific recreational user. *Cultee*, 95 Wn. App. at 521. Whether a condition is readily apparent to the general class of recreational users is a question of fact. *Id.* at 522. Generally, courts have held that a condition is not latent when the condition is "obvious." *See e.g. Ravenscroft*, 136 Wn.2d at 925.

The only recent case in which a court determined that a condition was latent is *Tennyson v. Plum Creek Timber Co.*, 73 Wn. App. 550, 872 P.2d 524 (1994). In that case, Tennyson was injured when he rode his motorcycle off the back side of a gravel mound, which had been recently excavated. *Id.* at 552-53. Tennyson argued that the condition was latent because it could not be seen by individuals approaching from the front side. *Id.* at 555. The court, however, held that the condition was not latent because (1) the excavation was readily apparent to anyone who viewed the mound as a whole, (2) the defendant was not required to anticipate that someone might ride up the mound without examining it, and (3) the plaintiff knew gravel from the mound could be removed at any time. *Id.* at 555-56.

§ 6.4.2 Formal Memo in Which the Writer Sets Out the Facts First and Organizes the Discussion Section Using a Script Format

For more on writing this type of memo, see Chapters 7, 8, and 9.

To: Christine Galeano
From: Legal Intern
Date: September 12, 2006
Re.   Elaine Olsen, Case No. 06-478
            Service of Process, Usual Place of Abode; Notification of Contents

Statement of Facts

Elaine Olsen has contacted our office asking for assistance in overturning an order terminating her parental rights. You have asked me to determine whether the service of process was valid.

On February 1, 2006, Ms. Olsen entered an inpatient drug treatment program in Miami, Florida. She remained in the program until March 27, 2006, when she moved into a residential treatment house for recovering addicts.

During April, May, and June 2006, Ms. Olsen was a full-time resident at the halfway house. She had a bedroom in the house, ate her meals there, and had some of her possessions there. In addition, when she applied for jobs, she listed the halfway house address as her address.

Beginning in July 2006, Ms. Olsen began spending less time at the halfway house and more time with her sister, Elizabeth Webster, who is 32. During July and August 2006, Ms. Olsen spent weeknights at the halfway house and Friday, Saturday, and Sunday nights at her sister's house. Because she was spending time at her sister's house, Ms. Olsen moved some of her clothing and personal effects into her sister's house. When she renewed her driver's license in August 2006, Ms. Olsen listed her sister's address as her address.

On Wednesday, July 26, 2006, a process server went to Ms. Webster's house and asked for Elaine Olsen. When Ms. Webster told the process server that "Elaine isn't here today," the process server handed the summons to Ms. Webster and told her that Ms. Olsen "needed to go to court."

Ms. Webster will testify that she never gave the summons to her sister. Because she thought that the papers related to some of Ms. Olsen's unpaid bills, she simply put the summons in a shoebox in the kitchen with a stack of Ms. Olsen's other mail. Ms. Olsen says she never received the summons and, as a result, did not respond. The return of service is regular on its face.

Ms. Olsen has been employed since August 1, 2006, and she has lived in her own apartment since September 1, 2006. Her voter's registration card lists the address she lived at before she entered the treatment program.

There is nothing in the record that indicates whether the State tried to personally serve Ms. Olsen or whether it tried to serve her at the halfway house.

Issue

Under Florida's service of process statute, was Ms. Olsen properly served when (1) service was made on Ms. Olsen's 32-year-old sister on a Wednesday at Ms. Olsen's sister's house; (2) during the month when service was made, Ms. Olsen spent weeknights at a halfway house where she had a room, ate meals, and kept belongings, and spent Friday, Saturday, and Sunday nights at her sister's house, where she had some belongings; (3) Ms. Olsen listed the halfway house address on job applications but her sister's address on her driver's license; (4) the process server told Ms. Olsen's sister that Ms. Olsen needed to go to court; and (5) Ms. Olsen's sister did not give the summons to Ms. Olsen, and Ms. Olsen states that she did not receive notice?

Brief Answer

Probably not. Because the summons and complaint were given to Ms. Olsen's adult sister at the sister's house, the court will decide that the service was made on a person 15 years or older who was living at the house at which the service was made. In addition, because the process server told Ms. Olsen's sister that Ms. Olsen needed to go to court, the court will, more likely than not, decide that the person served was informed of the contents of the documents. However, because Ms. Olsen was not actually living at her sister's house on the day that service was made, the court may decide that her sister's house was not her usual place of abode.

Discussion

The fundamental purpose of service of process is to give defendants notice of claims that have been filed against them and to provide defendants with an opportunity to defend their rights. *Shurman v. A. Mortg. & Inv. Corp.*, 795 So. 2d 952, 953-54 (Fla. 2001). Because it is important that litigants receive notice of actions against them, courts strictly construe and enforce statutes governing service of process. *Id.* at 954.

In Florida, substituted service can be made by "leaving the copies at [the defendant's] usual place of abode with any person residing therein who is 15 years of age or older and informing the person of their contents." Fla. Stat. § 48.031(a)(1) (2006).

Although the party seeking to invoke the jurisdiction of the court has the burden of proving that service was proper, if the return is regular on its face, the courts presume that the service was valid. *Thompson v. State, Dept. of Revenue*, 867 So. 2d 603, 605 (Fla. 1st DCA 2004); *Magazine v. Bedoya*, 475 So. 2d 1035, 1035 (Fla. 3rd DCA 1985). In such instances, the party challenging the service has the burden of presenting clear and convincing evidence that the service was invalid. *Id.*

In this case, Ms. Olsen will have to concede that the summons was left with a person 15 years or older who was residing at the house where the summons and complaint were served. In addition, it is unlikely that Ms. Olsen will be able to prove that her sister was not informed of the contents of the documents. Ms. Olsen may, however, be able to present clear and convincing evidence that the summons was not left at her usual place of abode.

A. Usual Place of Abode

If a defendant has more than one residence, the defendant's usual place of abode is the place where the defendant was actually living at the time of service. *Shurman v. A. Mortg. & Inv. Corp.*, 795 So. 2d 952, 953-54 (Fla. 2001). It is not enough that the summons and complaint are left with a relative. *Torres v. Arnco Const., Inc.*, 867 So. 2d 583, 586 (Fla. 5th DCA 2004).

The only case in which the Florida courts have held that the service was made at the defendant's usual place of abode is *State ex rel. Merritt v. Heffernan*, 195 So. 145 (Fla. 1940). In that case, the defendant was on a train en route to his permanent residence in Minnesota when his wife was served at the family's apartment in Florida, where the defendant had visited "twice during the season." *Id.* at 146. In its decision, the court stated that when a person has more than one residence, the summons and complaint must be served at the dwelling house in which the defendant is living at the time when the service is made. *Id.* In applying this rule to the facts of the case, the court concluded that the defendant was "not within the classification of persons who had at the time of service lost one place of residence and had not yet established another." *Id.* at 148. Thus, the court determined that, at the time of service, the defendant's then-place of abode was still the family's apartment in Florida. *Id.* at 147.

In contrast, in most of the cases in which the courts have held that the summons was not left at the defendant's usual place of abode, the defendant had not lived for a substantial period of time at the house where service was made. *See e.g Thompson*, 867 So. 2d at 605; *Shurman*, 795 So. 2d at 953-54. For example, in *Shurman*, the court held that the service had not been made at the defendant's usual place of abode when the summons was left with the defendant's wife at the family home but the defendant had been incarcerated for at least nine months. *Id.* at 955. Similarly, in *Thompson*, the court held that the summons had not been left at the defendant's usual place of abode when the summons was left with the defendant's wife at the family home. *Id.* at 605. In reaching its decision, the court relied on the defendant's affidavit in which the defendant stated that he was separated from his wife, that he had not resided at that address for over three years, and that he did not authorize anyone to accept service of process on his behalf. *Id.*

The only Florida case in which the summons was left with a relative with whom the defendant was visiting is *Torres*, 867 So. 2d at 585-86. In that case, the plaintiff tried, for more than a month, to serve Mr. Torres at the New York apartment where Mr. Torres had lived for twelve years. *Id.* at 585. Although all attempts at service were unsuccessful, the New York process server indicated in his affidavit that he had "verified" with a neighbor that "Mr. Torres lived at the New York address, but that he was often out of town, and was expected to return in two weeks." *Id.* Because it could not serve the defendant in New York, the plaintiff served Mr. Torres's mother at her residence in Florida. *Id.* In his affidavit, the Florida process server stated that Mr. Torres's mother told him that "he (presumably Mr. Torres) would be home soon." *Id.* Mr. Torres stated that he never received notice. *Id.* In holding that the service was not valid, the court noted that while the standard of review was gross abuse of discretion, the trial court had not heard live testimony, and the plaintiff had the burden of establishing that the service was valid. *Id.* at 587. It then went on to note that the evidence tended to support Mr. Torres's position that his usual place of abode was in New York and that Mr. Torres's mother's statement that Mr. Torres would be home soon was, at best, ambiguous. *Id.*

Ms. Olsen can make three arguments to support her assertion that her sister's house was not her usual place of abode. First, Ms. Olsen will argue that, under the plain language of the statute, her sister's house was not her usual place of abode. When a defendant has more than one residence, the service must be made at the place where the defendant was actually living at the time the summons and complaint were served. In this case, Ms. Olsen had more than one residence: during the week she lived at the half-way house, and on weekends she visited her sister. Because the summons and complaint were served on a Wednesday, a weekday, the service was not made at the place where Ms. Olsen was actually living.

Second, Ms. Olsen will argue that the facts in her case are more like the facts in *Torres* than the facts in *Heffernan*. Like Mr. Torres, who was only visiting his mother and who was not at his mother's house when service was made, Ms. Olsen only visited her sister and was not at her sister's house when the summons and complaint were served. However, while Mr. Torres's mother's statement that Mr. Torres "would be home soon" suggested that Mr. Torres would be returning to his mother's house that day, Ms. Olsen's sister told the process server that Ms. Olsen "isn't here today." In addition, while the plaintiff in *Torres* had tried on a number of occasions to serve Mr. Torres at his New York house, in our case we do not know whether the defendant tried to serve Ms. Olsen personally or at the halfway house. Finally *Heffernan* can be distinguished in two ways: (1) while Mr. Heffernan had been at his family's apartment only an hour before the summons and complaint were served, Ms. Olsen had not been at her sister's house for several days; and (2) while in *Heffernan* the summons and complaint were served on the defendant's wife, in our case the summons and complaint were served on Ms. Olsen's sister. It is also important to note that, since *Heffernan*, the courts have interpreted the service process statutes more narrowly.

Finally, Ms. Olsen can argue that, as a matter of public policy, the court should hold that the summons was not left at Ms. Olsen's usual place of abode. The courts have repeatedly held that the service of process statutes should be strictly construed and that service on a relative is not, by itself, enough. *Shurman*, 795 So. 2d at 953-54. In addition, in this case, Ms. Olsen did not receive notice.

In response, the State will argue that Ms. Olsen was served at one of her usual places of abode. In this case, Ms. Olsen was actually living at her sister's house at the time the summons and complaint were served.

The courts have not required that the plaintiff be living at the house on the day on which the summons was served. Instead, they require only that the defendant be living there "at the time of service." Therefore, while Ms. Olsen may not have been at her sister's house on the day that the summons and complaint were served, she had been there the previous weekend, and she was there the following weekend. In addition, Ms. Olsen had possessions at her sister's house, and she listed her sister's address as her own address when she applied for a driver's license.

Therefore, the State will argue that the facts in this case are much stronger than the facts in *Heffernan*. While in *Heffernan*, Mr. Heffernan visited his family only "twice during the season," Ms. Olsen lived at her sister's house three days a week. In addition, while Mr. Heffernan had another permanent residence, Ms. Olsen was staying at a halfway house, which, by definition, is only a temporary residence. Finally, while in *Heffernan* there was no indication that Mr. Heffernan listed the Florida address on any documents, Ms. Olsen listed her sister's address on her driver's license, and there is evidence indicating that Ms. Olsen received other types of a mail at her sister's house.

The State will use these same facts to distinguish *Torres*. While in *Torres*, Mr. Torres presented evidence establishing that his permanent residence was in New York, in our case, Ms. Olsen did not have a permanent residence. In the five months before service, she had been an inpatient in a treatment facility, she had lived at the halfway house, and she had lived with her sister. The plaintiff can also distinguish *Shurman* and *Thompson*. While in *Shurman* and *Thompson* the record indicated that the defendants had not lived at the house where service had been made for months or years, in this case, Ms. Olsen admits that she has stayed at her sister's house on the weekend before her sister was served.

Finally, the State will argue that, because the return was regular on its face, Ms. Olsen has the burden of proving, by clear and convincing evidence, that her sister's house was not her usual place of abode. In this instance, Ms. Olsen has not met that burden. In addition, when there is evidence that the defendant was in fact living at the house where service was made, the courts should not require plaintiffs to determine which house the defendant was living at on any particular day.

While both sides have strong arguments, the court will probably conclude that the summons was not left at Ms. Olsen's usual place of abode. In the more recent cases, the courts have strictly construed the statute, holding that the service was not made at the defendant's usual place of abode when the defendant had a more permanent place of abode. Thus, because the halfway house was Ms. Olsen's more permanent residence, the court will probably conclude that it was Ms. Olsen's usual place of abode. In addition, the court may be influenced by two key facts: the record does not indicate that the plaintiff tried to serve Ms. Olsen at the halfway house, and Ms. Olsen states that she did not receive notice.

B. Person 15 Years Old or Older Residing Therein

In addition to leaving the summons at the defendant's usual place of abode, the process server must leave the summons with a person 15 years old or older residing therein. If the court concludes that Ms. Olsen's sister's house was Ms. Olsen's usual place of abode, Ms. Olsen should concede that the summons was left with a person residing therein who is at least 15 years old: Ms. Webster is 32 years old, and the summons and complaint were left with her at her house.

C. Informed of Contents

[Not shown]

Conclusion

Because of the strong public policy in favor of ensuring that defendants receive notice of actions that have been filed against them, the court will probably decide that the substituted service of process was not valid and set aside the order terminating Ms. Olsen's parental rights.

Ms. Olsen will have to concede that her sister, Ms. Webster, is a person of suitable age and that Ms. Webster was residing at the house where the service was made. In addition, because the process server told Ms. Webster that Ms. Olsen needed to go to court, it seems unlikely that Ms. Olsen will be able prove that Ms. Webster was not informed of the contents.

Ms. Olsen may, however, be able to prove that the summons and complaint were not served at her usual place of abode. In the more recent cases, the courts have strictly construed the usual place of abode requirement, holding that the service was not made at the defendant's usual place of abode when the defendant had a more permanent residence. Therefore, because the halfway house was Ms. Olsen's more permanent residence, the court will probably conclude that it was Ms. Olsen's usual place of abode. In addition, the court may be influenced by two key facts: the record does not indicate that the plaintiff tried to serve Ms. Olsen at the halfway house, and Ms. Olsen states that she did not receive notice.

§ 6.4.3 Formal Memo in Which the Writer Sets Out the Issue Before the Statement of Facts, Does Not Include a Brief Answer, and Organizes the Discussion Section Using an Integrated Format

For more on writing this type of memo, see Chapters 7, 8, and 10.

TO: Julia Fishler
FROM: Legal Intern
DATE: November 1, 2006
RE: Michael Garcia
          Adverse possession; Washington law

Issue

Whether Doctors and Nurses Who Care (DNWC) has obtained a right to Mr. Garcia's land through adverse possession when (1) it has used Mr. Garcia's land for campouts several nights a week for eight weeks each summer since 1990; (2) to facilitate these campouts, the DNWC has maintained the campsites, fire area, outhouse, and dock; (3) in 1994, the DNWC sent a letter to Mr. Garcia asking him if it could continue using the land for campouts, but Mr. Garcia did not respond to the letter; and (4) Mr. Garcia has paid the taxes but did not visit the land from 1993 until August 2006.

Statement of Facts

Michael Garcia has contacted our office regarding property that he owns in Washington State. Mr. Garcia is concerned that the organization that owns the property next to his, Doctors and Nurses Who Care (DNWC), may be able to claim title to his property through adverse possession.

Mr. Garcia's property is on Lake Chelan, which is in the eastern part of Washington State. Mr. Garcia's grandfather, Eduardo Montoya, purchased the two-acre waterfront parcel in 1951, and the Montoya family used the land every summer from 1951 until Eduardo Montoya became ill in the late 1980s. When they used the land, the family would camp on the site and use a small dock for swimming, fishing, and boating. In 1992, Mr. Garcia's grandfather died and left the property to Mr. Garcia. Although Mr. Garcia spent one weekend at the property in fall of 1992, he moved to Texas in 1993 and did not visit the property until last August. He has, however, continued to pay all of the taxes and assessments.

In 1989, Doctors and Nurses Who Care (DNWC) purchased the five-acre parcel that adjoins Mr. Garcia's property. Since 1990, the DNWC has used its land as a summer camp for children with serious illnesses or disabilities. In a typical summer, the DNWC runs two one-week camps for children with cancer, two one-week camps for children who are blind, two one-week camps for autistic children, and two one-week camps for children with diabetes.

Most of the time the children stay in cabins located on the DNWC property. However, the DNWC uses Mr. Garcia's property for "campouts." On one night, one group of about ten children will camp out in tents on Mr. Garcia's property; the next night another group of ten will camp out on the property, and so on. Thus, the DNWC has been using the Garcia property four or five nights a week for eight weeks each summer since 1990. During these campouts, the children pitch and stay in tents, cook over a fire, and use the dock. To facilitate these campouts, the DNWC has maintained the campsite, the fire area, the outhouse, and the dock.

In February 1994, the DNWC set Mr. Garcia a letter asking him whether it could continue using his land for campouts. Mr. Garcia was busy and did not respond to the letter. Sometime during the summer of 1994, the DNWC posted a no trespassing sign on the dock, and the sign is still there.

Last August, Mr. Garcia visited the property with the intent of spending a few days camping on the lake. When he got there, he discovered children and their counselors on the property.

After discovering the children on his land, Mr. Garcia went to the DNWC's camp headquarters and talked to the director, Dr. Liu. Dr. Liu told Mr. Garcia that it was his understanding that the land belonged to the DNWC. Although Mr. Garcia did not spend that night at the property, he did spend the next night there after the children left. The DNWC did not ask him to leave.

Although over the years, the land around the lake has become more and more developed, the area in which the camp is located is still relatively undeveloped. Most of the property owners use their land only during the summer.

Discussion

The doctrine of adverse possession arose to assure maximum use of the land, to encourage the rejection of stale claims, and to quiet titles. *Chaplin v. Sanders,* 100 Wn.2d 853, 859-60, 676 P.2d 431 (1984); *see also* William B. Stoebuck, *The Law of Adverse Possession in Washington,* 35 Wash. L. Rev. 53, 53 (1960).

To establish title through adverse possession, the claimant must prove that its possession was (1) exclusive, (2) actual and uninterrupted, (3) open and notorious, and (4) hostile for the statutory period. *ITT Rayonier, Inc. v. Bell,* 112 Wn.2d 754, 757, 774 P.2d 6 (1989); *Chaplin v. Sanders,* 100 Wn.2d 853, 857, 676 P.2d 431 (1984). In this case, the statutory period is ten years. RCW 4.16.020(1).

Adverse possession is a mixed question of law and fact. *Chaplin,* 100 Wn.2d at 863. Whether the essential facts exist is for the trier of fact to decide; but whether the facts, as found, constitute adverse possession is for the court to determine as a matter of law. *Id.*

In this case, DNWC can easily prove that its possession was open and notorious and exclusive. In addition, it can probably prove that its possession is actual and uninterrupted. The only element that it may not be able to prove is that its possession was hostile.

A. Open and Notorious

A claimant can satisfy the open and notorious element by showing either (1) that the title owner had actual notice of the adverse use throughout the statutory period or (2) that the claimant used the land such that any reasonable person would have thought that the claimant owned it. *Riley v. Andres*, 107 Wn. 391, 396, 27 P.3d 618 (2001).

In this case, DNWC can prove both that Mr. Garcia had actual notice of its adverse use and that any reasonable person would have thought that DNWC owned the land. To prove that Mr. Garcia had actual knowledge of DNWC's use of the land, DNWC can offer the letter that it sent to Mr. Garcia in 1994 asking for continuing permission to use his land for campouts. To prove that a reasonable person would have thought that DNWC owned the land, DNWC will point out that it not only used the land for campouts but also maintained the campsites, fire area, outhouse, and dock and posted a no trespassing sign.

B. Actual and Uninterrupted

Although the Washington courts have not set out a test for actual possession, the cases illustrate the types of acts that are needed to establish actual possession. 17 *Wash. Prac., Real Estate: Property Law* § 8.10 (2d ed.).

The courts have held that the claimants had actual possession of rural land when the claimants built a fence and cultivated or pastured up to it, *Faubion v. Elder*, 49 Wn.2d 300, 301 P.2d 153 (1956); cleared the land, constructed and occupied buildings, and planted orchards, *Metro. Bldg. Co. v. Fitzgerald*, 122 Wash. 514, 210 P. 770 (1922); or cleared and fenced the land, planted an orchard and built a road, *Davies v. Wickstrom*, 56 Wash. 154, 105 P. 454 (1909). In contrast, the courts have held that the claimants did not have actual possession of rural land when they maintained a fence intended to be a cattle fence and not a line fence, *Roy v. Goerz*, 26 Wn. App. 807, 614 P.2d 1308 (1980); erected two signboards and a mailbox and ploughed weeds, *Slater v. Murphy*, 55 Wn.2d 892, 339 P.2d 457 (1959); or occasionally used the land for gardening, piling wood, and mowing hay, *Smith v. Chambers*, 112 Wash. 600, 192 P. 891 (1920). *See generally*, 17 *Wash. Prac., Real Estate: Property Law* § 8.10 (2d ed.).

If DNWC had only used the land for occasional campouts, it would have been difficult for it to prove that it had actual possession. However, in addition to using the land for campouts, DNWC maintained the campsites, the fire area, the outhouse, and the dock, and it posted a no trespassing sign. Because DNWC maintained permanent structures and posted the no trespassing sign, more likely than not a court will hold that it had actual possession.

In addition, DNWC's use and maintenance of the campsites, fire area, outhouse, and dock are probably enough to establish that its possession was uninterrupted. In all of the cases in which the claimants maintained and used permanent structures, the courts have held that the use was uninterrupted. In addition, in *Howard v. Kunto*, 3 Wn. App. 393, 477 P.2d 210 (1970), the court held that the claimants' use was continuous even though the claimants only used the property during the summer. As the court noted in that case, "the requisite possession requires such possession and dominion 'as ordinarily marks the conduct of owners in general in holding, managing, and caring for property of like nature and condition.'" *Id.* at 397. Consequently, while Mr. Garcia might be able to argue that the DNWC's use of the land was not uninterrupted because it only used the land during the summer months, this argument is a weak one. Because the land is recreational land, DNWC's use of the land only in summer is consistent with how the owners of similar land hold, manage, and care for their property.

C. Exclusive

To establish that its possession was exclusive, the claimant must show that its possession was "of a type that would be expected of an owner. . . ." *ITT-Rayonier*, 112 Wn.2d 754, 758, 774 P.2d 6 (1989). Therefore, while sharing possession of the land with the true owner will prevent a claimant from establishing that its possession was exclusive, sharing possession with a tenant or allowing occasional use by a neighbor does not. *Id.*

In this case, Mr. Garcia has stated that he did not visit the property between 1992 and 2006. Thus, during that period, DNWC did not share the property with the true owner. Although DNWC "shared" its use of Mr. Garcia's land with its campers, this fact should not prevent a court from finding that its possession was exclusive. Because the campers used the Garcia land under the supervision of the DNWC, they are analogous to tenants.

D. Hostile

While prior to 1984 the Washington courts considered the claimant's subjective intent in determining whether its use of the land was hostile, since 1984 the claimant's subjective intent has been irrelevant. *Chaplin*, 100 Wn.2d at 860-61 (overruling cases in which the courts had considered the claimant's subjective intent). Thus, under current Washington law, the claimant must prove only that it used the land as if it were its own for the statutory period. *Id.; Miller v. Anderson*, 91 Wn. App. 822, 828, 964 P.2d 365 (1998). If the claimant proves that it used the land as if it were its own, the use was hostile unless the true owner can prove that it gave the claimant permission to use the land. *Id.*

Permission can be express or implied. *Miller v. Anderson*, 91 Wn. App. at 829; *citing Granston v. Callahan*, 52 Wn. App. 288, 759 P.2d 462 (1988) (case dealt with a prescriptive easement and not adverse possession). The courts infer that the use was permissive if, under the circumstances, it is reasonable to assume that the use was permitted. *Id.* If there was permission, the party claiming adverse possession bears the burden of proving that permission terminated either because (1) the servient estate changed hands through death or alienation or (2) the claimant has asserted a hostile right. *Id.*

In deciding whether a claimant was using the land as if it were its own, the courts consider whether the claimant made improvements to the land, whether the claimant maintained the property; and whether the claimant used the land on a regular basis. *See e.g. Chaplin,* 100 Wn.2d at 855-56; *Timberlane,* 79 Wn. App at 310-11. For example, in *Chaplin,* the court held that the claimants were using the land as if it were their own when the claimants built a road across the disputed land, cleared and maintained the disputed land, installed utility lines, and used the area for recreational activities. *Id.* at 855-56. Similarly, in *Timberlane,* the court held that claimants had used land belonging to the homeowners' association as if it were their own when they built and maintained a fence and a concrete patio and the claimants' children played on the land. *Id.*

In deciding whether the claimants' use was permissive, the courts consider whether the parties are related or have a friendly relationship, whether the improvements benefited both the claimants' and the title owners' property, and whether the title owners allowed the claimants to use the land as a neighborly accommodation. *See e.g. Granston,* 52 Wn. App. at 294-95; *Miller v. Jarman,* 2 Wn. App. 994, 471 P.2d 704 (1970). For instance, in *Granston,* the court held that the claimants' use was permissive because the original owners of the two parcels were brothers who worked together to build driveways, walkways, and other improvements that benefited both properties. *Id.* at 294-95. Likewise, in *Miller,* the court held that the use was permissive because the title owners had allowed the claimants, who were their neighbors, to use their driveway as a neighborly accommodation. *Id.* at 998. In contrast, in *Lingvall v. Bartmess,* 97 Wn. App. 245, 256, 982 P.2d 690 (1999), the court held that the antagonistic relationship between two brothers negated a finding that the claimant's use of the land was permissive.

In the Garcia case, the court will probably conclude the DNWC's use of Mr. Garcia's land was hostile.

First, the court will probably conclude that DNWC used Mr. Garcia's land as if it were the true owner. Although the DNWC did not build any new structures on Mr. Garcia's land, it maintained the campsites, the fire area, the outhouse, and the dock. In addition, although the DNWC did not use the property year-round, it did use the property during the summer, which is how a typical owner would have used the land. As a result, this case is similar to *Chaplin* and *Timberlane,* in which the claimants maintained and used the disputed land as a true owner would have used the land. While in *Chaplin* and *Timberlane* the claimants built new structures (in *Chaplin,* the claimants built a road, and in *Timberlane,* they built a fence and a patio), the courts have held that the claimant does not have to do everything that a title owner might do.

Second, the court will probably conclude that DNWC's use of Mr. Garcia's land was not permissive. Unlike *Granston,* in which the parties were related and had a close relationship, there is no evidence that the members of the DNCW are related to Mr. Garcia. In addition, unlike *Miller,* in which the title owners allowed their neighbors to use their driveway as a neighborly accommodation, the typical owner of recreational land does not allow a neighboring property owner to use its land several days a week during the peak season.

While Mr. Garcia can argue that the letter that DNWC sent to him establishes that DNWC's use of the land was permissive, the court will probably reject this argument. First, the court will conclude that if Mr. Garcia's grandfather gave the DNWC permission to use his land, that permission terminated when his grandfather died. In addition, the court will probably conclude that even if the DNWC used Mr. Garcia's land with Mr. Garcia's implied permission from the time of his grandfather's death until it sent the letter in February of 1994, that permission terminated in the summer of 1994 when the DNWC posted the no trespassing sign and continued to use the property as its own.

Conclusion

More likely than not, DNWC will be able to establish title to Mr. Garcia's land through adverse possession.

To prove that its possession was open and notorious, DNWC only needs to show that Mr. Garcia had actual notice of its use of his land throughout the statutory period or that it used his land in such a way that any reasonable person would have thought that it owned this land. In this case, the DNWC can use the letter that it sent to Mr. Garcia to prove that he had actual notice, and it can show that its use of the land for campouts was such that any reasonable person would have thought that DNWC owned the land.

To prove that its possession was actual and uninterrupted, DNWC need only show that it actually used the land and that its use was consistent with how the true owner might have used the land. The case law suggests that DNWC's maintenance of the campsites, fire area, outhouse, and dock were sufficient to establish actual possession. In addition, although DNWC only used the land during the summer months, the court is likely to find that such use was uninterrupted because most owners of recreational land only use their land during certain seasons.

To prove that its use of the land was exclusive, DNWC will have to show that it did not share the land with anyone else. Although Garcia could try to argue that DNWC's use was not exclusive because it allowed campers to use the land, this argument is weak because the campers used the land under DNWC's supervision.

Finally, to prove that its use was hostile, DNWC will have to prove that it used the land as if it were its own and that it did not do so with Mr. Garcia's permission. DNWC's maintenance and use of the property is probably sufficient to establish that it used Mr. Garcia's land as if it were its own. In addition, DNWC will be able to prove that its use was not permissive. Even if DNWC's initial use of the property was with Mr. Garcia's grandfather's permission, that permission terminated when Mr. Garcia's grandfather died. In addition, although in its 1994 letter DNWC asked Mr. Garcia for permission to continue using the land, DNWC has a strong argument that it did a hostile act that terminated permission when, even after Mr. Garcia did not respond, it continued maintaining and using the property and it posted the no trespassing sign.

Because all of these elements have been met for the statutory period, which is ten years, DNWC has established a right to title to the land through adverse possession.

§ 6.4.4 Formal Memo Involving Three Issues, the Last of Which Is an Issue of First Impression

TO: Supervising Attorney
FROM: D. Elaine Conway, Legal Intern[2]
DATE: April 8, 2005
RE: Elder Care; Mary Smith; FMLA Leave

Statement of Facts

We represent Martha McLean, the owner of Elder Care, a small business that provides in-home care to elderly clients. You have asked me to determine whether Mary Smith, one of Ms. McLean's employees, has a claim under the Family and Medical Leave Act (FMLA).

Elder Care is a small business that employs approximately 60-65 employees who provide daily in-home care to elderly clients. Mary Smith was a specialist at Elder Care for two years and, while generally a good worker, Ms. Smith was late to work several times and used all of her sick and vacation time. Three weeks ago, Ms. McLean received an email from Ms. Smith, in which Ms. Smith stated (1) that she had "been at the hospital all night"; (2) that she "needed to take care of some family matters"; and (3) that she was sorry, but that she would be gone for about a month. Ms. Smith also asked Ms. McLean to respond to the email because Ms. Smith could not be reached by phone. Ms. McLean did not respond to the email. Instead, she hired a replacement to take over Ms. Smith's clients.

There was no contact between Ms. Smith and Ms. McLean until two days ago when Ms. Smith returned to work. At that point, Ms. Smith told Ms. McLean that she had missed work because her husband had physically abused her. Ms. Smith's husband had hit Ms. Smith so hard that Ms. Smith had gone to the emergency room. Ms. Smith spent the night at the emergency room, meeting with both a doctor and a clinical social worker. Although Ms. Smith was not admitted to the hospital, the doctor told her that she should not work for a week. In addition, the social worker told Ms. Smith that she had to leave home before her husband killed her. Ms. Smith immediately went into hiding at a women's shelter; it is not, however, clear

---

[2] Elaine Conway wrote this memo as a first-year law student at Seattle University School of Law. The memo is reprinted in this book with her permission.

whether the social worker specifically recommended that she check in to such a shelter.

Because of Ms. Smith's lengthy absence, Ms. McLean was unable to hold Ms. Smith's position open for Ms. Smith. Thus, when Ms. Smith returned to work, Ms. McLean told Ms. Smith that she had filled her position. Ms. McLean did, however, offer to hire Ms. Smith as a part-time office coordinator. In this new position, Ms. Smith would make approximately 75 percent of her previous salary and receive partial benefits. Ms. Smith says that an advocate at the shelter told her that she was entitled to FMLA leave and that Elder Care has to give her job back to her.

Issues

1. Under the FMLA, is Elder Care a covered employer and is Mary Smith a covered employee when (1) Elder Care has between 60-65 employees; (2) more likely than not, Elder Care's employees all work within seventy-five miles of the main office; and (3) Mary Smith has worked for Elder Care for at least twelve months and probably worked at least 1,250 hours in the previous twelve months?
2. Under the FMLA, did Mary Smith give Elder Care sufficient notice when (1) Ms. Smith notified Elder Care of her unforeseeable absence the day after the injury occurred; (2) Ms. Smith's email stated that "she had been at the hospital all night" and "needed to take care of some family matters"; and (3) Ms. McLean did not respond to Ms. Smith's email to inquire further into the details of Ms. Smith's leave request?
3. Under the FMLA, does Mary have a serious health condition when (1) domestic violence is not specifically mentioned as a qualifying condition in the text of the FMLA or the governing regulations; (2) Ms. Smith was not admitted to the hospital the night of her injury; (3) Ms. Smith met with both a doctor and a clinical social worker while at the hospital and was told not to work for the rest of the week; and (4) the social worker told Ms. Smith she had to get out of the situation at home right away?

Brief Answers

1. Probably. Elder Care and Mary Smith probably meet the requirements for coverage under the FMLA.
2. Probably not. Although Ms. Smith gave notice within the required timeframe, the substance of her notice was insufficient to create a reasonable belief that the she was taking FMLA leave.
3. Probably not. Domestic violence is not mentioned specifically in the FMLA, and a court will probably determine that it is not a serious health condition under the FMLA.

Discussion

In 1993, Congress enacted the Family and Medical Leave Act (FMLA) to provide job security for employees who have serious health conditions that prevent them from working for temporary periods. 29 U.S.C. § 2601(a)(4)

(2000). The Act is intended to balance the "demands of the workplace with the needs of families" as well as entitle "employees to take reasonable leave for medical reasons." 29 U.S.C. § 2601(b)(1) (2000). The Act seeks to accomplish its purposes "in a manner that accommodates the legitimate interests of employers." 29 U.S.C. § 2601(b)(3) (2000).

Issue 1: Is Elder Care a covered employer and is Ms. Smith a covered employee?

Under the FMLA, an employer is a covered employer if it (1) is engaged in commerce and (2) employs fifty or more employees working within seventy-five miles of the worksite. 29 C.F.R. § 825.104 (2004). In this instance, Elder Care is a covered employer because it is engaged in commerce and employs fifty or more employees. We should, however, verify that at least fifty of these employees work within a seventy-five-mile radius of the worksite.

Under the FMLA, an employee is a covered employee if he or she (1) has been employed by the employer for at least twelve months, and (2) has been employed for at least 1,250 hours of service during the twelve-month period immediately preceding the commencement of the leave. 29 C.F.R. § 835.110(a)(1) (2004). Thus, in this case, Ms. Smith is a covered employee if she worked at least 1,250 hours during the preceding twelve months and has not already used twelve weeks of FMLA leave.

Issue 2: Did Ms. Smith provide Elder Care with appropriate notice?

The FMLA's notice requirement is met when the employee gives notice to the employer as soon as practicable, or within no more than one or two working days of learning of the need for leave. 29 C.F.R. § 825.303 (2004). If there is a medical emergency, the employee need not follow the employer's usual procedures for requesting leave. *Id.* The regulations further state that the notice requirement is met if the employee provides notice to the employer either in person or by some electronic means. *Id.* When the employee gives this notice, the employee does not have to request FMLA leave or even mention the FMLA; the employee only needs to state that he or she needs leave. *Id.* Once the employee has given notice, the burden then shifts to the employer to obtain any additional required information. *Id.*

Courts have not required employees to use the specific language of the FMLA to invoke FMLA rights and benefits. Instead, the notice requirement is met if an employee's notice to his or her employer is sufficient to create a reasonable belief that the employee is requesting FMLA leave. *See e.g. Aubuchon v. Knauf Fiberglass, GMBH*, 359 F.3d 950, 952 (7th Cir. 2004); *Collins v. NTN-Bower Corp.*, 272 F.3d 1006, 1008 (7th Cir. 2001); *Stoops v. One Call Communications, Inc.*, 141 F.3d 309, 312-13 (7th Cir. 1998).

In the cases in which the notice requirement was met, the employee told his or her employer that he or she had received medical care and that he or she needed to take medical leave. *See e.g. Price v. City of Fort Wayne*, 117 F.3d 1022, 1025 (7th Cir. 1997); *Haschmann v. Time Warner Entertain-*

ment Co., L.P., 151 F.3d 591, 595 (7th Cir. 1998). For instance, in *Price,* a decision vacating a district court's grant of summary judgment for the employer, the court held that an employee's notice was sufficient when the employee's request for medical leave was accompanied by a physician's note requiring the employee to take time off. *Price,* 117 F.3d at 1025. In contrast, in the cases in which courts have held that the notice requirement was not met, the employee's statements were vague. *See e.g. Collins,* 272 F.3d at 1008; *Hauge v. Equistar Chem. Co.,* 2002 U.S. Dist. LEXIS 15822 (D. Ill. 2002). For example, in *Collins,* the court held that the notice requirement was not met when the employee merely "called in sick" for two days without giving the employer additional information. *Collins,* 272 F.3d at 1008. In its opinion, the court stated that employers "are entitled to the sort of notice that will inform them not only that the FMLA may apply but also when a given employee will return to work." *Id.*

Although it is possible that a court would determine that Ms. Smith's need for leave was foreseeable, it seems unlikely that a court would make that determination. Even if Ms. Smith's husband has abused her before, more likely than not, the court would decide that this particular incident was not foreseeable. In addition, more likely than not, the court would determine that Ms. Smith provided Elder Care with notice as soon as was practicable: Ms. Smith sent an email message to Ms. McLean the day after she had gone to the hospital.

The court will, however, probably determine that Ms. Smith's email was not sufficient to put Elder Care on notice that Ms. Smith was requesting or was entitled to FMLA leave. While in her email Ms. Smith stated that she had been at the hospital and that she needed to take care of some family matters, she did not say why she had been at the hospital or what type of family matters she needed to take care of. Consequently, the court will probably determine that this case is more similar to *Collins* than it is to *Price.* Although Ms. Smith gave Elder Care more information than Collins gave her employer, Ms. Smith did not go into the detail that Price did. For example, Ms. Smith did not say that she had been injured, that she had received treatment at the hospital, or that she needed to leave home. Although as a matter of public policy the courts may not want to require employees to tell their employers that they have been the victim of domestic violence, employers should not be required to investigate every employee absence to determine whether the employee is entitled to FMLA leave.

Issue 3: Did Ms. Smith have a serious health condition?

The FMLA defines the term "serious health condition" as "an illness, injury, impairment, or physical or mental condition that involves A) inpatient care in a hospital, hospice, or residential medical care facility or B) continuing treatment by a health care provider". 29 U.S.C. § 2611(11) (2000). Therefore, to establish that she had a serious health condition, Ms. Smith must prove the following: (1) that she had an illness, injury, impairment, or physical or mental condition that prevented her from working for three weeks and (2) either (a) that she received inpatient care or (b) that she received continuing treatment.

1. Did Ms. Smith have an illness, injury, impairment, or physical or mental condition that prevented her for working for three weeks?

Under the FMLA, the employer may require that a request for leave be supported by "a certification issued by the health care provider" that states that the employee or eligible relative has a qualifying illness, injury, impairment, or physical or mental condition. 29 U.S.C. § 2613 (2000). Although neither the statute nor the applicable regulations state what does and does not constitute an illness, injury, impairment, or physical or medical condition, the courts have held that cancer, severe depression and a terminal illness fall within the definition. *See e.g. Ragsdale v. Wolverine World Wide, Inc.,* 535 U.S. 81, 84 (2002); *Collins,* 272 F.3d at 1008; *Sherry v. Protection, Inc.,* 981 F. Supp. 1133, 1135 (D. Ill. 1997). Thus, Ms. Smith's head injury would constitute an injury. However, that injury lasted, at most, one week, and Ms. Smith missed three weeks of work. Therefore, Ms. Smith may try to argue that domestic violence falls within the definition of an illness, injury, impairment, or physical or medical condition or that she suffers from post traumatic stress disorder.

Although Ms. Smith will make a number of public policy arguments about the need for FMLA coverage for victims of domestic violence, at this time she does not have a strong analogous case or statutory argument. Although not binding in our circuit, the Alaska Supreme Court has decided a case involving an FMLA claim based partially on domestic abuse. *Municipality of Anchorage v. Gregg,* 101 P.3d 181 (Alaska 2004). In *Gregg,* the Alaska Supreme Court affirmed the trial court's decision for the employee, concluding that the employee suffered from the cumulative effect of several physical and mental conditions that constituted a serious health condition. *Id.* The court further stated that, while a victim of domestic violence is not automatically entitled to FMLA protection, a victim who meets the test for a serious health condition has a right to the statutory leave. *Id.*

Additionally, Congress is currently considering a proposed amendment to the FMLA. The Family and Medical Leave Expansion Act of 2005 includes language that would allow employees to take FMLA qualifying leave due to domestic violence. The Family and Medical Leave Expansion Act, S. 282, 109th Cong. (2005). This proposed amendment helps our client in that it indicates that the FMLA does not currently cover domestic violence. If the FMLA currently covered domestic violence, there would be no need for an amendment. However, if this Act passes, our case will deteriorate rapidly.

2. Did Ms. Smith receive either inpatient care or continuing treatment?

In addition to proving that she had an illness, injury, impairment, or physical or mental condition that prevented her from working for three weeks, Ms. Smith must also prove that she received either (a) inpatient care or (b) continuing treatment. 29 C.F.R. § 825.800(1) (2004).[3]

a.   Did Ms. Smith receive inpatient care?

The regulations require that a qualifying condition involve inpatient care in a hospital, hospice, or residential medical care facility. 29 C.F.R. § 825.800(1)(i) (2004). In this instance, Ms. Smith will not be able to prove that she received inpatient care in a hospital. Although Ms. Smith spent the night at the emergency room, she was not admitted and, therefore, never received inpatient care. Telephone Interview with John Doe, Hospital Administrator, Providence Hospital (Feb. 5, 2005).

It also seems unlikely that Ms. Smith will be able to prove that the shelter was a residential medical care facility. Whether this particular requirement is met depends on the composition of the staff at the women's shelter. If the shelter employs qualified medical professionals, Ms. Smith's claim that it should be considered a residential care facility might be successful. If the shelter does not offer continuing treatment by health care providers as defined in the regulations, this requirement will not be met.

From the information we have thus far about the facility, it does not appear to employ a health care provider such as a doctor. Although Ms. Smith will likely argue that she felt dizzy while at the shelter as evidence that she was suffering from continued symptoms, this argument will, in fact, benefit Elder Care. Ms. Smith states that she did not return to the doctor because she was afraid to leave the shelter. This statement indicates that there was no doctor present at the shelter that she could see, and thus the statement strengthens Elder Care's argument that the shelter was not a residential care facility.

b.   Did Ms. Smith receive continuing treatment?

In the alternative, Ms. Smith can try to prove that she received continuing treatment. To do this, she will have to prove that she was incapacitated for three or more days and at least one of the following: (i) she received treatment two or more times by a health care provider, by a nurse or physician's assistant under direct supervision of a health care provider, or by a provider of health care services under orders of, or on referral by, a health care provider; or (ii) she received treatment by a health care provider on at least one occasion that results in a regimen of continuing treatment under the supervision of the health care provider; or (iii) she suffered from a chronic health condition. 29 C.F.R. § 825.800(1)(iii) (2004).

c.   Was Ms. Smith incapacitated for three or more days?

The regulations define incapacity as an inability to work, attend school, or perform other regular daily activities because of the serious health con-

---

[3] Information found in 29 C.F.R. § 825.800 can also be found in 29 C.F.R. § 825.114.

dition, treatment therefore, or recovery therefrom, or any subsequent treatment in connection with such inpatient care. 29 C.F.R. § 825.800(1)(i) (2004). Elder Care should concede that Ms. Smith suffered a period of incapacity of three or more days. The doctor who examined her at the emergency room told her not to work the rest of the week and to get as much bed rest as possible.

(i)   Did Ms. Smith receive two or more treatments?

While conceding that Ms. Smith was incapacitated for three or more days, Elder Care can argue that the other requirements are not met. Although Ms. Smith will argue that she meets the first requirement because she met with both a doctor and a social worker while in the emergency room, the court will likely reject that argument because consulting with two health care providers during the same visit to the emergency room does not constitute two or more treatments. In reaching this conclusion, the court may rely on a Ninth Circuit case involving a boy who was treated in the emergency room and then sent home without being admitted to the hospital. *Marchisheck v. San Mateo County*, 199 F.3d 1068 (9th Cir. 1999). In that case, the court concluded that the boy had not been treated two or more times by a health care provider because he had been to the emergency room only once. *Id.* at 1075. While Ms. Smith will attempt to distinguish *Marchisheck* by arguing that during her visit to the emergency room she was treated by two different health care providers, more likely than not, the Marchisheck boy was also seen by at least two health care providers while he was at the emergency room. For example, he was probably seen by both a nurse and a doctor. Because most individuals see more than one health care provider during a single visit, it is unlikely that a court will decide that Ms. Smith's single visit to the emergency room counts as two or more treatments by a health care provider. In the alternative, Ms. Smith may argue that she received two or more treatments because she went to the emergency room and she was seen by a health care provider while she was at the shelter. If it turns out that Ms. Smith consulted a qualified health care provider at the shelter on more than one occasion, a court will likely find that Ms. Smith had continuing treatment by a health care provider.

(ii) Did Ms. Smith receive treatment once combined with a regimen of continuing treatment under the supervision of the health care provider?

Ms. Smith may also argue that she received treatment once combined with a regimen of continuing treatment under the supervision of a health care provider. In making this argument, Ms. Smith will argue that she received one treatment at the emergency room and that she then received a regimen of continuing treatment when, on the recommendation of the social worker, she went to the shelter. However, based on what we now know, it appears that the social worker only told Ms. Smith that she needed to get out of the situation at home. It does not appear that she told Ms.

Smith to go to a shelter. If it is true that the social worker did not tell Ms. Smith to go to the shelter, the court will reject this argument.

(iii) Did Ms. Smith suffer from a chronic health condition?

Finally, the regulations consider any period of incapacity or treatment for such incapacity due to a chronic serious health condition as a qualifying condition. A chronic serious health condition is one which (1) requires periodic visits for treatment by a health care provider, or by a nurse or physician's assistant under direct supervision of a health care provider; (2) continues over an extended period of time (including recurring episodes of a single underlying condition); and (3) may cause episodic rather than a continuing period of incapacity (e.g., asthma, diabetes, epilepsy, etc.).

Ms. Smith will make a public policy argument that domestic violence is a chronic, serious health condition. Ms. Smith may try to point to her use of her vacation and sick leave to deal with the abusive situation at home as an indicator that the condition was chronic. In addition, she will attempt to compare herself to the employee in *Price,* who had multiple illnesses. *See Price*, 117 F.3d at 1025. In *Price,* the court decided that, although none of the employee's individual illnesses constituted a serious health condition, the combination of them could. *Id.* at 1023; *accord Municipality of Anchorage v. Gregg,* 101 P.3d 181 (Alaska 2004). Similarly, Ms. Smith may try to persuade the court that it should take into consideration that her physical disabilities resulted not only from the assault but also from prior incidences of domestic violence. However, there are important differences between Ms. Smith and the employee in *Price.* For example, in *Price*, the employee saw her doctor on many occasions and was under his continuing supervision. *Id.* at 1025. In addition, while the doctor in *Price* ordered the employee not to work for three weeks, *id.,* in the present case the doctor told Ms. Smith not to work for the rest of the week. In addition, while the employee in *Price* suffered from reoccurring physical ailments, Ms. Smith suffered from only one physical injury.

Conclusion

Although Elder Care is a covered employer and Ms. Smith is a covered employee, Ms. Smith did not provide Elder Care with the required notice. In addition, it seems unlikely that Ms. Smith will be able to prove that she had a serious health condition as that term is defined under the FMLA.

Elder Care is a covered employer because it is engaged in commerce and employs fifty or more employees. We should, however, verify that at least fifty of these employees work within a seventy-five-mile radius of Elder Care's office. It also appears that Ms. Smith is a covered employee. We should, though check Elder Care's records to make sure that Ms. Smith worked at least 1,250 hours during the previous twelve months and that she has not already used twelve weeks of FMLA leave.

The court will probably determine that Ms. Smith's email was not sufficient to put Elder Care on notice that Ms. Smith was requesting or was entitled to FMLA leave. While in her email Ms. Smith stated that she had been at the hospital and that she needed to take care of some family matters, she did not say why she had been at the hospital or what type of family matters she needed to take care of. Although as a matter of public policy the courts may not want to require that employees tell their employers that they have been the victim of domestic violence, employers should not be required to investigate every employee absence to determine whether the employee is entitled to FMLA leave.

If, however, the court determines that Ms. Smith did give Elder Care adequate notice, Ms. Smith will have to prove that she had a "serious health condition," which is defined as "an illness, injury, impairment, or physical or mental condition that involves A) inpatient care in a hospital, hospice, or residential medical care facility or B) continuing treatment by a health care provider." Because no court has held that domestic violence is a serious health condition, this case would present an issue of first impression. Although Ms. Smith missed more than three weeks of work, she may have a difficult time proving that she was unable to work. In addition, because she was treated at the emergency room, she will have a difficult time proving that she received inpatient care or that she received continuing treatment.

Although it appears unlikely that Ms. Smith will be able to prove that Elder Care violated the FMLA, litigation can be expensive. Therefore, we should talk to Elder Care about settling. For example, if turnover is high, it may be possible for Elder Care to reinstate Ms. Smith sometime in the near future.

§ 6.4.5 Bench Memo Involving an Issue of First Impression

For more on writing this type of memo, see Chapter 11.

To: United States District Court Judge, Northern District of Illinois
From: Chad Kirby[4]
Date: April 3, 2005
Re: Tamil Welfare and Human Rights Committee v. John Ashcroft et al.

Statement of Facts

On January 28, 2005, the Tamil Welfare and Human Rights Committee (TWHRC), a non-profit organization based in Illinois, filed a complaint in this court. The TWHRC alleges that 18 U.S.C. § 2339B of the Antiterrorism and Effective Death Penalty Act (AEDPA) violates the Fifth Amendment

---

[4] Chad Kirby wrote this memo as a first-year law student at Seattle University School of Law. The memo is reprinted in this book with his permission.

Due Process Clause insofar as it criminalizes the provision of "communications equipment" to a "foreign terrorist organization" (FTO) without proof that the individual making the donation intended to further the organization's terrorist agenda. To help you decide this issue, you have asked me to research and analyze what type of intent is required to violate 18 U.S.C. § 2339B.

The TWHRC wants to provide a tsunami warning system to the Liberation Tigers of Tamil Eelam (LTTE), an organization that operates in Sri Lanka and has been designated as an FTO. *See* Designation of Foreign Terrorist Organizations, 62 Fed. Reg. 52,650 (Oct. 8, 1997). The tsunami warning system would consist of a series of interconnected sirens and would be considered "communications equipment" under the AEDPA. Even though it intends that the warning system would be used only to save the lives of coastal dwellers in Sri Lanka, the TWHRC fears that it would be subject to criminal prosecution under the AEDPA if it provides this equipment to the LTTE.

The TWHRC's proposed donation would violate 18 U.S.C. § 2339B if a violation of that statute requires only general intent to provide prohibited equipment to an FTO. On the other hand, the donation would probably not violate 18 U.S.C. § 2339B if a violation of that statute requires a specific intent to further an FTO's terrorist agenda (if the statute has a scienter requirement).

Issue

To convict the TWHRC under 18 U.S.C. § 2339B for providing a tsunami warning system to the LTTE, would the government need to prove merely that the TWHRC knew that it had provided material support and that the LTTE had been designated as an FTO, or would the government also need to prove that the TWHRC intended or knew it was likely that the LTTE would use the system to further its terrorist agenda?

Discussion

Two years before enacting the AEDPA, Congress enacted 18 U.S.C. § 2339A as part of the Violent Crime Control and Law Enforcement Act of 1994. Pub. L. No. 103-322, § 120005, 108 Stat. 1796 (1994). Section 2339A makes it a crime to provide "material support or resources" knowing or intending that they will be used "in preparation for, or in carrying out" crimes of terrorism. 18 U.S.C. § 2339A (2000). "Material support or resources" is defined very broadly; the current definition reads as follows (emphasis added):

> (1) the term "material support or resources" means any property . . . or service, including currency or monetary instruments . . . , lodging, training, expert advice or assistance, . . . *communications equipment*, facilities, weapons, lethal substances, explosives, personnel

(1 or more individuals who may be or include oneself), and transportation, except medicine or religious materials;

18 U.S.C.A. § 2339A (West, Westlaw through P.L. 109-4).

Congress enacted 18 U.S.C. § 2339B two years later as part of the Antiterrorism and Effective Death Penalty Act (AEDPA). Like § 2339A, § 2339B made it a crime, punishable by a ten-year imprisonment, to knowingly provide "material support or resources"; unlike § 2339A, § 2339B encompassed a broad range of behavior, criminalizing all knowing provisions of material support to any organization that had been designated as a "foreign terrorist organization" by the Secretary of State, whether the provider intended that the support be used for terrorist purposes or for humanitarian (or any other) purposes. Section 2339B uses the same broad definition of "material support or resources" as § 2339A.

The USA PATRIOT Act of 2001 amended § 2339B, increasing the prison term to fifteen years and adding a life sentence if any death resulted from the violation. Pub. L. 107-56, § 810(d), 115 Stat. 272 (2001). Two years later, the Ninth Circuit Court of Appeals struck down portions of § 2339B on First and Fifth Amendment grounds. See *Humanitarian Law Project v. United States Dept. of Justice* 352 F.3d 382, 403 (9th Cir. 2003), *vacated by* 393 F.3d 902 (9th Cir. 2004) (*Humanitarian 2003*). In response, Congress adopted the Intelligence Reform and Terrorism Prevention Act of 2004, which, among other things, clarified the definition of "material support or resources" and made the intent requirement more explicit. Pub. L. 108-458, § 6603, 118 Stat. 3638 (2004). The relevant text of the current version of § 2339B reads as follows:

§ 2339B. Providing material support or resources to designated foreign terrorist organizations

(a) Prohibited activities.
     (1) Unlawful conduct. Whoever knowingly provides material support or resources to a foreign terrorist organization, or attempts or conspires to do so, shall be fined under this title or imprisoned not more than 15 years, or both, and, if the death of any person results, shall be imprisoned for any term of years or for life. *To violate this paragraph, a person must have knowledge that the organization is a designated terrorist organization. . . , that the organization has engaged or engages in terrorist activity. . . , or that the organization has engaged or engages in terrorism. . . .*
     . . . .

(g) Definitions. As used in this section—
     . . . .
     (4) the term "material support or resources" has the same meaning given that term in section 2339A (including the definitions of "training" and "expert advice or assistance" in that section);
     . . . .

> (i) Rule of construction. *Nothing in this section shall be con-*
> *strued or applied so as to abridge the exercise of rights guaranteed*
> *under the First Amendment to the Constitution of the United States.*

18 U.S.C.A. § 2339B (West, Westlaw through P.L. 109-3) (emphasis added).

In determining what intent the government would have to prove to convict under § 2339B, the Court should look to the plain language of the statute before considering its legislative history and underlying public policy. The court should also consider how other courts have analyzed this issue.

I. Plain Language

The starting point in all statutory analysis is the plain language of the statute itself. *Boim v. Quranic Literacy Inst.,* 291 F.3d 1000, 1009 (7th Cir. 2002). The courts look to the language to determine what Congress intended, and they also look to the statute's structure, subject matter, context, and history for this same purpose. *Id.* While the plain language and legislative history of § 2339B tends to favor a holding that, to convict under the statute, the government would need to prove only that defendants knew they were providing material support to an organization that they knew was an FTO, the plain language and legislative history also provide some justification for the proposition that the government would also need to prove that defendants knew or intended that their support would be used to further the FTO's terrorist agenda.

The original text of § 2339B, however, provided little support for this proposition: The 1996 version of the statute made it a crime to "knowingly [provide] material support or resources to a foreign terrorist organization," 18 U.S.C. 2339B (2000), leading courts to consider whether Congress intended § 2339B to be essentially a strict liability offense. *See Humanitarian Law Project v. United States Dept. of Justice,* 352 F.3d 382, 398-403 (9th Cir. 2003), *vacated by* 393 F.3d 902 (9th Cir. 2004). In other words, the plain language of § 2339B as originally enacted seemed to require only that defendants knew that they were providing material support without even requiring that they knew they were providing support to an FTO. Courts ultimately rejected this interpretation, *id.*, and in 2004, Congress followed suit: the 2004 amendments to § 2339B state that to convict under that statute, the government must prove that a defendant knowingly provided material support to an organization and that he or she had "knowledge that the organization [was] a designated terrorist organization . . . , that the organization has engaged or engages in terrorist activity . . . , or that the organization has engaged or engages in terrorism. . . ." 18 U.S.C. § 2339B. A scienter requirement is notably absent from the statute; nowhere in the plain language of § 2339B is the government required to prove that defendants knew or intended that the material support they provided was to be used for terrorist purposes.

A comparison between the language of § 2339B and that of its sister statute, § 2339A, supports this interpretation. Congress demonstrated that it knew how to write a scienter requirement into an antiterrorism statute when it wrote § 2339A: "Whoever provides material support or resources . . . *knowing or intending* that they are to be used in preparation for, or in carrying out . . . [an act of terrorism] . . . shall be fined under this title. . . ." 18 U.S.C. § 2339A (emphasis added). If Congress had intended § 2339B to have a scienter requirement, it could have amended the statute to add similar language. On the contrary, not only did the 2004 amendments not use such language, but Congress would also have had a difficult time writing text that more clearly stated its intention that §2339B **not** have a scienter requirement: "To violate this paragraph, a person must have knowledge that the organization is a designated terrorist organization . . . , that the organization has engaged or engages in terrorist activity . . . , or that the organization has engaged or engages in terrorism. . . ." 18 U.S.C. § 2339B.

While subsection (a) of § 2339B offers little opportunity to read in a scienter requirement, subsection (i) ("[the statute] shall [not] be construed or applied so as to abridge the exercise of rights guaranteed under the First Amendment to the Constitution") explicitly instructs the court to construe the statute so as to be constitutional. *Id.* Although subsection (i) mentions only the First Amendment, it is evidence from which the court could infer that Congress realized that the statute must not abridge rights guaranteed by **any** amendment if § 2339B is to effectively stop material support from reaching FTOs. As will be discussed later in section IV, this provision of the statute provides some justification for construing § 2339B to have a scienter requirement.

II. Legislative History

The *Congressional Record* contains few statements that relate to whether Congress intended that § 2339B have a scienter requirement. In introducing the Senate Conference Report on the AEDPA, Senator Hatch, who co-sponsored the bill, stated, "[t]his bill also includes provisions making it a crime to knowingly provide material support *to the terrorist functions* of foreign groups designated . . . to be engaged in terrorist activities." 142 Cong. Rec. S3354 (daily ed. April 16, 1996) (statement of Sen. Hatch) (emphasis added). While this statement suggests that Congress intended § 2339B to prohibit only contributions that are intended to further an FTO's terrorist agenda, Senator Hatch immediately went on to say, "I am convinced we have crafted a narrow but effective designation provision which meets these obligations while safeguarding the freedom to associate, which none of us would willingly give up." *Id.* This second sentence alters the context in which the first sentence should be interpreted, making it less likely that Senator Hatch was speaking about scienter and more likely that he was speaking about the distinction between punishing mere association with an FTO (which would likely abridge a right granted by the First Amendment) and punishing the conduct of providing material support to an FTO (which would have fewer constitutional implications). These statements do, however, provide evidence that Congress intended to craft a statute that did not criminalize an overly broad range of behavior and did not abridge any constitutionally protected rights.

On the same day that Senator Hatch made his comments, Senator Snowe said, "this bill . . . will cut off the ability of terrorist groups . . . to raise huge sums in the United States for supposedly 'humanitarian' purposes, where in reality a large part of those funds go toward conducting terrorist activities." 142 Cong. Rec. S3380 (daily ed. April 16, 1996) (statement of Sen. Snowe). This statement can be interpreted at least two ways. On one hand, this comment provides some evidence that Congress intended to cut off all support from the United States to FTOs, regardless of the ostensible purpose of the donation. On the other hand, this comment could also be read as evidence that Congress intended to prohibit only support for terrorist activities that was cloaked behind a fraudulent façade of humanitarianism. It is not clear from Senator Snowe's statement whether Congress intended to criminalize donations of support that in reality go towards conducting humanitarian activities.

The Congressional statement of findings and purpose regarding § 2339B provides some clarification on this point: "foreign organizations that engage in terrorist activity are so tainted by their criminal conduct that *any contribution* to such an organization facilitates that conduct." Antiterrorism and Effective Death Penalty Act of 1996, Pub. L. No. 104-132, § 301, 110 Stat. 1214 (1996) (emphasis added). This finding provides unequivocal evidence that Congress did in fact intend to criminalize all donations made to FTOs, regardless of the intent of the donor or of the actual use to which the support would be put. Supporting this interpretation, the House Conference Report for the Comprehensive Antiterrorism Act of 1995 (a predecessor of the AEDPA) provides further evidence of Congress's approach to controlling contributions to terrorist organizations:

> There is no other mechanism, other than an *outright prohibition on contributions*, to effectively prevent such organizations from using funds raised in the United States to further their terrorist activities abroad. . . . The prohibition is absolutely necessary to achieve the government's compelling interest in protecting the nation's safety from the very real and growing terrorist threat.

H.R. Rep. No. 104-383 at 45 (emphasis added).

In conclusion, the *Congressional Record* contains some support for a holding that § 2339B has a scienter requirement. However, less equivocal evidence in the record supports a holding that to convict under § 2339B, the government would need only to prove that defendants knew they were providing material support to an organization that they knew had been designated as an FTO.

III. Public Policy

The legislative history of § 2339B will also factor into the court's public policy analysis as it considers whether to construe that statute so as to have a scienter requirement. While the public policy of "protecting the nation's safety from the very real and growing terrorist threat," *id.*, is compelling and should not be undermined, that policy is not absolute: It must be balanced against the goals of encouraging humanitarian charitable donations and (more importantly) not punishing innocent conduct.

A. The Medicine Exemption

While the list of items and services that constitute prohibited "material support" is long and broad, Congress chose not to prohibit donations of "medicine or religious material" to FTOs. 18 U.S.C. § 2339A. While this exemption might be interpreted so as to allow the donation of humanitarian aid in general, the legislative history behind the medicine exemption clearly indicates that it was not intended to apply so broadly. First, the medicine exemption is not a clear indicator of a legislative intent to allow humanitarian aid as a matter of policy because the amendment that added the medicine exemption to § 2339A was passed by only one vote in committee. H.R. Rep. No. 104-383 at 73. Furthermore, the report from that committee states, "'Medicine' should be understood to be limited to the medicine itself, and does not include the vast array of medical supplies." H.R. Rep. No. 104-518 at 114, 1996 U.S.C.C.A.N. (110 Stat. 1214) 947. Thus, the medicine exemption was not intended to be a general-purpose humanitarian aid exemption.

Congress's actual intent behind the medicine exemption is more difficult to infer. Because it is relatively easily sold, donated medicine could certainly be converted to non-humanitarian use. Thus, the medicine exemption would appear to provide a bad-faith medicine donor with a potential route around § 2339B's prohibitions. However, because Congress has not done away with the exemption on any of the occasions it has amended § 2339A, it seems content to live with this potential loophole.

Even if the medicine exemption was not intended to allow groups to provide humanitarian aid to FTOs, it could be interpreted as evidence that, as a matter of policy, § 2339B should not prohibit humanitarian aid given without any intent to further an FTO's terrorist agenda. A narrow interpretation of the medicine exemption would, in fact, create the absurd situation where it would be permissible to donate Viagra to an FTO, but a felony to donate band-aids, permissible to donate Prozac, but a felony to donate water purification tablets. In addition, the court might allow the donation of humanitarian aid on policy grounds because groups designated as FTOs "often do much more than commit terrorist acts. They also undertake important and worthwhile charitable, humanitarian, educational, or political activities." Randolph N. Jonakait, *The Mens Rea For the Crime of Providing Material Resources to a Foreign Terrorist Organization*, 56 Baylor L. Rev. 861, 873 (2004). If the court holds that § 2339B has no scienter requirement, charitable giving that ought to be encouraged by a rich country like the United States "will have taken on previously unknown risks," because donors who seek only to support an FTO's humanitarian agenda could be subjected to criminal penalties. *Id.*

On the other hand, any broadening of the medicine exemption would conflict with Congress's intent to make an outright prohibition on contributions from the United States to FTOs and interfere with Congress's larger goal of combating terrorism. *See* H.R. Rep. No. 104-383 at 45. In addition, any exemption for humanitarian aid would be extremely difficult to administer so as to ensure that the humanitarian aid was not subverted to further the FTO's terrorist agenda:

> [T]errorist organizations do not maintain organizational structures or "firewalls" to prevent resources donated for humanitarian purposes from being used to commit or support terrorist acts. . . . [E]ven if funds or goods raised for charitable purposes are in fact so used, the addition of such items to the coffers of terrorist groups frees funds raised from other sources for use in facilitating terrorist acts. Thus, humanitarian support, however well-intentioned, increases the resources that a terrorist organization can devote to terrorist ends.

Brief for the Appellees/Cross-Appellants at 16-17, *Humanitarian Law Project v. United States Dept. of Justice,* 352 F.3d 382 (9th Cir. 2003) (No. 02-55082). As a matter of policy, the government recognizes that any material support, training, or donations made to an FTO are "dangerous quite apart from the specific intent of the donor." *Id.* at 9-10. In other words, a humanitarian intent on the part of the donor does not restrict an FTO's use of the donated goods to peaceful purposes.

Congress's stated policy of preventing all contributions to FTOs is certainly undermined by the medicine exemption, and it may be that the medicine exemption cannot be completely reconciled with the policy behind the antiterrorism statutes. But the mere fact that § 2339B is not completely consistent between its language and the policies it seeks to further is not grounds for effectively abandoning those policies by creating a loophole as large as the one that would be created if the court interprets the medicine exemption broadly. Even so, without creating a large loophole, the court should interpret the policies behind § 2339B as allowing only those humanitarian donations that would not serve to further an FTO's terrorist agenda.

B. Wrongdoing Must Be Conscious to Be Criminal

Also supporting a holding that would allow certain blame-free donations of humanitarian aid, the policy that "wrongdoing must be conscious to be criminal" is fundamental to our justice system. *Morissette v. United States,* 342 U.S. 246, 252 (1952). The courts have long required proof of some kind of criminal intent to "protect those who were not blameworthy in mind from conviction." *Id.* The latest amendment to § 2339B (to violate the statute, a person must "have knowledge that the organization is a designated terrorist organization," 18 U.S.C. § 2339B) purports to adhere to this concept because, to be convicted, defendants must have known that they provided material support to an organization and must have known that the organization was an FTO (or had engaged in or engages in acts of terrorism). *See e.g. Humanitarian II,* 352 F.3d at 399; Jonakait, supra, at 875. This interpretation of the statute, however, leads to absurd results insofar as it means that a cab driver could be guilty for giving a ride to an FTO member if the cab driver knew that the person was a member of an FTO or that the person was a member of an organization that had engaged in terrorist activity. *United States v. Al-Arian,* 329 F. Supp. 2d 1294, 1337-38, *modification denied,* 329 F. Supp. 2d 1294 (M.D. Fla. 2004).

To avoid similar problems of absurdity, some courts have held that statutes should not be interpreted "so as to sweep within a crime otherwise significant innocent activities." *Staples v. United States,* 511 U.S. 600, 610 (1994) (quoting *Liparota v. United States,* 471 U.S. 419, 426 (1985)); *see also United States v. X-Citement Video,* 513 U.S. 64, 69 (1994); Jonakait, supra, at 876-877. Accordingly, "the Supreme Court and [the ninth] circuit have construed Congress' [sic] inclusion of the word 'knowingly' to require proof of knowledge of the law and an intent to further the proscribed act." *Humanitarian 2003,* 352 F.3d at 399.

IV. Cases

The question of whether to read a scienter requirement into § 2339B involves balancing policies designed to protect the United States from terrorism against policies designed to protect innocent behavior from criminal prosecution. To illuminate this balancing test, it is instructive to consider next how various courts have analyzed the question of what kind of intent § 2339B requires.

A. *Humanitarian Law Project*

The Ninth Circuit addressed the question of what intent § 2339B requires in a set of cases descending from a civil action for declaratory and injunctive relief. That suit was brought by a number of organizations and individuals who wished to provide two FTOs, the Kurdistan Workers' Party and the LTTE, with support for the political and nonviolent humanitarian activities of each organization. *See Humanitarian Law Project v. United States Dept. of Justice,* 393 F.3d 902 (9th Cir. Cal. 2004) (*Humanitarian 2004*); *Humanitarian 2003,* 352 F.3d 382, 403-05; *Humanitarian Law Project v. Reno,* 205 F.3d 1130, 1137-38 (9th Cir. 2000), *reasoning adopted in Humanitarian Law Project v. United States Dept. of Justice,* 393 F.3d 902 (9th Cir. 2004) (*Humanitarian 2000*).

In *Humanitarian 2000*, the plaintiffs challenged § 2339B on freedom of association, freedom of speech, and vagueness grounds. *See Humanitarian 2000,* 205 F.3d at 1133-38. The Ninth Circuit held that § 2339B did not restrict the plaintiffs' rights to association or speech, *see id.* at 1133-36, but also held that the "personnel" and "training" elements of "material support" were unconstitutionally vague, *see id.* at 1137-38. That court refused to cure the vagueness problems by imposing a stricter scienter requirement than it felt was warranted by the language of § 2339B, holding that

the term "knowingly" modified only "provides" and that the intent requirement was satisfied if the defendants knew only that they were providing
something. *See id.* at 1138.

On appeal, the Ninth Circuit upheld its prior vagueness analysis, *see
Humanitarian 2003*, 352 F.3d at 403-05, but reconsidered its interpretation
of § 2339B's intent requirement after the plaintiffs argued that the statute
lacked a personal guilt requirement and was therefore unconstitutional on
Fifth Amendment grounds. *Id.* at 385. Where punishment is imposed for a
person's conduct because of that conduct's *relationship* to other criminal
activity, the concept of personal guilt requires that the relationship be substantial enough to withstand attack under the Due Process Clause. *Id.* at
394. Faced with this Fifth Amendment argument, the *Humanitarian 2003*
court concluded that its prior interpretation of the statute contravened the
personal guilt requirement because it could severely punish persons who
acted with innocent intent (as in the case of a person who contributes
money solely to support the lawful purposes of an organization that turns
out to have been an FTO). *Id.* at 399, 403. That court then held that to
convict defendants under § 2339B, the government must prove that the
defendants either knew that an organization was an FTO or knew of an
organization's unlawful activities that caused it to be designated as an FTO.
See id. at 403. The *Humanitarian 2003* court reasoned that with this intent
requirement, the relationship between the conduct prohibited by § 2339B
(providing material support to an FTO) and the criminal terrorist activity of
that FTO was sufficiently substantial to satisfy the Fifth Amendment's personal guilt requirement. *See id.* at 394-403.

Shortly after Congress amended § 2339B, the Ninth Circuit, appearing
to be satisfied that the statute as it now reads meets constitutional muster,
vacated its judgment in *Humanitarian 2003* regarding the vagueness of the
terms "personnel" and "training." *See Humanitarian 2004*, 393 F.3d at 903.
The Ninth Circuit is thus willing to presume that defendants act with guilty
intent when they provide material support to an organization that they
know is an FTO or has committed acts of terrorism. *See id; Humanitarian
2003*, 352 F.3d at 394-404.

B. *Boim*

The *Humanitarian* courts, however, are not the only courts to have addressed the scienter requirement of § 2339B; this circuit has addressed (if
only obliquely) the scienter requirement of § 2339B in a civil case involving a violation of 18 U.S.C. § 2333 ("Any national of the United States
injured . . . by reason of an act of international terrorism . . . may sue
therefor . . . and shall recover threefold the damages he or she sustains . . . .").
In that case, the parents of a man killed by Palestinian terrorists sued a
number of organizations, alleging that the organizations were civilly liable
for the murder under § 2333 because the organizations had provided material support to Hamas (an FTO) in violation of § 2339B. *Boim*, 291 F.3d at
1001-06.

That court held that a violation of § 2339B would serve as the basis for civil liability under § 2333 "so long as knowledge and intent are also shown." *Id.* at 1015. While this statement is susceptible to multiple interpretations, it arguably means that the *Boim* court believed that § 2339B lacked a scienter requirement and that a plaintiff alleging civil liability under § 2333 based on a violation of § 2339B must prove knowledge and intent in addition to proving a § 2339B violation (which could be proven without knowledge and intent). Supporting this interpretation, the *Boim* court later indicated that § 2339B does not require intent to further an FTO's criminal activities when that court stated the following: "Terrorist organizations use funds for illegal activities *regardless of the intent of the donor*, and Congress thus was compelled to attach liability [under § 2339B] to *all* donations to foreign terrorist organizations." *Id.* at 1027 (emphasis added).

C. Al-Arian

The problem with the *Boim* court's interpretation, however, is that it uses a stricter intent requirement for civil liability under § 2333 than it does for criminal liability under § 2339B. A district court in the Eleventh Circuit noted this anomaly as it was constructing § 2339B. *Al-Arian*, 308 F. Supp. 2d at 1339 (note 33). In that case, the defendants were alleged members of a designated FTO (the Palestinian Islamic Jihad-Shiqaqi Faction) and purportedly had been conducting fund-raising and other supporting activities on behalf of the FTO for twenty years. *Id.* at 1328. Among the fifty counts in that indictment were two counts of conspiring to provide material support to an FTO. *Id.*

In ruling on a pretrial motion to dismiss the counts involving violations of § 2339B, the *Al-Arian* court rejected the *Humanitarian 2003* court's construction of that statute's scienter requirement because the *Humanitarian 2003* construction still criminalized otherwise innocent conduct (under *Humanitarian 2003*, a cab driver could be guilty for giving a ride to an FTO member if the driver knew the person was a member of an FTO). *Id.* at 1337-38. That court also noted that the *Humanitarian 2003* court did not properly apply the Supreme Court's holding that a scienter requirement "should apply to each of the statutory elements that criminalize otherwise innocent conduct" because *Humanitarian 2003* did not impose a scienter requirement on the "material support" element. *Id.* (quoting *X-Citement Video*, 513 U.S. at 69 (constructing a statute that prohibits "knowingly" transporting, shipping, receiving, distributing, or reproducing a visual depiction of a minor engaging in sexually explicit conduct to require that the defendant also know the minor's age)).

Applying the *X-Citement Video* analysis, the *Al-Arian* court concluded that the most effective way to carry out Congress's intention that material support be withheld from FTOs was to impose intent requirements on not only the "FTO" element of § 2339B (as in *Humanitarian 2003*), but also the "material support" element. *See id.* at 1338-39. Consequently, that court held that to convict a person under § 2339B, the government would have to prove not only that defendants knew that the organization they were supporting was an FTO or had committed unlawful activities, but also that they knew that they were providing material support and knew (had a specific intent) that the support would further the illegal activities of the FTO. *Id.* at 1338-39. Thus, the *Al-Arian* court held that § 2339B had the same scienter requirement as the requirement that the *Boim* court constructed for § 2333, thereby avoiding the anomaly of "civil liability being more narrow than criminal liability based on the same statutory language." *Id.* at 1339 (note 33).

At first glance, this holding seems to make § 2339B a less useful tool for promoting the underlying policy of hindering international terrorism because the broader scienter requirement created a "charitable intent" loophole, making it more difficult for the government to win convictions under the statute. The *Al-Arian* court, however, did not see its holding in this light; that court believed that the burden of proving specific intent would not be so great as to undermine the purpose of § 2339B because a jury can easily infer such intent where appropriate. *See id.* at 1339. For example, "a jury could infer a specific intent when a defendant knows that the organization continues to commit illegal acts and the defendant provides funds to that organization knowing that money is fungible and, once received, the donee can use the funds for any purpose it chooses." *Id.* Far from ignoring congressional purpose when creating section 2339B, the *Al-Arian* court believed that "[its] holding work[ed] to avoid potential constitutional problems and fully accomplish congressional intent." *Id.*

D. Summary of Cases

In summary, the *Humanitarian 2003* court essentially held that the government need only prove that defendants knew that they were providing material support to an organization that had been designated as an FTO or that had committed acts of terrorism. *Humanitarian 2003,* 352 F.3d at 385. In this case, the government argues that this interpretation of § 2339B's scienter requirement is proper and urges the Court to adopt the rules set out in *Humanitarian 2003*. The *Al-Arian* court, on the other hand, held that in addition to proving the intent required by *Humanitarian 2003*, the government must also prove (by inference or otherwise) that defendants had a specific intent to aid the organization's illegal activities. *Al-Arian,* 308 F. Supp 2d at 1339. The *Boim* court (the only court in this circuit that has addressed this issue) seems to have assumed that no proof of specific intent was required for criminal liability under § 2339B but chose to require proof of intent for civil liability under § 2333. *Boim,* 291 F.3d at 1015, 1025.

The *Boim* court, however, did not do an in-depth analysis of § 2339B's intent requirement because the defendants in that case were not charged with a criminal violation of that statute; the *Boim* court only *prima facie* analyzed § 2339B for evidence of what conduct Congress intended to include in its definition of "international terrorism." *See id.* at 1025. Because the *Boim* case did not require the court to look beyond the face of § 2339B, it is entirely possible that the Seventh Circuit could reach a different conclusion as to the intent requirement of that statute if this case, which puts the intent requirement of § 2339B squarely at issue, reached that court on appeal. As the *Al-Arian* court pointed out, it would make little sense for the Seventh Circuit to require proof of specific intent for civil liability but no proof of specific intent for criminal liability based on the same conduct (providing material support to an FTO). *See Al-Arian* 308 F. Supp. 2d at 1339. To avoid that anomalous result, it is arguable that the Seventh Circuit's holding in *Boim* indicates that that court might be inclined to hold that § 2339B has a scienter requirement if it had to construct § 2339B.

Conclusion

This Court has already decided that § 2339B would be unconstitutional without a scienter requirement; therefore, the Court must decide whether to strike down the statute or to read a scienter requirement into the statute. The *Al-Arain* court's analysis and conclusion (applying a scienter requirement to the "material support" element of § 2339B is the best way to avoid punishing innocent behavior) are persuasive. *See id.* at 1335-39. In this case, the Court should hold that § 2339B has a scienter requirement: to convict the TWHRC under § 2339B for providing material support to an FTO, the government would need to prove that the TWHRC intended or knew it was likely that the LTTE (an FTO) would have used the donated tsunami warning equipment to further its terrorist agenda. This holding is likely to stand up on appeal because this circuit was willing to construct a similar intent requirement for § 2333 and because to hold otherwise would result in civil liability under § 2333 being narrower than criminal liability under § 2339B. *See Boim*, 291 F.3d at 1012-15; *Al-Arian* 308 F. Supp. 2d at 1339. The Court will also be able to find support for this holding in the plain language, legislative history, and public policy of § 2339B.

I.   Plain Language

Reading a scienter requirement into § 2339B appears at first to be at odds with the relatively clear plain language of subsection (a) of the statute, "To violate this paragraph, a person must have knowledge that the organization is a designated terrorist organization . . . , that the organization has engaged or engages in terrorist activity . . . , or that the organization has engaged or engages in terrorism. . . ." 18 U.S.C. § 2339B. Subsection (i), however, also states that the statute "shall [not] be construed or applied so as to abridge the exercise of rights guaranteed under the First Amendment to the Constitution," *id.*, indicating that Congress realized that the statute must be free from constitutional defects if it is to be effective at all. Because § 2339B will not prevent any material support from reaching any FTOs if it is unconstitutional under either the First or Fifth Amendments, and because (as this court has already decided) the statute faces constitutional problems if it is constructed without a scienter requirement, *see also Al-Arian* 308 F. Supp. 2d at 1338-39, reading a scienter requirement into the statute is not inconsistent with the plain language of the statute.

II. Legislative Intent

Reading a scienter requirement into § 2339B also appears at first to be counter to Congress's intention to make an outright prohibition on contributions to FTOs. *See e.g.* Antiterrorism and Effective Death Penalty Act § 301. However, Senator Snowe's statement in the *Congressional Record*, wherein she notes that the statute will prevent donations "for supposedly 'humanitarian' purposes, where in reality a large part of those funds go toward conducting terrorist activities," 142 Cong. Rec. S3380, could easily be interpreted to mean merely that Congress did not want to create a "loophole" that would allow terrorism-supporting donations to hide behind a façade of humanitarianism. It is difficult to infer from this statement that Congress intended to prohibit actual humanitarian donations; it is more likely that Congress intended to prohibit all donations only because it could not legislatively distinguish between good-faith and bad-faith "humanitarian" donations. Therefore, if the *Al-Arian* court is correct in its belief that juries are capable of seeing a defendant's true intent even if it is hidden behind a false façade of humanitarianism, then Congress's intent would not be thwarted by allowing donations made with genuine humanitarian intent. *See Al-Arian*, 308 F. Supp. 2d at 1339; *see also* Paul Rosenzweig, *Aiding Terrorists—An Examination of the Material Support Statute* (2004), at http://www.heritage.org/ Research/LegalIssues/tst050504a.cfm ("Our collective American experience is that juries are quite good at sorting the sham claims of innocence from the legitimate ones."). Furthermore, the Court should reiterate that the government may often prove specific intent by inference and that this burden should not be that great in the typical case. *See Al-Arian*, 308 F. Supp. 2d at 1339.

By contrast, Congress's intent would be thwarted if the Court does not require proof of specific intent, and § 2339B were thereby rendered unconstitutional for punishing innocent conduct. *See id.* at 1337-38. Constructing § 2339B to have a scienter requirement is the only option that avoids this constitutional problem and is, therefore, the only option that works to accomplish congressional intent.

III. Public Policy

Finally, it is difficult to conceive of a legitimate policy interest that would be hindered by allowing donations of nonfungible equipment, such as a tsunami warning system, that could not easily be subverted to further an FTO's terrorist agenda. While it may be that a humanitarian intent on the part of the donor does not generally restrict an FTO's use of the contributed goods to peaceful purposes, in this case, the nature of the goods themselves is evidence from which a jury could infer that the TWHRC contributed the tsunami warning system with a genuine humanitarian intent. It is not even plausible to argue that this donation should be prohibited because giving the tsunami warning system to the LTTE would free up other resources that the LTTE could then use for illegal activities. That argument is not plausible because it is highly unlikely that the LTTE would ever choose to expend its limited resources on a costly system that may or may not have any benefit to the population it serves in the short- or medium-term. In other words, it is difficult to argue that any of the LTTE's resources would be "freed up" by the donation of equipment that the LTTE would not otherwise have expended its own resources to acquire.

It would be a different matter if the TWHRC wished to donate *money* to be used for the purchase of a tsunami warning system; in that case, a jury could infer that the TWHRC had a specific intent to further the illegal activities of the LTTE because the TWHRC knows that the LTTE is an FTO, that the LTTE continues to commit illegal acts, and that money is fungible and the LTTE could use the donated funds for any purpose it chose.

IV. Conclusion

In conclusion, there are no insurmountable plain language, legislative history, public policy, or case law barriers to prevent the Court from holding that a conviction under § 2339B would require proof of intent with respect to both the "FTO" element and the "material support" element. If the Court holds that § 2339B has such a scienter requirement, it will be constructing a workable standard that will continue to prevent FTOs from using the United States as a base of support, thus remaining true to the purpose of the statute, while also leaving innocent charitable giving free from the threat of criminal prosecution and allowing legitimate humanitarian aid to reach at-risk populations.

CHAPTER

7

Drafting the
Statement of Facts

Just as every case starts with a story, so do most memos. Thus, if you are writing a formal memo, include a statement of facts.

For the purposes of this chapter, presume that you have been asked to write a formal memo in which the attorney wants you to both summarize and apply the applicable law. Also presume that, instead of having to go through the case file to find facts, the attorney has set them out in the memo assigning the project.

To see the memo based on this fact pattern, see section 6.4.2.

To: Legal Intern
From: Christina Galeano
Date: September 12, 2006
Re: Elaine Olsen, Case No. 06-478

Elaine Olsen has requested our help in overturning an order terminating her parental rights.

- Ms. Olsen says she never received the summons and, as a result, did not respond.
- On Wednesday, July 26, 2006, a process server went to Ms. Webster's house and asked for Elaine Olsen. (Ms. Webster is Ms. Olsen's sister.) When Ms. Webster told the process server

that "Elaine isn't here today," the process server handed what was probably a summons and complaint to Ms. Webster and told Ms. Webster that Ms. Olsen "needed to go to court."

- On February 1, 2006, Ms. Olsen entered an inpatient drug treatment program in Miami, Florida. She remained in the program until March 27, 2006, when she moved into a "half-way" house. The halfway house was a four-bedroom house in a residential neighborhood. Up to eight women live in the house for three to twelve months while they make the transition from inpatient treatment to living on their own. There is always a staff member at the house, who makes sure that the women do not use drugs or engage in any other illegal activities and who provides counseling.

- During April, May, and June, Ms. Olsen was a full-time resident at the halfway house. She had a bedroom in the house, ate her meals there, and had some of her possessions there.

- When Ms. Olsen renewed her driver's license in August 2006, she listed Ms. Webster's address as her address.

- Beginning in July 2006, Ms. Olsen began spending less time at the halfway house and more time with her sister, Elizabeth Webster. During July and August 2006, Ms. Olsen usually spent weeknights at the halfway house and Friday, Saturday, and Sunday nights at her sister's house. Because she was spending time at her sister's house, Ms. Olsen moved some of her clothing and personal effects into her sister's house.

- Ms. Webster is 32. She will testify that she never gave the summons to her sister. Because she thought that paper related to some of Ms. Olsen's unpaid bills, she simply put the summons in a shoebox in the kitchen with a stack of Ms. Olsen's other mail.

- From April and May 2006, Ms. Olsen put the halfway house address on employment applications. However, her driver's license showed her sister's address as her address. Her voter registration shows the address where she lived before entering the treatment program.

- On September 1, 2006, Ms. Olsen moved into her own apartment. Since August 1, 2006, she has worked part-time.

- I looked at the return on the service of process and everything appears to be in order. Thus, please assume that the return of service is regular on its face.

- There is nothing in the record that indicates whether the defendant tried to personally serve Ms. Olsen or whether it tried to serve her at the halfway house.

As the first step, I would like to determine if the service of process is valid under the applicable Florida statute or statutes. Thus, please research the service of process issue for me.

§ 7.1 Decide What Facts to Include

In a typical statement of facts, there are three types of facts: the legally significant facts, the emotionally significant facts, and the background facts. In addition, the writer usually identifies those facts that are unknown.

§ 7.1.1 Legally Significant Facts

A legally significant fact is a fact that a court would consider in deciding whether a statute or rule is applicable or in applying that statute or rule. For instance, in the Olsen case, the legally significant facts are those facts that the court would consider in determining whether service of process was valid. More specifically, the legally significant facts are the facts that the court would consider in determining (1) whether the summons was left at the defendant's usual place of abode, (2) whether the summons was left with person residing therein who is 15 years old or older, and (3) whether the process server notified the person being served of the contents of the documents.

You can use either of two techniques to determine whether a fact is legally significant. Before you write the discussion section, you can prepare a two-column chart in which you list the elements in the first column and the facts that relate to those elements in the second column. See Chart 7.1.

Chart 7.1	Elements and Facts the Court Would Consider in Deciding Whether the Elements Are Met
Element	**Facts the court would consider in deciding whether element is met**
Usual Place of Abode	Ms. Webster told the process server that "Elaine isn't here today."
	On February 1, 2006, Ms. Olsen entered an inpatient drug treatment program in Miami. She remained in the program until March 27, 2006, when she moved into a residential treatment house for recovering addicts.
	During April, May, and June 2006, Ms. Olsen was a full-time resident at the halfway house. She had a bedroom in the house, ate her meals there, and had some of her possessions there.

(continues)

Continued

	Beginning in July 2006, Ms. Olsen began spending less time at the halfway house and more time with her sister, Elizabeth Webster.
	During July and August 2006, Ms. Olsen spent weeknights at the halfway house and Friday, Saturday, and Sunday nights at her sister's house. Because she was spending time at her sister's house, she moved some of her clothing and personal effects into her sister's house.
	When Ms. Olsen renewed her driver's license in August 2006, she listed her sister's address as her address.
	From April and May 2006, Ms. Olsen put the halfway house address on employment applications. However, her driver's license showed her sister's address as her address.
	Her voter registration shows the address where she lived before entering the treatment program.
	Since August 1, 2006, Ms. Olsen has worked. On September 1, 2006, Ms. Olsen moved into her own apartment.
	The return on the service of process appears to be in order.
Person residing therein who is 15 years old or older	Ms. Webster lives in the house where the summons was left.
	Ms. Webster is 32.
Informing person of contents	The process server handed what was probably a summons and complaint to Ms. Webster and told Ms. Webster that Ms. Olsen "needed to go to court."

The second technique is used after the discussion section has been completed. To ensure that you have included all of the legally significant facts in your statement of facts, go through your discussion section, checking to make sure that each of the facts that you used in setting out the arguments is in your statement of facts. If you used a fact in the arguments, that fact is legally significant and should be included in the statement of facts. (Remember, writing a memo is a recursive process. Even though you may write the statement of facts first, you will need to revise it after you have completed the discussion section.)

§ 7.1.2 Emotionally Significant Facts

An emotionally significant fact is one that, while not legally significant, may affect the way the judge or jury decides the case.

For example, in the Olsen case, while it is not legally significant that Ms. Olsen was in a drug treatment program, that fact may color the way the judge views her. Therefore, this fact is an emotionally significant fact and should be included in the statement of facts. In addition, while it is not legally significant that Ms. Olsen was applying for jobs and obtained a job, those facts may also color the way in which the judge views her and should, therefore, be included in the statement of facts.

§ 7.1.3 Background Facts

In addition to including the legally and emotionally significant facts, also include those facts that are needed to tell the story and that provide the context for the legally and emotionally significant facts.

§ 7.1.4 Unknown Facts

Sometimes you are not given all of the facts needed to analyze an issue. For instance, because the attorney did not know the law, he or she may not have asked the right questions, or the documents containing the unknown facts are in the possession of the opposing party. If the unknown facts are legally significant and you can obtain them, try to do so before writing the memo. If, however, the unknown facts are not legally significant or if you cannot obtain them, write the memo, but tell the attorney, either in the statement of facts or in the discussion section, what facts are unknown.

PRACTICE POINTER   You may not realize a fact is unknown until you have read the cases. For instance, in our example problem, at the time that she interviewed Ms. Olsen, the attorney did not ask Ms. Olsen whether the process server had tried to serve her at the halfway house or on any other occasions. However, after doing the research, you know that these facts may be legally significant.

---

§ 7.2 Select an Organizational Scheme

As a general rule, begin your statement of facts with an introductory sentence or paragraph that identifies the parties and the issue. Then present the facts using one of three organizational schemes: a chronological organizational scheme, a topical organizational scheme, or a combination of the two, for example, a scheme in which you organize the facts by topic and then, within each topic, in chronological order.

Most of the time, the facts dictate which organizational scheme will work best. If the case involves a series of events related by date, then the facts should be presented chronologically. If, however, there are a number of facts that are not related by date (for example, the description of several different pieces of property) or a number of unrelated events that occurred during the same time period (for example, four unrelated crimes committed by the defendant over the same two-day period), the facts should be organized by topic.

Sometimes, though, the facts can be presented in more than one way. For example, in the Olsen case, the facts can be presented using either a scheme that is primarily chronological or a scheme that is primarily topical. See Examples 1 and 2.

EXAMPLE 1 **Statement of Facts with Facts Presented in Chronological Order**

Elaine Olsen has contacted our office asking for assistance in overturning an order terminating her parental rights. You have asked me to determine whether the service of process was valid.

On February 1, 2006, Ms. Olsen entered an inpatient drug treatment program in Miami, Florida. She remained in the program until March 27, 2006, when she moved into a residential treatment house for recovering addicts.

During April, May, and June 2006, Ms. Olsen was a full-time resident at the halfway house. She had a bedroom in the house, ate her meals there, and had some of her possessions there. In addition, when she applied for jobs in May and June, she listed the halfway house address as her address.

Beginning in July 2006, Ms. Olsen began spending less time at the halfway house and more time with her sister, Elizabeth Webster, who is 32. During July and August 2006, Ms. Olsen usually spent weeknights at the halfway house and Friday, Saturday, and Sunday nights at her sister's house. Because she was spending time at her sister's house, Ms. Olsen moved some of her clothing and personal effects into her sister's house. When she renewed her driver's license in August 2006, Ms. Olsen listed her sister's address as her address.

On Wednesday, July 26, 2006, a process server went to Ms. Webster's house and asked for Elaine Olsen. When Ms. Webster told the process server that "Elaine isn't here today," the process server handed the summons to Ms. Webster and told her that Ms. Olsen "needed to go to court."

Ms. Webster will testify that she never gave the summons to her sister. Because she thought that papers related to some of Ms. Olsen's unpaid bills, she simply put the summons in a shoebox in the kitchen with a stack of Ms. Olsen's other mail. Ms. Olsen says she never received the summons and, as a result, did not respond. You have asked me to presume that the return of service—that is, the affidavit completed by the process server—is regular on its face.

Ms. Olsen has been employed since August 1, 2006, and she has lived in her own apartment since September 1, 2006. Her voter registration card lists the address where she lived before she entered the treatment program.

There is nothing in the record that indicates whether the State tried to personally serve Ms. Olsen or whether it tried to serve her at the halfway house.

EXAMPLE 2 Statement of Facts with Facts Organized by Topic

You have asked me to determine whether the service of process on one of our clients, Elaine Olsen, is valid.

During the past six months, Ms. Olsen has lived in three places. From February 1, 2006, until March 27, 2006, Ms. Olsen was a patient in an in-patient drug treatment program in Miami, Florida. On March 27, 2006, she moved into a halfway house for recovering addicts. During April, May, and June, Ms. Olsen was a full-time resident at the halfway house. She had a bedroom in the house, ate her meals there, and had some of her possessions there. In addition, Ms. Olsen listed the halfway house address on job applications. Beginning in July 2006, Ms. Olsen began spending more time at her sister's house. During July and August 2006, Ms. Olsen spent weeknights at the halfway house and Friday, Saturday, and Sunday nights at her sister's house. Because she was spending time at her sister's house, Ms. Olsen moved some of her clothing and personal effects into her sister's house. When she renewed her driver's license in August 2006, Ms. Olsen listed her sister's address as her address.

On Wednesday, July 26, 2006, a process server went to Ms. Olsen's sister's house and asked for Elaine Olsen. When Ms. Olsen's sister, Ms. Webster, told the process server that "Elaine isn't here today," the process server handed the summons to Ms. Webster and told her that Ms. Olsen "needed to go to court."

Ms. Webster, who is 32, will testify that she never gave the summons to her sister. Because she thought that the papers related to some of Ms. Olsen's unpaid bills, she simply put the summons in a shoebox in the kitchen with a stack of Ms. Olsen's other mail. Ms. Olsen says she never received the summons and complaint, and as a result, she did not respond. You have asked me to presume that the return of service is regular on its face. There is nothing in the record that indicates whether the State tried to personally serve Ms. Olsen or whether it tried to serve her at the halfway house.

PRACTICE

POINTER

If you are using a chronological organizational scheme, try to start the sentence that follows your introduction with a date. In addition, start many but not all of the subsequent sentences with dates. In contrast, if you are using a topical organizational scheme, try to use topic sentences that identify the topics. Do not, however, include law or argue the facts in the Statement of Facts; both belong in the Discussion section, which will be explained in Chapters 9, 10, and 11.

§ 7.3 Present the Facts Concisely but Clearly

Most United States attorneys prefer statements of fact that are short and to the point. This does not, however, mean that they want the facts set out using bullet points. While bullet points are common in other types of business writing and in documents submitted to courts in other legal systems, most U.S. attorneys want the facts presented in easy-to-read sentences in well-constructed paragraphs. (For more on writing effective sentences and paragraphs, see Chapters 3 and 5 in *Just Writing, 2d ed.*)

Well-written sentences and paragraphs have several advantages over bullet points. First, most readers have an easier time understanding what happened when the facts are presented in the form of a "story." The narrative quality of a story helps readers understand the "cast of characters" in a legal story and follow a sequence of events. Unlike the choppiness of bullet points, paragraphs convey how a story unfolds, making it more memorable for readers. Second, setting out the facts in story form makes it easier to convert the statement of facts in the memo to a statement of facts for a brief to a U.S. court.

The key thing to remember when writing a statement of facts for an office memo, then, is that the facts must be clear and easy to follow without a lot of extra verbiage or irrelevant detail.

§ 7.4 Present the Facts Accurately and Objectively

In writing the statement of facts for an objective memorandum, present the facts accurately and objectively. Do not include facts that are not in your file, and do not set out legal conclusions, misstate facts, leave out facts that are legally significant, or present the facts so that they favor one side over the other.

In the following example, the author has violated all of these "rules."

EXAMPLE   **Writer Has Not Presented the Facts Accurately and Objectively**

Hoping to obtain a default judgment against Ms. Olsen, the plaintiff had the sheriff serve the summons and complaint at Ms. Olsen's sister's house and not at the halfway house where Ms. Olsen was actually living. Although Ms. Olsen occasionally visited her sister at her sister's house, she did not keep any of personal belongings at her sister's house.

In the first sentence, the author violates the first two rules. First, she sets out facts that are not in the record when she states that the plaintiff hoped to get a default judgment and when she states that the plaintiff had a sheriff serve Ms. Olsen at her sister's house and not at the halfway house. Second, she sets out legal conclusions when she states that the defendant was actually living at the halfway house. Because a person's usual place of abode is the place where the defendant is actually living, in the context of this case, the statement that the defendant was actually living in the halfway house is a legal conclusion.

In the second sentence, the author violates the last three rules. The author misstates the facts when she states that Ms. Olsen did not keep any personal belongings at her sister's house; she leaves out legally significant facts when she does not include the fact that Ms. Olsen used her sister's address when she renewed her driver's license, and she presents the facts in a light favorable to her client when she states that Ms. Olsen only occasionally visited her sister.

PRACTICE POINTER   As a general rule, do not refer to individuals by just their first names. Instead, use the appropriate title and last name. For instance, instead of referring to Elaine Olsen as "Elaine," use "Elaine Olsen" or "Ms. Olsen." For information on bias-free language, see section 6.5.2 in *Just Writing, 2d ed.*

---

§ 7.5   Checklist for Critiquing the First Draft of the Statement of Facts

A. Content

- The writer has included all of the legally significant facts.
- When appropriate, the writer included emotionally significant facts.
- The writer included enough background facts so that a person who is not familiar with the case can understand what happened.

- The writer has identified the unknown facts.
- The writer presented the facts accurately.
- The writer presented the facts objectively.
- The writer has not included legal conclusions in the statement of facts.

B. Organization

- The writer has included an introductory sentence or paragraph that identifies the parties and the nature of the dispute.
- The writer has used one of the conventional organizational schemes: chronological, topical, or a combination of chronological and topical.

C. Writing

- The attorney can understand the facts of the case after reading the statement of facts once.
- The paragraph divisions are logical, and the paragraphs are neither too long nor too short. (See Chapter 3 in *Just Writing, 2d ed.*)
- Transitions and dovetailing have been used to make the connection between ideas clear. (See section 13.1 in this book and Chapter 4 in *Just Writing, 2d ed.*)
- In most sentences, the writer has used the actor as the subject of the sentence, and the subject and verb are close together. (See section 13.2.1 in this book and Chapter 5 in *Just Writing, 2d ed.*)
- The writer has varied the length of the sentences and the sentence patterns so that each sentence flows smoothly from the prior sentence. (See section 13.2.1 in this book and Chapter 5 in *Just Writing, 2d ed.*)
- The writing is concise and precise. (See sections 13.2 and 13.3 in this book and Chapter 6 in *Just Writing, 2d ed.*)
- The writing is grammatically correct and correctly punctuated. (See section 13.2.4 in this book and Chapters 8 and 9 in *Just Writing, 2d ed.*)
- The statement of facts has been proofread. (See section 13.3 in this book and Chapter 1 in *Just Writing, 2d ed.*)

8

Drafting the Issue Statement and Brief Answer

In a formal memo, the issue statement provides the focus for the memo, and the brief answer provides the quick answer.

§ 8.1 The Issue Statement

A well-written issue statement, or question presented, identifies the applicable statute or common law rule, sets out the legal question, and summarizes the facts that will be significant in deciding that legal question.

By convention, you should have the same number of issue statements as you have "parts" to the discussion section. Accordingly, if you have three issue statements—(1) whether service of process was adequate, (2) whether the statute of limitations has run, and (3) whether the defendant is entitled to judgment as a matter of law—you should also have three parts to the discussion section, one corresponding to each of the three issues. If, however, you have only one issue statement, for example, whether service of process is valid, your discussion section will have only one part.

As a general rule, do not treat each element as a separate issue. For example, if the issue is whether the service of process was valid, do not treat the first element, usual place of abode, as one issue; the second element, person residing therein who is 15 or older, as a second issue; and the third element, informing about the contents, as a third issue.

Convention also dictates that in a multi-issue memo you list the issues in the same order in which you discuss those issues in the discussion section. The first issue statement will correspond to the first part of the discussion section, the second will correspond to the second part, and so on. For an example of a multi-issue discussion section, see the memo set out in section 6.4.4.

The two most common formats for an issue statement are the "under-does-when" format and the "whether" format.

§ 8.2 The "Under-Does-When" Format

The under-does-when format is easy to use because the format forces you to include all the essential information. After the "under," insert a reference to the applicable law; after the verb (for example, "does," "is," or "may"), insert the legal question; and after "when," insert the most important of the legally significant facts. Because the format is written as a question, add a question mark at the end.

Under   [insert reference to applicable law],

does/is/may   [insert legal question]

when   [insert the key facts]?

§ 8.2.1 Reference to the Applicable Law

To be useful to the reader, the reference to the rule of law cannot be too specific or too general. For example, in the service of process problem, a reference only to the statute would be too specific: very few attorneys would know that Fla. Stat. § 48.031 (2006) deals with service of process. Similarly, a reference to "Florida law" is too broad; hundreds of cases are filed each year in which the issue is governed by Florida law.

EXAMPLE 1   Reference to the Rule of Law Too Specific

Under Fla. Stat. § 48.031 (2006) . . . .

EXAMPLE 2   **Reference to the Rule of Law Too General**

Under Florida law . . . .

EXAMPLE 3   **Appropriate References**

Under Florida's service of process statute . . . .
Under Florida's service of process statute, Fla. Stat. § 48.031 (2006) . . . .

PRACTICE POINTER If you identify the statute in your statement of the legal question, you can refer to the statute by number in your reference to the rule of law. For example, in some instances, the following format works well:

Under Fla. Stat. § 48.031 (2006), was the service of process valid when . . . .

---

§ 8.2.2 Statement of the Legal Question

After identifying the applicable law, set out the legal question. In doing so, make sure that your statement of the legal question is neither too narrow nor too broad. If stated too narrowly, your statement of the legal question will not cover all of the issues and subissues; if stated too broadly, the question does not serve its function of focusing the reader's attention on the real issue.

To see a copy of the memo from which these examples are drawn, see the memo set out in section 6.4.2.

EXAMPLE 1   **Legal Questions that Are Too Narrow**

was the summons left at Ms. Olsen's usual place of abode . . . .
was the summons left at the place where Ms. Olsen was actually living . . . .
did the process server inform Ms. Webster about the contents of the summons . . . .

EXAMPLE 2   **Legal Questions that Are Too Broad**

did the court properly terminate Ms. Olsen's parental rights . . . .
were Ms. Olsen's rights violated . . . .

EXAMPLE 3   **Legal Questions that Are Properly Framed**

---

was service valid . . . .

was Ms. Olsen properly served . . . .

was service at Ms. Olsen's sister's house valid . . . .

was the substituted service on the defendant's sister at the sister's house
    valid . . . .

---

§ 8.2.3 The Key Facts

Unless the issue that you have been asked to research involves only a question of law, you will want to end your issue statement by setting out the key facts. How will the court apply the rule of law to the facts in your client's case?

How many facts you include depends on how many facts are legally significant. If there are only a few legally significant facts, you will usually want to include all of them. If, however, there are a large number of legally significant facts, you will need to be more selective. Either list only the most important of the legally significant facts, or list only the facts that relate to the disputed element or elements.

In Example 1 set out below, the author has not included enough facts: while he has included the facts that the court would consider in deciding whether the process server informed the person served of the contents of the documents, he has not included facts that the court would consider in deciding whether the summons was left at Ms. Olsen's usual place of abode with a person 15 or older residing therein.

EXAMPLE 1   **Author Has Not Included Enough Facts**

Under Florida's service of process statute, Fla. Stat. § 48.031 (2006), was the service valid when the process server told Ms. Webster that Ms. Olsen "needed to go to court"?

In contrast, in Example 2, the author has included too many facts. As a result, the issue statement is too long, and many attorneys would not take the time to read through it.

EXAMPLE 2   **Author Has Included Too Many Facts**

Under Florida's service of process statute, was substituted service on Ms. Olsen's sister at the sister's house valid when (1) Ms. Olsen was a patient in an in-patient drug treatment program in Miami from February 1, 2006, until March 27, 2006; (2) Ms. Olsen moved into a halfway house for recovering addicts on March 27, 2006; (3) during April, May, and June 2006, Ms. Olsen was a full-time resident at the halfway house, where she had a bedroom, where she ate her meals, and where she had some possessions; (4) during April and May 2006, Ms. Olsen listed the halfway house address on job applications; (5) beginning in July 2006, Ms. Olsen began spending less time at the halfway house and more time with her sister, Ms. Webster; (6) during July and August 2006, Ms. Olsen usually spent weeknights at the halfway house and Friday, Saturday, and Sunday nights at her sister's house; (7) when Ms. Olsen renewed her driver's license in August 2006, she listed her sister's address as her address; (8) on July 26, 2006, a process server went to Ms. Webster's house and asked for Elaine Olsen; (9) when Ms. Webster told the process server that "Elaine isn't here today," the process server handed the summons to Ms. Webster and told her that Ms. Olsen "needed to go to court"; and (10) Ms. Webster is 32 years old and lives at the house where she received the summons?

Examples 3 and 4 are better: They include the key facts without going into too much detail.

EXAMPLE 3   Better Example

Under Florida's service of process statute, was Ms. Olsen properly served when (1) service was made on Ms. Olsen's 32-year-old sister on a Wednesday at the sister's house; (2) during the month when service was made, Ms. Olsen spent weeknights at a halfway house, where she had a room, ate meals, and kept belongings, and weekends at her sister's house, where she also had some belongings; (3) Ms. Olsen listed the halfway house address on job applications but her sister's address on her driver's license; (4) the process server told Ms. Olsen's sister that Ms. Olsen "needed to go to court"; and (5) Ms. Olsen's sister did not give the summons to Ms. Olsen, and Ms. Olsen states that she did not receive notice?

EXAMPLE 4   Better Example

Under Florida's statute authorizing substituted service of process, was service on the defendant's adult sister at the sister's house valid when the defendant spent weeknights at a halfway house and weekends at her sister's house; when the service was made on a weekday; when the process server told the defendant's sister that the defendant "needed to go to court"; and when the defendant states that she did not receive notice?

PRACTICE POINTER   While some attorneys will want you to "personalize" your issue statements by using the parties' names, other attorneys will want you to write issue statements that are more generic. Compare Example 3 above in which the writer used Ms. Olsen's name with Example 4 in which the writer uses the word, "the defendant."

In setting out the facts, make sure you set out facts and not legal conclusions. While what is a fact and what is a legal conclusion will vary from case to case, saying or implying that an element is or is not met will always be a legal conclusion. In the following example, the author has set out legal conclusions. Instead of setting out the facts that the court would consider in deciding whether an element is met, she has simply listed the elements.

EXAMPLE   **Writer Has Incorrectly Set Out Legal Conclusions Rather than Facts**

Under Florida's statute authorizing substituted service of process, was the service valid when the process server left the summons with a person of suitable age and discretion at one of the defendant's usual places of abode and told the person about the contents of the notice?

Finally, make sure that you set out the facts accurately and objectively. Do not misstate a fact, and do not include only those facts that favor your client. While in a brief to a court you will want to present the facts in the light most favorable to your client, in an office memo you need to be objective.

EXAMPLE   **Writer Has Not Set Out Facts Accurately and Objectively**

Under Florida's service of process statute, was the service invalid when (1) at the time that service was made, Ms. Olsen's permanent residence was a halfway house where she had a room, ate meals, and kept belongings; (2) Ms. Olsen listed the halfway house address on job applications; (3) the process server did not tell Ms. Olsen's sister that the State was planning to terminate Ms. Olsen's parental rights; and (4) Ms. Olsen's sister did not give the summons to Ms. Olsen, and Ms. Olsen states that she did not receive notice?

---

§ 8.3 The "Whether" Format

Although the under-does-when format is often easier to use, some attorneys prefer the more traditional whether format. When you use the whether format, begin your issue statement with the word "whether," and then set out the legal question and the key facts. In this format, the issue is written as a statement and not a question, so it ends with a period.

PRACTICE
POINTER

Issue statements written using the whether format are incomplete sentences. For the issue statement to be a complete sentence, you need to "read in" the phrase "The issue is": "The issue is whether . . . ."

While you do not need to include a reference to the rule of law, you may incorporate one into your statement of the legal question.

EXAMPLE 1   **Whether Format**

Whether Ms. Olsen was properly served when (1) service was made on Ms. Olsen's 32-year-old sister on a Wednesday at Ms. Olsen's sister's house; (2) during the month when service was made, Ms. Olsen spent weeknights at a halfway house where she had a room, ate meals, and kept belongings, and weekends at her sister's house, where she also had some belongings; (3) Ms. Olsen listed the halfway house address on job applications but her sister's address on her driver's license; (4) the process server told Ms. Olsen's sister that Ms. Olsen "needed to go to court"; and (5) Ms. Olsen's sister did not give the summons to Ms. Olsen, and Ms. Olsen states that she did not receive notice.

EXAMPLE 2   **Whether Format**

Whether service on the defendant's adult sister at the sister's house was valid under Florida's service of process statute when the defendant spent weeknights at a halfway house and weekends at her sister's house; when the service was made on a weekday; when the process server told the defendant's sister that the defendant "needed to go to court"; and when the defendant states that she did not receive notice.

PRACTICE POINTER   There are a number of techniques that you can use to make the list of facts easier to read. The most frequently used technique is enumeration: simply "number" each item in your list. See Example 1 above. Another technique is to repeat key structural terms, for example "that" or "when": "**when** the defendant spent weekend nights at a halfway house and weekends at her sister's house, **when** the process server told the defendant's sister that the defendant "needed to go to court"; and **when** the defendant states that she did not receive notice. See Example 2 above.

If the issue you have been asked to research involves only an issue of law, your issue statement will not include facts. For example, if you have been asked to determine whether commercial websites are a place of public accommodation under the Americans with Disabilities Act, you could frame the issue as follows:

EXAMPLE   **Issue Statement for an Issue of Law**

Under the Americans with Disabilities Act, are commercial websites places of public accommodation?

EXAMPLE   **Issue Statement for an Issue of Law**

Whether commercial websites are places of public accommodation under the Americans with Disabilities Act.

---

§ 8.4 Readibility

It is not enough to include the right information in your issue statement. You must also present that information in such a way that your issue statement is easy to read.

The "under-does-when" format helps you write a readable issue statement by forcing you to use the three slots in a sentence: The reference to the rule of law goes into the introductory phrase or clause, the legal question goes into the main clause, and the key facts go into the list of modifiers.

_____, _____ _____

introductory phrase or clause,   main clause   modifiers

Because issue statements written using the whether format have only two slots, the slot for the whether statement and the slot for the facts, you need to take more care in writing them. First, edit out any unnecessary information. Second, in drafting the "whether" clause, try to use a concrete subject and action verb. Third, in listing the facts, use parallel constructions for each item in your list. Finally, if there are more than a few items in your list of facts, use enumeration or start each item in the list with the same word, for example, start each item in your list with "that" or "when."

PRACTICE    End issue statements written using the under-does-when format with a question mark. End issue statement written using the whether format with a period.

---

§ 8.5 Checklist for Critiquing the Issue Statement

A. Content

- The reference to the rule of law is neither too broad nor too narrow.
- The legal question is properly focused.
- The most significant of the legally significant facts have been included.
- Legal conclusions have not been set out as facts.

B. Format

- The writer has used one of the conventional formats, for example, the "under-does-when" format or the "whether" format.

C. Writing

- The issue statement is easy to read and understand.
- In setting out the legal question, the writer has used a concrete subject and an action verb. (See Chapter 5 in *Just Writing, 2d ed.*)
- In listing the facts, the writer has used parallel constructions for all of the items in the list. (See section 8.7 in *Just Writing, 2d ed.*)
- If the list of facts is long, the writer has used enumeration or has repeated key structural cues, for examples, words like "when" and "that." (See section 8.7 in *Just Writing, 2d ed.*)

§ 8.6 The Brief Answer

The brief answer serves a purpose similar to that served by the formal conclusion: it tells the attorney how you think a court will decide an issue and why. The brief answer is not, however, as detailed as the formal conclusion. In drafting your brief answer, think about what you would tell the attorney if he or she stopped you in the hallway and asked for a one-sentence answer to the question you were asked to research.

Convention dictates that you should include a separate brief answer for each issue statement. In addition, convention dictates that you should start each of your brief answers with a one- or two-word short answer. The words that are typically used are "probably," and "probably not." After this one- or two-word answer, briefly explain your answer.

In writing your brief answers, keep a couple of things in mind. First, remember your audience and purpose. You are writing to an attorney who needs an objective evaluation of the client's case. Second, make sure that you answer the question you set out in your issue statement and that you match the style you used in your issue statement. For example, if you used the parties' names in your issue statement, also use them in your brief answer. Third, be specific. Tell the attorney which elements you or the other side will or will not be able to prove. Finally, make sure that you get the burden of proof right. If you have personalized your issue statement and your client has the burden of proof, talk about what your client can and cannot prove. If, however, the other side has the burden of proof, talk about what it can and cannot prove. In contrast, if you wrote a more generic issue statement, talk about what the court will and will not conclude. As a general rule, you do not need to discuss the elements that are not in dispute.

EXAMPLE 1   Issue Statement and Brief Answer in Which the Writer Uses the Parties' Names

Issue

Under Florida's service of process statute, was Ms. Olsen properly served when (1) service was made on Ms. Olsen's 32-year-old sister on a Wednesday at Ms. Olsen's sister's house; (2) during the month when service was made, Ms. Olsen spent weeknights at a halfway house, where she had a room, ate meals, and kept belongings, and weekends at her sister's house, where she also had some belongings; (3) Ms. Olsen listed the halfway house address on job applications but her sister's address on her driver's license; (4) the process server told Ms. Olsen's sister that Ms. Olsen "needed to go to court"; and (5) Ms. Olsen's sister did not give the summons to Ms. Olsen, and Ms. Olsen states that she did not receive notice?

Brief Answer

Probably not. Because the summons and complaint were given to Ms. Olsen's adult sister at the sister's house, Ms. Olsen will have to concede that the service was made on a person 15 years or older who was living at the house at which the service was made. In addition, because the process server told Ms. Olsen's sister that Ms. Olsen needed to go to court, Ms. Olsen cannot meet her burden of proving that the person served was not informed of the contents of the documents. However, because Ms. Olsen was not actually living at her sister's house on the day that service was made, she can probably meet her burden of proving that her sister's house was not her usual place of abode.

EXAMPLE 2   Issue Statement and Brief Answer in Which the Writer Does Not Use the Parties' Names

Issue

Under Florida's statute authorizing substituted service of process, was service at the defendant's adult sister's house valid when the defendant spent weeknights at a halfway house and weekends at her sister's house; the service was made on a Wednesday; the process server told the defendant's sister that the defendant "needed to go to court"; and the defendant states that she did not receive notice?

Brief Answer

Probably not. The court will conclude that the service was made on a person 15 years old or older living at the place where service was made and that the process server informed the person served of the contents of the documents. However, the court will probably conclude that the service was not made at the defendant's usual place of abode because the defendant was not actually living at the house on the day service was made.

---

§ 8.7 Checklist for Critiquing the Brief Answer

A. Content

- The writer has predicted but not guaranteed how the issue will be decided.
- The writer has briefly explained his or her prediction, for example, the writer has explained which elements will be easy to prove and which will be more difficult and why.

B. Format

- A separate brief answer has been included for each issue statement.
- The answer begins with a one- or two-word short answer. This one- or two-word short answer is then followed by a short explanation.

C. Writing

- The brief answer is easy to read and understand.
- Most of the sentences have concrete subjects and action verbs. (See Chapter 5 in *Just Writing, 2d ed.*)
- There are no grammatical or punctuation errors. (See Chapters 8 and 9 in *Just Writing, 2d ed.*)

Drafting the Discussion Section Using a Script Format

Expectations. We all have them, and we have them about a variety of things. If we go to the symphony, we expect to be handed a program, have an usher show us to our seats, wait until the hall is darkened, hear the orchestra members tuning their instruments, and then applaud the conductor as he or she takes the podium. We expect these things to be in a certain order, and there is a sense of satisfaction when our expectations are met.

We even have expectations about the organization of the most mundane things in our lives. If you walk into a house, you expect to see certain types of rooms (kitchen, bedrooms, bathroom, living or family room), and you expect those rooms to be in specific places. Dining rooms should be near kitchens; bathrooms should be near bedrooms, and so on. We even expect certain things to be in each room. Stoves should be in kitchens, not in dining rooms, and desks are usually in bedrooms, offices, or studies, not in bathrooms.

The same is true of discussion sections. When attorneys read a discussion section, they expect to see specific types of information. For example, in a formal memo, the attorney expects to see the applicable rules, examples of how those rules have been applied in analogous cases, each side's arguments, and a conclusion. In addition, the attorney expects to see each of those types of information in specific places. In most instances, the rules should be before, and not after, the descriptions of the analogous cases, and the descriptions of analogous cases should be before, and not after, the arguments. Finally, the attorney expects to see specific things in each section. Just as you would be surprised to see a stove in a bedroom, an attorney would be surprised to see arguments in the rules section.

These expectations are not born of whim. Instead, they reflect the way United States attorneys think about legal questions. In most instances, attorneys begin their analysis by identifying the applicable statute or common law rule and by determining who has the burden of proof and what that burden is. If this "general rule" sets out a list of elements, the attorney then goes through those elements one by one, determining which elements the party with the burden of proof can easily prove and which elements will be more difficult to prove.

In most situations, the attorney spends very little time on the elements that the party with the burden of proof can easily prove: For these "undisputed elements," the attorney simply applies the law to the facts. Instead of focusing on the undisputed elements, the attorney focuses on the elements that will be more difficult to prove. For each of these "disputed elements," the attorney looks at the definitions or tests the courts apply in determining whether the element is met, looks at examples of how those definitions or tests have been applied in analogous cases, and looks at each side's arguments. What factual arguments will the parties make? How will each side use the analogous cases? Given the purpose and policies underlying the statute or rule, what types of policy arguments might each side make? Finally, most attorneys make a prediction. Given the facts, rules, cases, and arguments, how will a court decide each element?

The discussion section reflects this process. It contains the same components—rules, analogous cases, arguments, and mini-conclusions—in the same order. At its simplest—and at its best—the discussion section analyzes the problem, walking the attorney step-by-step through the law, cases, and arguments to the probable outcome.

§ 9.1 The Script Format

Just as different people prefer different styles of houses, some attorneys prefer different styles of discussion sections: some prefer discussion sections written using a script format, and others prefer discussion sections written using a more integrated format. Although neither format is inherently better than the other, the script format tends to be a bit easier to use. Thus, in this chapter we show you how to write a discussion section using that format. Then, once you have mastered the script format, you can turn to the next chapter, Chapter 10, for a description of how to write a discussion section using a more integrated format.

In studying Chart 9.1, note how the template reflects the way attorneys think about problems involving an elements analysis. The first section is an introductory section in which the writer introduces and sets out the applicable statute or common law rule, the burden of proof, and any other general rules. At the end of this introductory section, the writer provides the attorney with a roadmap that tells the attorney which elements the party with the burden of proof can easily prove and which elements that party will have more difficulty proving. The writer then walks the attorney through the elements one by one, For the elements that the party with the burden of proof can easily prove, that is, for the elements that are not likely to be in dispute, the writer simply sets out the specific rules for that element and applies them to the client's case. For the elements that will be more difficult to prove, the attorney sets out the specific rules for those elements, provides the attorney with descriptions of cases in which those rules have been applied, and then writes the "script" for the oral arguments related to that element. If that element were litigated, what would the party with the burden of proof argue? What would the other side argue? How would the court decide the question?

Chart 9.1	Template for Discussion Section Written Using a Script Format

Discussion

Introductory section *[do not include this subheading]*

- If one or both sides will make a policy argument, describe the policies underlying the statute or rule.
- Introduce and set out the applicable statute(s) or common law rule.
- Explain which side has the burden of proof and what that burden is.
- Set out any other rules that apply to all of the elements.
- End by providing the attorney with a roadmap for the rest of the discussion.

A. First Element *[include a subheading that identifies the element]*

- If the first element is not likely to be in dispute, simply set out and apply applicable rule.
- If, however, first element will be in dispute, set out the following information:

    1. Specific rules for the first element
    2. Examples showing how the specific rules have been applied in analogous cases
    3. Arguments
    4. Mini-conclusion for the first element

B. Second Element *[include a subheading that identifies the element]*

- If the second element is not likely to be in dispute, simply set out and apply applicable rule.
- If, however, the second element will be in dispute, set out the following information:

(continues)

Continued

1. Specific rules for second element
2. Examples of how specific rules have been applied in analogous cases
3. Arguments
4. Mini-conclusion for the second element

C. Third Element *[include a subheading that identifies the element]*

- If the third element is not likely to be in dispute, simply set out and apply applicable rule.
- If, however, third element will be in dispute, set out the following information:

1. Specific rules for the third element
2. Examples of how specific rules have been applied in analogous cases
3. Arguments
4. Mini-conclusion for the third element

D. Fourth Element *[include a subheading that identifies the element]*

- If the fourth element is not likely to be in dispute, simply set out and apply applicable rule.
- If, however, the fourth element will be in dispute, set out the following information:

1. Specific rules for fourth element
2. Examples of how specific rules have been applied in analogous cases
3. Arguments
4. Mini-conclusion for the fourth element

The template set out in Chart 9.1 is, however, only a template. Just as a builder may need to modify a standard blueprint so that the house fits on the lot and satisfies the buyer's preferences, you may need to modify the template set out in Chart 9.1 so that it works for your problem and your reader. For example, if the general rule, that is, the applicable statute or common law rule, sets out only two elements, you would need to modify the template so that it has only two subsections. Similarly, if the statute or common law rules has five elements, you would need to modify the template so that it has five subsections.

In the service of process problem that we used as an example in Chapters 7 and 8, the statute and the cases applying that statute set out three elements: (1) whether the summons was left at Ms. Olsen's usual place of abode, (2) whether the summons was left with a person who was 15 years old or older; residing therein; and (3) whether the process server informed the person served of the contents. Thus, we need to modify the template so that it has three subsections. See Chart 9.2.

Chart 9.2   **Revised Template**

Discussion

Introductory section:

Set out policies underlying Fla. Stat. § 48.031.

- Introduce and set out Fla. Stat. § 48.031.
- Explain which side has the burden of proof and what that burden is.
- Set out any other rules that apply to all of the elements.
- End with a roadmap that tells the attorney that the State can easily prove the second element but that it may not be able to prove the first and third elements.

A. Usual Place of Abode *[disputed element]*

1. Specific rules
2. Examples of how specific rules have been applied in analogous cases
3. Arguments

   - The State's arguments
   - Ms. Olsen's arguments

4. Mini-conclusion

B. Age and Residing Therein *[undisputed element]*

1. Set out applicable rules
2. Apply applicable rules

C. Informing of Contents *[disputed element]*

1. Specific rules
2. Examples of how specific rules have been applied in analogous cases
3. Arguments

   - The State's arguments
   - Ms. Olsen's arguments

4. Mini-conclusion

PRACTICE

POINTER

Frequently, there is more than one way to list the elements. In these situations, the safest approach is to list the elements in the same way that they are listed in the pattern jury instruction or the way the majority of the courts have listed them.

---

§ 9.2 The Introductory, or General Rule, Section

Drafting the introductory, or general rule, section is a three-step process. Decide what information to include, order that information, and draft the section.

§ 9.2.1 Decide What Information You Need to Include

The first step is to list the information that you want to include in your introductory section. In preparing this list, keep two things in mind. First, remember your audience. If the attorney for whom you are preparing the memo knows little or nothing about the area of law, provide the attorney with an overview of the area of law, distinguishing closely related doctrines and defining key terms. If, however, the attorney knows the area of law, do not include this type of information. Second, distinguish between general rules (that is, rules that apply to all of the elements) and specific rules (that is, rules that apply to only one of the elements). Include only general rules in your introductory section. Save the specific rules for the discussion of the element to which they apply.

In the service of process problem, you can presume that the attorney will have taken civil procedure as a law student and will, therefore, know the basics. Therefore, in drafting the introductory section, you do not need to explain the difference between personal service and substituted service or define those terms. You do, however, need to set out the applicable portion of the statute, the rules relating to the burden of proof, the policies underlying the statute, and the fact that the courts have said that the statute should be narrowly construed to assure due process. In addition, you will want to include a roadmap, which is what the name suggests: a map for the rest of the discussion.

§ 9.2.2 Order the Information

The next step is to order the items on the list. Most of the time, you will want to set out more general information before more specific information. Therefore, in drafting the introductory section, you will usually want to use an inverted pyramid: broad rules first, narrower rules next, and exceptions last. (For more on this paragraph pattern, see section 3.2 in *Just Writing, 2d ed.*)

More general information

More specific information

Exceptions

In the service of process problem, most attorneys would agree that the policies that underlie the statute are the most general piece of information, that the applicable portion of the statute is the next most general piece of information, and that the most specific rules are the rules relating to the burden of proof. Consequently, in the service of process problem, you would want to present the information in the following order.

Policies underlying statute

Text of applicable portion of statute

Rules relating to burden of proof

Roadmap

PRACTICE POINTER

If you are not sure which rules are the more general rules and which rules are the more specific rules, look at the cases. In most instances, the courts set out more general rules before more specific rules.

The approach is similar when there is more than one applicable statutory section: Instead of setting out the statutes in the order in which they appear in the code, set out the more general statutory sections first. For example, set out the section that explains the statute's purpose before the section that sets out the rule, and set out the section that contains the rule before the section that contains the definitions.

§ 9.2.3 Prepare the First Draft

In preparing the first draft, do not do what the writer of the following example, Example 1, did, which is to string together a series of quotes, at least some of which set out the same rules using slightly different language.

EXAMPLE 1   Poor Draft: Writer Has Simply Strung Together a Series of Quotes

Discussion

"The purpose of service of process is to advise the defendant that an action has been commenced and to warn the defendant that he or she must appear in a timely manner to state such defenses as are available." *Torres v. Arnco Constr., Inc.*, 867 So. 2d 583 (Fla. 5th DCA 2004), *citing Shurman v. A. Mortg. & Inv. Corp.*, 795 So. 2d 952 (Fla. 2001); *Abbate v. Provident Nat'l. Bank*, 631 So. 2d 312 (Fla. 5th DCA 1994). "It is well settled that the fundamental purpose of service is 'to give proper notice to the defendant in the case that he is answerable to the claim of plaintiff and, therefore, to vest jurisdiction in the court entertaining the controversy.'" *Shurman*, 795 So. 2d 952, 953-54 (Fla. 2001), *citing*

State ex rel. Merritt v. Heffernan, 142 Fla. 496, 195 So. 145, 147 (1940). Therefore, "a judgment entered without due service of process is void." *Torres,* 867
So. 2d at 586.

The statute specifically states:

> Service of original process is made by delivering a copy of it to the
> person to be served with a copy of the complaint, petition, or other
> initial pleading or paper or by leaving the copies at his or her usual
> place of abode with any person residing therein who is 15 years of age
> or older and informing the person of their contents. Minors who are
> or have been married shall be served as provided in this section.

Fla. Stat. § 48.031(1)(a) (2006).

"The statutes regulating service of process are to be strictly construed to
assure that a defendant is notified of the proceedings." *Torres,* 867 So. 2d at
586. "Indeed, because statutes authorizing substituted service are exceptions
to the general rule requiring a defendant to be served personally, due process
requires strict compliance with their statutory requirements." *Id.*

Thus, because Ms. Olsen is challenging the validity of the service, she will
have the burden of proof. Ms. Olsen will concede that the summons was left
with a person who is 15 years old or older residing therein. In addition, she
will probably concede that her sister was informed of the contents of the documents. She may, however, be able to prove that the summons was not left at
her usual place of abode.

Instead of just cutting and pasting the rules from your research notes
into your first draft, take the time to read, analyze, and synthesize the rules.
Once you understand the rules, determine which rules apply to your case,
and then set out each of the applicable rules once and only once.

PRACTICE POINTER   Almost all attorneys will want you to quote
the relevant portions of statutes. However, when it
comes to other rules (for example, common law
rules or rules that the courts have developed in
applying a statute), different attorneys prefer different things. While some
attorneys will want you to quote all of the rules, others find a series of
quotes annoying and prefer that you set out close paraphrases of the rules.
Therefore, before you do your first draft, check with your supervising
attorney to see which style he or she prefers.

**EXAMPLE 2   Better Draft: Writer Has Set Out Each Rule Only
Once**

Discussion

The fundamental purpose of service of process is to give defendants notice
of claims that have been filed against them and to provide them with an oppor-

tunity to defend their rights. *Shurman v. A. Mortg. & Inv. Corp.*, 795 So. 2d 952, 953-54 (Fla. 2001). Because it is important that litigants receive notice of actions against them, courts strictly construe and enforce statutes governing service of process. *Id.* at 954. In this case, the applicable section of the statute reads as follows:

> Service of original process is made by delivering a copy of it to the person to be served with a copy of the complaint, petition, or other initial pleading or paper or by leaving the copies at his or her usual place of abode with any person residing therein who is 15 years of age or older and informing the person of their contents. Minors who are or have been married shall be served as provided in this section.

Fla. Stat. § 48.031(a)(1) (2006).

Although the party seeking to invoke the jurisdiction of the court has the burden of proving that service was proper, if the return is regular on its face, the courts presume that the service was valid. *Thompson v. State, Dept. of Revenue*, 867 So. 2d 603, 605 (Fla. 1st DCA 2004); *Magazine v. Bedoya*, 475 So. 2d 1035, 1035 (Fla. 3d DCA 1985). In such instances, the party challenging the service has the burden of presenting clear and convincing evidence that the service was invalid. *Id.*

In this case, Ms. Olsen will have to concede that the summons was left with a person 15 years or older who was residing at the house where the summons and complaint were served. In addition, it is unlikely that Ms. Olsen will be able to prove that her sister was not informed of the contents of the documents. Ms. Olsen may, however, be able to present clear and convincing evidence that the summons was not left at her usual place of abode.

You do not, however, have to set out the entire statute. If only part of the statute is applicable, you can set out only that part.

EXAMPLE 3   **Better Draft: Writer Has Quoted Only the Applicable Portion of the Statute**

Discussion

The fundamental purpose of service of process is to give defendants notice of claims that have been filed against them and to provide defendants with an opportunity to defend their rights. *Shurman v. A. Mortg. & Inv. Corp.*, 795 So. 2d 952, 953-54 (Fla. 2001). Because it is important that litigants receive notice of actions against them, courts strictly construe and enforce statutes governing service of process. *Id.* at 954.

In Florida, substituted service can be made by leaving the copies at defendant's "usual place of abode with any person residing therein who is 15 years of age or older and informing the person of their contents." Fla. Stat. § 48.031(a)(1) (2006).

Although the party seeking to invoke the jurisdiction of the court has the burden of proving that service was proper, if the return is regular on its face, the courts presume that the service was valid. *Thompson v. State, Dept. of Revenue,* 867 So. 2d 603, 605 (Fla. 1st DCA 2004); *Magazine v. Bedoya,* 475 So. 2d 1035, 1035 (Fla. 3d DCA 1985). In such instances, the party challenging the service has the burden of presenting clear and convincing evidence that the service was invalid. *Id.*

In this case, Ms. Olsen will have to concede that the summons was left with a person 15 years or older who was residing at the house where the summons and complaint were served. In addition, it is unlikely that Ms. Olsen will be able to prove that her sister was not informed of the contents of the documents. Ms. Olsen may, however, be able to present clear and convincing evidence that the summons was not left at her usual place of abode.

PRACTICE
   If your quotation has fifty words or more, you need to set it out as a block quote, indenting five spaces on the left and five spaces on the right and dropping the quotation marks. In contrast, if the quote has fewer than fifty words, you can include it in the text of your sentence. See Rules 47.4 and 47.5 in the *ALWD Citation Manual, 3d ed.* and Rule 5.1 in *The Bluebook, 18th ed.* If you use Word, you can determine how many words are in your quote by highlighting the quoted language, selecting "Tools" and then selecting "Word Count."

---

§ 9.2.4 Include a Citation to Authority for Each Rule

You must include a citation to authority for each rule that you set out in your memo. This authority may be a constitutional provision, a statute, a regulation, a court rule, or a case.

In choosing an authority always choose mandatory, or binding authority, over persuasive authority. (See sections 2.6 and 2.7.) For example, in choosing a case, always choose cases from your jurisdiction over cases from other jurisdictions. In addition, you will usually want to choose decisions from higher courts over decisions from lower courts and more recent decisions over older decisions. The exception might be when the decisions of the jurisdiction's highest court, for example your state's highest court, are quite old and there are more recent decisions from your state's intermediate court of appeals. If the decisions from both your state's highest court and intermediate court are mandatory authority, you can choose to cite the more recent decision from the state intermediate court of appeals. Although there may be times when you want to list more than one case to show the attorney that the rule is well established, avoid long string cites, that is, listing more than two or three cases. In addition, you do not need to tell the attorney what case the case that you are citing cited. Compare Example 1 above with Examples 2 and 3 above.

PRACTICE POINTER   As a general rule, do not cite unpublished or unreported decisions as authority for a rule. Instead, cite a published decision, for example, the case or cases that the unpublished or unreported decision cited as authority for the rule.

§ 9.3 The Undisputed Elements

More likely than not, one or more of the elements will not be in dispute. Although you cannot ignore these undisputed elements, you do not need to devote much space to them.

§ 9.3.1 Decide Where to Put Your Discussion of the Undisputed Elements

While some attorneys choose to raise and dismiss the undisputed elements at the end of their introductory section, others choose to discuss all of the elements in order. Compare the following examples. In Example 1, the writer has raised and dismissed the undisputed element in her roadmap at the end of her introductory section. In contrast, in Example 2, the writer has raised and dismissed the undisputed elements in their own subsections.

EXAMPLE 1 Undisputed Elements Raised and Dismissed at the End of the Introductory Section

[The text of the first part of the introductory section is not shown.]

In this case, Ms. Olsen will have to concede that the summons and complaint were left with a person 15 years or older who was residing at the house where the summons and complaint were served. Ms. Olsen's sister is 32 years old, and she was served at her house. Ms. Olsen may, however, be able to present clear and convincing evidence that the summons and complaint were not left at her usual place of abode and that her sister was not informed of the contents.

EXAMPLE 2 Undisputed Elements Raised in Separate Subsections

Introductory section

[The text of the introductory section is not shown.]

A. Usual Place of Abode

[Disputed element; text not included in this example.]

B. Person 15 Years Old or Older Residing Therein

In addition to leaving the summons at the defendant's usual place of abode, the process server must leave the summons with a person 15 years old or older residing therein. If the court concludes that Ms. Olsen's sister's house was Ms. Olsen's usual place of abode, Ms. Olsen should concede that the summons was left with a person residing therein who is at least 15 years old: Ms. Webster is 32 years old, and the summons and complaint were left with her at her house.

C. Notified of Contents

[Disputed element; text not included in this example.]

To see the full text of this example, see the memo set out in section 6.4.2.

---

§ 9.3.2 Prepare the First Draft of Your Discussion of the Undisputed Elements

In most instances, your discussion of an undisputed element will be very short. Identify the element, set out any applicable specific rules, and apply those rules to the facts of your case. Typically, you will not include descriptions of analogous cases. Compare the following examples.

EXAMPLE 1   **Poor Draft of Undisputed Element: Writer Has Set Out Conclusion Without Setting Out Facts that Support that Conclusion**

Ms. Olsen should concede that the second element, that the summons and complaint be left with a person 15 years or older residing therein, is met.

EXAMPLE 2   **Poor Draft of Undisputed Element: Writer Has Gone into Too Much Depth on Undisputed Element**

For substitute service of process to be valid at a defendant's "usual place of abode," the papers must be left with a person residing therein who is 15 years of age or older. Fla. Stat. § 48.031 (2006). Although the statute does not specify the period of time an individual must occupy a home to be regarded as "residing therein," the courts do not require extended habitation. *Compare Magazine v. Bedoya*, 475 So. 2d 1035 (Fla. Dist. Ct. App. 1985) (six-week stay long enough to establish residency) *with Gamboa v. Jones*, 455 So. 2d 613 (Fla. Dist. Ct. App. 1985) (ten-day visit not sufficient to establish residency). Because she is 32, Ms. Webster satisfies the age requirement. From the facts given, it is unclear how long Ms. Webster has lived at the home in question; however, the memo indicated that she was served at "her house." Thus, unless other facts are presented, Ms. Webster appears to be the owner and primary resident of the house, and she has lived there long enough to establish residency. Therefore, the re-siding therein requirement is met.

EXAMPLE 3   **Better Draft of Undisputed Element**

In addition to leaving the summons at the defendant's usual place of abode, the process server must leave the summons with a person 15 years old or older residing therein. If the court concludes that Ms. Olsen's sister's house was Ms. Olsen's usual place of abode, Ms. Olsen should concede that the summons was left with a person residing therein who is at least 15 years old: Ms. Webster is 32 years old, and the summons and complaint were left with her at her house.

EXAMPLE 4   **Better Draft of Undisputed Element**

In this case, Ms. Olsen will have to concede that the summons and complaint were left with a person 15 years or older who was residing therein: the summons was left with Ms. Olsen's 32-year-old sister, who lives at the house where the summons was left.

EXAMPLE 5   **Better Draft of Undisputed Element**

A court will find that the second element is met. Because the summons and complaint were left with Ms. Olsen's 32-year-old sister, the age requirement is met. In addition, because Ms. Olsen's sister lives at the house where the sum-mons and complaint were left, the residing therein requirement is met.

PRACTICE
POINTER

While some elements are clearly not in dispute and some are clearly in dispute, there may be elements that fall somewhere in between these two categories.

```
_____ X _____
Not in dispute                              In dispute
```

When you have an element that falls into this "in between" category, you will usually do more than raise and dismiss the element but less than a full analysis. Alert the attorney to the fact that one side might have a weak argument, set out that argument, explain why the argument is weak, and then move on.

---

§ 9.4 The Disputed Elements

You will usually want to create a separate subsection for each disputed element. Include a subheading that identifies the element and then set out, in paragraph form, the following information:

(1) the specific rules for that element;
(2) cases that illustrate how those specific rules have been applied;
(3) each side's arguments; and
(4) your prediction about how the court is likely to decide the element.

§ 9.4.1 Set Out the Specific Rules

Begin your discussion of a disputed element by setting out the rules that relate to that element. For example, if the courts apply a particular test in determining whether the element is met, set out that test. Similarly, if the courts have defined any terms, set out those definitions.

In drafting your specific rule paragraphs, use the same process that you used in drafting the introductory section. Begin by listing all of the information that you want to include in your specific rule paragraph, and then order that information setting out more general information before more specific information. Finally, draft the specific rule paragraph or paragraphs.

In drafting these paragraphs, keep the following in mind. First, include only those rules that apply to the element that you are currently discussing. Do not repeat general rules that you set out in your introductory section, and do not set out rules that apply to other elements. Second, do not simply cut and paste the rules from your research notes into your draft. Instead, determine what the rules are, and then set out each rule once, and only once, using clear and concise language. Finally, remember to include a citation to authority for each rule that you set out. Compare the following examples, both of which are examples of the specific rule paragraph for the usual place of abode element.

EXAMPLE 1 **Poor Draft of Specific Rule Paragraph: Writer Has Simply Cut and Pasted Rules from Research Notes into Draft**

The Florida courts have defined "usual place of abode" as "the fixed place of residence for the time being when the service is made." *Shurman v. A. Mortg. & Inv. Corp.*, 795 So. 2d 952, 953-54 (Fla. 2001). "If a person has more than one residence, a summons must be served at the residence at which the defendant is actually living at the time of service." *Id.* at 954. As the Florida Supreme Court noted in *Shurman*, "the courts have frequently invalidated substituted service of process in cases where the defendant was not actually living at the place where service was made, even though process might have been delivered to a relative." *Torres v. Arnco Const., Inc.*, 867 So. 2d 583, 586 (Fla. 5th DCA 2004).

EXAMPLE 2   **Better Draft of Specific Rule Paragraph: Writer Has Identified the Rules and Then Set Out Each Rule Once, Using Language that Is Clear and Concise**

If a defendant has more than one residence, the defendant's usual place of abode is the place where the defendant was actually living at the time of service. *Shurman v. A. Mortg. & Inv. Corp.*, 795 So. 2d 952, 953-54 (Fla. 2001). It is not enough that the summons and complaint are left with a relative. *Torres v. Arnco Const., Inc.*, 867 So. 2d 583, 586 (Fla. 5th DCA 2004).

---

§ 9.4.2 Describe the Analogous Cases

When an element is in dispute, most attorneys want to see not only the specific rules but also examples of how those specific rules have been applied in analogous cases. Thus, if an element is in dispute and there are analogous cases, you will usually want to describe at least some of those cases.

In drafting the analogous case section, always keep in mind why you are including cases. Do not include analogous cases descriptions just to prove to the attorney that you located and read cases. The analogous case section is not there so that you can prove that you did a lot of work. Instead, include analogous case descriptions because the case descriptions will help the attorney understand the rules or because either your side or the other side is likely to use the cases to support its position.

Step 1: Identify the analogous cases

The first step is to go back through your research notes and identify the cases in which the court discussed the disputed element. In the service of process problem, there are five cases that discussed usual place of abode: a 1940 Florida Supreme Court case, a 2001 Florida Supreme Court Case, and three Florida District Court of Appeals cases.

PRACTICE POINTER   In looking for analogous cases, look first for cases from your jurisdiction. If you do not find any, you can then look for analogous cases from other jurisdictions. However, before deciding to use an out-of-state case, make sure that the other state's specific rules are the same as your state's specific rules.

Step 2: Sort the cases

Once you have identified the analogous cases, sort those cases. Put the cases in which the court held that the element was met in one stack and the cases in which the court held that the element was not met in a different stack.

 **Sort the Cases**

Cases in which element was met	Cases in which element was not met
State ex rel. Merritt v. Heffernan	*Alvarez v. State Farm Mut. Auto. Ins.*
	Shurman v. A. Mortg. & Inv. Corp.
	Torres v. Arnco Constr., Inc.
	Thompson v. State, Dept. of Revenue

PRACTICE POINTER   If you were not born and educated in the United States, it may take you a while to get used to the way U.S. attorneys approach problems. For example, you may find it surprising that U.S. attorneys go through the elements one by one and that U.S. attorneys divide the analogous cases into two stacks. These preferences reflect the fact that people from different cultures approach problems differently. For example, while people born and educated in the United States tend to divide problems into parts, create principles, and sort items according to those principles, people born and educated in Asian countries often take a more holistic approach. For more on the different ways in which people from different cultures view and solve problems, see *The Geography of Thought* by Ronald E. Nisbett.

Step 3: Analyze and synthesize the cases

It is at this step that the real work begins. Because you want to do more than provide the attorney with "book reports" on the cases that you have located and read, you need to analyze each of the cases and then synthesize the group.

Analysis requires you to read the cases carefully and critically, identifying the issue that was before the court, the standard of review that the court applied, the facts that the court considered, the court's holding, and the court's reasoning. For more on understanding and reading cases, see Chapters 4 and 5 in this book.

PRACTICE POINTER   The standard of review is the standard that an appellate court uses in reviewing a trial court's decision.

Once you have analyzed the cases, synthesize them. What do the cases in which the courts have held that the element is met have in common? What do the cases in which the courts have held that the element is not met have in common? What do the cases in which the courts have discussed a particular part of the rule have in common?

One way of doing this analysis and synthesis is to prepare a chart for each set of cases in which you identify the court, the date of the decision, the key facts, and the court's reasoning. Note that in the following examples, there is not a column for the holding. This column is not necessary because the cases are grouped based on their holdings. Chart 9.3 contains the case in which the element was met, and Chart 9.4 contains the cases in which the element was not met.

Chart 9.3	Case in Which Court Held that Service Was Made at the Defendant's Usual Place of Abode			
Case	**Court**	**Date**	**Facts**	**Reasoning**
Merritt v. Heffernan	Florida Supreme Court	1940	• Wife served one hour after D left to go back to Minn. • D had an office, voted, and paid taxes in Minn. • D had moved family to Florida two months earlier. • D had visited family twice "during season." • Summons was left with D's wife and, apparently, D received actual notice.	• Ct acknowledges that D's permanent residence was in Minn. • However, ct seems to think that it was more important that his family was in Florida, that D was on a train and not in Minn. at the time of service, and that the evidence suggested that D intended to return to Minn.

Chart 9.4	Cases in Which Court Held that Service Was Not Made at the Defendant's Usual Place of Abode			
Case	**Court**	**Date**	**Facts**	**Reasoning**
Alvarez v. State Farm	Fla. 3d DCA	1994	• Service was left with D's cousin at cousin's residence. • Affidavits, telephone bill,	• Uncontradicted evidence established that D was not living at that address on the date of

(continues)

Continued

Case	Court	Date	Facts	Reasoning
			and marriage license established that D was not living with cousin at time of service and that she had not lived there for some time.	service or for some time before. Therefore, service of process was ineffective as a matter of law.
Shurman v. A. Mortg. & Inv. Co.	Florida Supreme Court	2001	• Service left with D's wife. • D had been incarcerated for at least 9 months.	• D was actually living at the prison. • Substituted service, being in derogation of the common law, must be strictly construed. • In general, the courts presume that D will receive notice of process if the summons is left with a competent member of his household who lives in his house. This presumption is not, however, valid when the head of the household is in prison.
Torres v. Arnco Const.	Fla. 5th DCA	2004	• Summons left with D's mother. • D had resided in NY for 57 years and at NY address for 12 years. • NY neighbors verified that D lived in house but that he traveled	• Although standard of review is gross abuse of discretion, no live testimony. • P has the burden of proof. • P did not meet burden. • Mother's statement was ambiguous.

(continues)

Continued

Case	Court	Date	Facts	Reasoning
			a lot. • Mother said that D would be home soon.	• Dissent argues that D had burden of proof and that his statements were not sufficient. If D were visiting his family in Florida for substantial periods of time, the Florida house was his "usual abode" when he was served in Florida. It would also be consistent with the affidavit of the Florida process server who said that D's mother remarked that Torres "would be home soon, and she would see to it that he received the papers."
Thompson v. State, Dept. of Revenue	Fla. 1st DCA	2004	• Service was made on D's wife. • Child support case. • In affidavit D stated that he has been separated from his wife, that he has not resided at that address for over three years, and that he did not authorize anyone to accept service of process on his behalf.	• D's affidavit sufficient to establish *prima facie* case that he was not served at his usual place of abode. • Court cites other Fla. cases. • Having raised the issue of personal jurisdiction, D's motion and accompanying affidavit placed the burden on the Dept. to establish the validity of service of process.

 **PRACTICE POINTER**   Just as it is unlikely that anyone other than you will see your research notes, it is also unlikely that anyone other than you will see your charts. Thus, use the format and abbreviations that make sense to you. Do not waste time creating charts that "look nice."

In creating and examining your chart, you might discover that the cases in which the element was met (or not met) have one of the following in common:

(1) that all of the cases in which the element is met (or not met) have a particular fact or set of facts in common;
(2) that in all of the cases in which the element is met (or not met) the courts seem to focus on a particular policy underlying the rule;
(3) that different courts or different divisions of the same court seem to take a particular approach;
(4) that the rules seem to be evolving; or
(5) that the decisions seem to be result oriented.

When you determine what the cases have in common or that they do not have anything in common, you have done synthesis.

Step 4: Introduce the cases

When writing for U.S. attorneys, assume that it is your responsibility to let them know why you have included a particular case or group of cases in your memo. Do not make them guess what a case or group of cases contributes to the overall analysis. Instead, introduce each case or group of cases. How you introduce the case or cases will depend on a number of factors, including the issue that you are researching, the number of analogous cases that you located, and what you discovered in analyzing and synthesizing each group of cases.

If you are using a case to illustrate a part of a rule, a transition may be enough. For instance, in the following example, the writer uses the transition "for example" to introduce a case that illustrates the rule that, if the return is regular on its face, the court presumes that the service is valid unless the defendant presents clear and convincing evidence to the contrary. (In the following example, the transition is in boldface type.)

EXAMPLE   **Using a Transition to Introduce a Case that Illustrates the Application of a Particular Rule**

Although the party seeking to invoke the jurisdiction of the court has the burden of proving that service was proper, if the return is regular on its face, the courts presume that the service was valid. *Thompson v. State, Dept. of Revenue,* 867 So. 2d 603, 605 (Fla 1st DCA 2004); *Magazine v. Bedoya,* 475 So. 2d 1035, 1035 (Fla 3d DCA 1985). **For example,** in a case involving a default judgment obtained by a bank, the District Court of Appeals held that the trial court had erred in overturning a default judgment because the return of service was regular on its face and the defendant did not "present 'clear and convincing evidence' to corroborate his denial of service." *Florida Nat'l. Bank v. Halphen*, 641 So. 2d 495, 495 (Fla. 3d DCA 1994).

If there is only one case that has applied your statute, you can use a topic sentence that sets out that fact. (In the following example, the topic sentence is in boldface type.)

EXAMPLE   **Using a Topic Sentence to Introduce the Only Case that Has Applied a Particular Statute**

The only case in which the Florida courts have discussed usual place of abode and held that the service was made at the defendant's usual place of abode is a 1940 case: *State ex rel. Merritt v. Heffernan*, 195 So. 145 (Fla. 1940). In *Heffernan*, the defendant's wife was served at the family's apartment in Florida. However, one hour before service was made, the defendant had left the apartment to return to . . . .

P R A C T I C E
POINTER

In most instances, when you refer to a case by only one of the parties' names, you should use the plaintiff's name. For example, when you refer to *Thompson v. State, Dept. of Revenue*, 867 So. 2d 603, 605 (Fla. 1st DCA 2004), you would say "in *Thompson*," and when you refer to *Magazine v. Bedoya*, 475 So. 2d 1035, 1035 (Fla 3d DCA 1985), you would say, "in *Magazine*." There are, however, some exceptions to this general rule. When the plaintiff is the state, you will refer to the case using the defendant's name: "*State v. Smith*" becomes "*Smith*," and "*Commonwealth v. Jones*" becomes "*Jones*." In addition, if the courts typically refer to a case using the defendant's name, you should use that name. For instance, because the Florida courts refer to *State ex rel. Merritt v. Heffernan* as "*Heffernan*," you should use "*Heffernan*" and not "*Merritt*." For more on short cites, see Rule 12.21(b) in the *ALWD Citation Manual, 3d ed.* and Rule 10.9 in *The Bluebook, 18th ed.*

A more sophisticated type of analysis is, however, principle-based analysis. If, in analyzing and synthesizing the cases in which the courts held that a particular element was met you determined that all of the cases had a particular fact in common, use this fact to introduce that group of cases. In contrast, if in analyzing and synthesizing the cases you determined that, in each case, the court gave considerable weight to one of the policies underlying the statute, use this policy to introduce the group of cases.

While sometimes everyone who reads the group of cases draws the same principle from those cases, at other times different readers draw different principles or they focus on different aspects of the principle. In the examples set out below, the writers set out essentially the same principle but emphasize different aspects of that principle. In Example 1, the writer emphasizes the length of time; in Example 2, the writer emphasizes that the summons was left with a relative; and in Example 3, the writer empha- sizes that the defendant produced evidence that indicated that he or she was not living at the house where the summons was served. In the fourth example, however, the writer takes a different approach: she notes that in the more recent cases, the courts have emphasized that it is the plaintiff who has the burden of proof.

EXAMPLE 1   Principle-Based Topic Sentence Used to Introduce a Group of Analogous Cases

In most of the cases in which the courts have held that the summons was not left at the defendant's usual place of abode, the defendant had not lived at the house where service was made for a substantial period of time. *See e.g. Shurman v. A. Mortg. & Inv. Corp.*, 795 So. 2d 952 (Fla. 2001); *Alvarez v. State Farm Mut. Auto Ins. Co.*, 635 So. 2d 131, 132 (Fla. 3d DCA 1994).

EXAMPLE 2   Principle-Based Topic Sentence Used to Introduce a Group of Analogous Cases

In cases in which the courts have held that substituted service was not made at the defendant's usual place of abode, service was made at the resi- dence of a relative of the defendant, but the defendant produced evidence to show that he or she did not actually live with the relative at the time. *See e.g. Shurman v. A. Mortg.& Inv. Corp.*, 795 So. 2d 952 (Fla. 2001); *Alvarez v. State Farm Mut. Auto Ins. Co.*, 635 So. 2d 131, 132 (Fla. 3d DCA 1994).

EXAMPLE 3   Principle-Based Topic Sentence Used to Introduce a Group of Analogous Cases

In the cases in which the courts have held that the service was not left at the defendant's usual place of abode, the defendant produced evidence that he or she was not living at the house where service was made. *See e.g. Shurman v. A. Mortg. & Inv. Corp.*, 795 So. 2d 952 (Fla. 2001); *Alvarez v. State Farm Mut. Auto Ins. Co.*, 635 So. 2d 131, 132 (Fla. 3d DCA 1994).

EXAMPLE 4   Principle-Based Topic Sentence Used to Introduce a Group of Analogous Cases

In the more recent cases, the courts have emphasized that the plaintiff has the burden of proving that the service was made at the defendant's usual place of abode. Therefore, if the defendant produced at least some evidence that he or she was not living at the house where the service was made, the court either held that the service was invalid or remanded the case for an evidentiary hearing. *See e.g. Thompson v. State, Dept. of Revenue*, 867 So. 2d 603, 605 (Fla 1st DCA 2004); *Torres v. Arnco Const., Inc.*, 867 So. 2d 583 (Fla. 5th DCA 2004).

P R A C T I C E

POINTER

In introducing the cases, use the phrase "In the cases **in which** the courts have held" and not the phrase "In the cases **where** the courts have held." Use the word "where" when referring to a place. In addition, set out citations to authority after your introductory sentences. Because, in most cases, you will have made an inference, include the signal "*see*." If, in drawing the principle you relied on cases other than the ones that you cite, also include an "e.g." See Rule 44 in the *ALWD Citation Manual, 3d ed.* and Rule 2.1 in *The Bluebook, 18th ed.*

Step 5: Draft your descriptions of the cases

In drafting case descriptions, remember why you are including case descriptions. You include case descriptions not to prove to your professor, the attorney that you work for, or the client that you have located and read cases but to illustrate how the courts have applied a rule or set of rules or because you believe that either you or opposing counsel will use the cases that you describe to support an assertion.

If there are only two or three analogous cases, you can describe all of them. If, however, there are a number of cases, describe only the "best" cases. In selecting these cases, use the following criteria:

- Select cases from your jurisdiction over cases from other jurisdictions.
- Select cases with published decisions over cases with unpublished, or unreported, decisions.
- Select cases that are more factually similar to your case over cases that are less factually similar.
- Select more recent cases over older cases.
- Select cases from higher courts over cases from lower courts.

In addition, most of the time you will be using the cases to see where your case falls along the continuum of decided cases. Is your case more like the cases in which the court held that the element was met or more like the cases in which the court held that the element was not met?

??←my case→??

Cases in which element met   Cases in which element not met

How much you say about a case will depend on the point that you are using the case to illustrate. If you are using the case to illustrate a small point, a sentence or even a clause, a phrase, or a word may be enough. In contrast, if you expect that one or both sides will rely heavily on the case, your description will be longer. The bottom line is that you need include only that information that is relevant to the rule or principle that you are using the case to illustrate and to set up the arguments based on that case.

Compare the following examples. In Example 1, the case descriptions are very short because the writer is using the cases to illustrate a small point. In contrast, in Example 2, the description is longer because the writer wants to use the case to illustrate several points and because the writer expects that both sides will use the case. In Example 3, the writer sets out two medium-length case descriptions.

EXAMPLE 1   **Short Descriptions of Two Cases**

Although the statute does not specify how long the person who received the service must have been "residing therein," the courts do not require extended habitation. While in *Gamboa*, the court determined that a ten-day visit was not sufficient to establish residency, *id.* at 64, in *Magazine*, the court determined that a six-week stay was sufficient, *id.* at 1035.

EXAMPLE 2   **Longer Description in Which Writer Sets Out Facts and Court's Holding and Reasoning**

The only case in which the Florida courts have held that the service was made at the defendant's usual place of abode is *State ex rel. Merritt v. Heffernan*, 195 So. 145 (Fla. 1940). In that case, the defendant's wife was served at the family's apartment in Florida. *Id.* at 146. However, one hour before service was made, the defendant had left the apartment to return to his permanent residence in Minnesota, where he had an office, voted, and paid taxes. *Id.* The court noted that many persons have several residences that they permanently maintain, occupying one at one period of the year and another during another period. *Id.* at 147. In such situations, the summons and complaint must be served at the dwelling house at which the defendant is living at the time when the service is made. *Id.* Although the defendant was on a train heading toward Minnesota at the time service was made, the court stated that he was not within the classification of persons "who had at the time of service lost one place of residence and had not yet established another." *Id.* at 148. Instead, the court held that the defendant's then place of abode was the apartment in Florida. *Id.* at 147. The court also pointed out that the defendant had visited his family in Florida "twice during the season" and that there was no convincing proof that he did not intend to return to Florida. *Id.*

EXAMPLE 3   **Two Descriptions in Which Writer Sets Out Facts and Courts' Holdings and Reasoning**

In contrast, in most of the cases in which the courts have held that the summons was not left at the defendant's usual place of abode, the defendant had not lived at the house where service was made for a substantial period of time. *See e.g. Shurman v. A. Mortg. & Inv. Corp.*, 795 So. 2d 952 (Fla. 2001); *Thompson v. State, Dept. of Revenue*, 867 So. 2d 603, 605 (Fla. 1st DCA 2004); For example, in *Shurman*, the court held that the service had not been made at the defendant's usual place of abode when the summons was left with the defendant's wife at the family home but the defendant had been incarcerated for at least nine months. *Id.* at 955. Similarly, in *Thompson*, the court held that the summons had not been left at the defendant's usual place of abode when the summons was left with the defendant's wife at the family home. *Id.* at 605. In reaching its decision, the *Thompson* court relied on the defendant's affidavit in which the defendant stated that he was separated from his wife, that he had not resided at that address for over three years, and that he did not authorize anyone to accept service of process on his behalf. *Id.* at 605. In both cases, the plaintiff did not present evidence contradicting the defendant's statements.

Occasionally, you will not need to include a full description of an analogous case. For instance, you may not need to include a full description of a case if you are using the case to illustrate a single point or if you have already given full descriptions of one or two cases but want to tell the attorney about a third or fourth case or when you simply want to illustrate one aspect of a rule. In these situations you can use parentheticals.

EXAMPLE 4   **Cases Described in Parentheticals**

Although the statute does not specify the period of time an individual must occupy a home to be regarded as "residing therein," the courts do not require extended habitation. *Compare Magazine v. Bedoya*, 475 So. 2d 1035 (Fla. 3d DCA 1985) (six-week stay sufficient to establish residency), *with Gamboa v. Jones*, 455 So. 2d 613 (Fla. 3d DCA 1985) (ten-day visit not sufficient to establish residency).

EXAMPLE 5   **Additional Cases Described in Parentheticals**

In cases in which the courts have held that substituted service was not made at the defendant's usual place of abode, service was made at the residence of a relative of the defendant, but the defendant produced evidence to show that he or she was not actually living with the relative at the time service was made. *See e.g. Shurman v. A. Mortg. & Inv. Corp.*, 795 So. 2d 952 (Fla. 2001); *Alvarez v. State Farm Mut. Auto Ins. Co.*, 635 So. 2d 131, 132 (Fla. 3d DCA 1994). For instance, in *Shurman*, the Florida Supreme Court held that service of process upon the defendant, who had been incarcerated for nine months, did not comply with section 48.031(1)(a) when service of process occurred at the residence of the defendant's wife, which is where the defendant lived prior to incarceration. In that case, the court held that because the defendant was "actually living" in prison at the time of service, service at the residence of his wife was invalid. *Id.* at 955.

Similarly, in *Alvarez*, the defendant established by means of affidavits and supporting documentation (including a telephone bill and a marriage license) that she had not been living with her cousin for some time before process was served at her cousin's residence. *Id.* at 132; *accord Milanes,* 507 So. 2d at 778 (service of process on defendant's ex-wife at her residence was not service at the defendant's usual place of abode); *Gonzalez v. Totalbank,* 472 So. 2d 861, 864 (Fla. 3d DCA 1985) (service of process on defendant's wife at her residence not valid when wife was separated from husband and defendant was no longer living at address where service was attempted).

§ 9.4.3 Draft the Arguments

It is at this point that your role changes dramatically. No longer are you just a "reporter" telling the attorney what you found in doing your research. To do a good job presenting each side's arguments, you must become an advocate, using your training and mental resources to construct the arguments each side is likely to make. You must think like the plaintiff's attorney and then like the defendant's attorney.

When you use the script format, you write a "script" for the oral arguments on the issue. You begin by putting yourself in the shoes of the party with the burden of proof, setting out the arguments that side might make. You then step into the other side's shoes and set out that side's arguments. Finally, you assume the role of the judge, predicting how the court would decide the element and how it would justify its decision. Thus, your "script' looks something like this.

EXAMPLE   **"Script" for Arguments**

- Party with the burden of proof's arguments
- Responding party's arguments
- Party with the burden of proof's rebuttal (optional)
- Court's decision + rationale

Step 1: Identify each side's arguments

The first step is to identify each side's arguments. If you wrote down possible arguments as you did your research, start with that list.

| EXAMPLE | **List of Arguments from Research Notes** |

Ms. Olsen's arguments

- During the week she lived at the halfway house and not at her sister's house.
- Service on a relative is not sufficient.
- Her more permanent address was the halfway house address. She had a room, etc. at the halfway house.
- *Heffernan* is an old case.
- In *Torres*, the court held that the defendant's mother's house was not the defendant's usual place of abode even though the mother indicated that the defendant would be home later.

The State's arguments

- Ms. Olsen stayed at her sister's house three nights a week.
- Ms. Olsen apparently received mail at her sister's house—the shoebox.
- Ms. Olsen listed her sister's address on her driver's license.
- In *Heffernan*, the court held that the apartment was the defendant's usual place of abode even though the defendant had left the apartment and was on a train back to his permanent residence.
- In *Torres*, the defendant had a permanent residence where he had lived for twelve years. He was just visiting his mother.

Do not, however, stop with the list that you came up with while researching the issue. Push yourself further, asking yourself whether the parties can make any of the other standard types of arguments. For example, can one or both of the parties make plain language arguments, arguments based on the analogous cases, or policy arguments?

(a) Plain Language Arguments

A plain language argument is an argument in which you apply the plain language of a statute or rule to the facts of your case. For instance, in the service of process problem, you would make a plain language argument if you argued that, under the plain language of the statute, the service was not made at Ms. Olsen's "usual" place of abode because her sister's house was not the place where she "usually" stayed. During the month in which service was made, Ms. Olsen spent four nights a week at the halfway house and only three nights a week at her sister's house. Similarly, you would be making a plain language argument if you argued that, under the plain language of the rule that the courts have set out, Ms. Olsen was not "actually living" at her sister's house because the summons and complaint were served on a weekday and, during the week, Ms. Olsen "actually lived" at the halfway house. Note that a plain language argument has two components: a word or phrase from the statute or rule and facts that show that that requirement is or is not met.

To make sure that you have considered all the plain language arguments, do two things. First, think about each word or phrase in the applicable part of the statute and/or rules, asking yourself what the plain meaning of that word or phrase requires. Second, go through each of your facts, asking yourself how each side might be able to use that fact.

(b) Analogous Case Arguments

Under our system of law, judges usually decide like cases in a like manner. Thus, if the analogous cases support the conclusion that you want the court to reach, you need to argue that your case is like the analogous cases and, therefore, the court should reach the same result as the courts reached in those decisions. In contrast, if the analogous cases do not support the conclusion that you want the court to reach, you need to distinguish those cases. For example, in Ms. Olsen's case, she will want to argue that her case is like *Thompson*, *Torres*, and *Alvarez*, and she will want to distinguish *Heffernan*. Conversely, the defendant will want to distinguish *Thompson*, *Torres*, and *Alvarez* and argue that its case is more like *Heffernan*.

To make sure that you have considered all analogous case arguments, think about rules and principles you drew from the cases and how each side might be able to use those rules or principles to support their respective positions. In addition, go through the analogous cases one by one, thinking about how each side might be able to use each case.

PRACTICE POINTER   In constructing analogous case arguments, ask yourself the following questions:

- In what ways is the analogous case similar to my case?
- In what ways is it different?
- Is the case a relatively old case? If it is, how can each side use that fact?
- Is the case from an intermediate court of appeals or from the state's highest court? How can each side use that fact?
- Is the case well reasoned or poorly reasoned? How can each side use that fact?
- How have other cases used or distinguished the case?

(c) Policy Arguments

In making a policy argument, look at the reasons why the legislature enacted a particular statute or a court adopted a particular rule and use those underlying reasons to support your client's position. For example, in the service of process case you could use the policy behind the service of process statutes—to ensure that defendants had notice of actions that had been filed against them—to argue that service was invalid because Ms. Olsen did not receive notice.

When your issue is one that is governed by a statute, you may be able to find the policies underlying the statute in a "finding" or "purpose" section of the act of which your statute is a part, or a legislative history may tell you what the legislature intended when it enacted the statute. In addition, in applying a statute, the courts frequently set out what they believe are the policies underlying the statutes. Thus, to come up with policy arguments, look at the text of the statute, the statute's legislative history, and those parts of other courts' decisions that discuss the policies underlying the statute. Once you identify the various policies, determine how each side might be able to use those policies to support its position.

In situations in which the underlying reason for the statute is not explicitly laid out in the act, in its legislative history, or in court decisions, use common sense to determine why the statute was enacted. Ask yourself "what good was the legislature trying to promote" or "what harm was the legislature trying to prevent" when it created this law.

PRACTICE POINTER

At this initial stage, list all of the arguments (plain language, analogous case, and policy), no matter how weak they may seem. Later, you can go through these arguments, weeding out those that don't pass "the giggle test," that is, those that you could not make to a court without giggling.

You can use a chart like the one set out in Chapter 9.5 to keep track of the arguments that each side makes.

Chart 9.5	List of Arguments	
Element	**Olsen's arguments**	**Other side's arguments**
Usual Place of Abode [in dispute]	Plain language arguments:	Plain language arguments:
	Analogous case arguments:	Analogous case arguments:
	Policy arguments:	Policy arguments:
Age and Residing Therein [not in dispute]		

(continues)

Continued

Element	Olsen's arguments	Other side's arguments
Informing of Contents [in dispute]	Plain language arguments:	Plain language arguments:
	Analogous case arguments:	Analogous case arguments:
	Policy arguments:	Policy arguments:

Step 2: Order the arguments

After you have identified each side's arguments, you are ready to move to the second step: deciding how you want to present those arguments. Once again, you have some choices. For instance, you can organize the arguments by type of arguments. If you choose this organizational scheme, set out the party with the burden of proof's plain language arguments in one paragraph, its analogous cases arguments in another paragraph or block of paragraphs, and its policy arguments in a third paragraph. Then set out the other side's arguments: set out the other side's plain language arguments in one paragraph, its analogous case arguments in another paragraph or block of paragraphs, and its policy arguments in a third paragraph.

PRACTICE POINTER   If you organize your arguments around types of arguments, you will usually set out the plain language arguments first, analogous cases arguments second, and policy arguments third. This ordering reflects the weight that courts typically give to the different types of arguments. If a court can decide an issue by applying the plain language of the statute or rule to the facts of the case, it will usually do so. If, however, the court cannot decide the issue based on the plain language, it will look to the cases to see how the cases have applied the statutory language. If the cases do not resolve the issue, the court will then look to the policies underlying the statute.

Another way to organize the arguments is around the principles that you identified when you analyzed and synthesized the cases. For example, if you determined that all of the cases have three factors in common, you could organize your arguments around those three factors. In setting out the party with the burden of proof's arguments, you would discuss the first factor in one paragraph or block of paragraphs, the second factor in a second paragraph or block of paragraphs, and the third factor in a third paragraph or block of paragraphs. Similarly, in setting out the other side's arguments, you would discuss the first factor in one paragraph or block of paragraphs, the second factor is a second paragraph or block of paragraphs, and the third factor in a third paragraph or block of paragraphs. Within the paragraphs discussing these factors, you would set out any plain language, analogous case, and/or policy arguments that relate to that factor.

A third, and similar, approach is to organize your arguments around "lines of argument." For example, if you have a burden of proof argument and an argument on the merits, you could organize the arguments around these two lines of argument. In setting out your arguments, set out the party with the burden of proof's arguments relating to the first line of argument in one paragraph or block of paragraphs and its arguments relating to the second line of argument in a second paragraph or block of paragraphs. Then set out the other side's arguments, putting the other side's points relating to the first line of argument in one paragraph and its points relating to the second line of argument in a second paragraph or block of paragraphs. In setting out these lines of argument, include the plain language, analogous case, or policy arguments that relate to that line of argument.

PRACTICE POINTER

If you use the second option—organizing your arguments around the principles you identified when you analyzed and synthesized the cases— you will usually want to discuss the factors in the same order that you set them out and illustrated them in your analogous case section. If you use the third approach—organizing your arguments around "lines of argument"—you should discuss threshold arguments first. In other words, if one argument builds upon another argument, set out the foundational argument first.

Chart 9.6 illustrates the differences between these three organizational schemes.

Chart 9.6	Three Ways of Organizing the Arguments	
Arguments organized by type of argument	Arguments organized by principles, for example, common factors	Arguments organized by lines of argument
Party with burden of proof's arguments	**Party with burden of proof's arguments**	**Party with burden of proof's arguments**
• Plain language arguments	• Arguments relating to first factor (include any plain language, analogous case, and policy arguments)	• First line of argument (include any plain language, analogous case, and policy arguments)

(continues)

Continued

Party with burden of proof's arguments	Party with burden of proof's arguments	Party with burden of proof's arguments
• Analogous case arguments • Policy arguments	• Arguments relating to second factor (include any plain language, analogous case, and policy arguments) • Arguments relating to third factor (include any plain language, analogous case, and policy arguments)	• Second line of argument (include any plain language, analogous case, and policy arguments)
Responding party's arguments	**Responding party's arguments**	**Responding party's arguments**
• Plain language arguments • Analogous case arguments • Policy arguments	• Arguments relating to first factor (include any plain language, analogous case, and policy arguments) • Arguments relating to second factor (include any plain language, analogous case, and policy arguments) • Arguments relating to third factor (include any plain language, analogous case, and policy arguments)	• First line of argument (include any plain language, analogous case, and policy arguments) • Second line of argument (include any plain language, analogous case, and policy arguments)

Step 3: Draft the arguments

In most instances, you should start your discussion of each side's arguments by setting out that side's general assertion. For example, in the Olsen case, start the usual place of abode arguments by setting out Ms. Olsen's general assertion: that her sister's house was not her usual place of abode. Similarly, start your discussion of the State's arguments by setting out the State's assertion: Ms. Olsen's sister's house was Ms Olsen's usual place of abode or it was one of her usual places of abode. In addition, if you are going to make a number of different arguments, you may want to alert the attorney to that fact.

| EXAMPLE 1 | **Three Ways of Setting Out Ms. Olsen's General Assertion Relating to Usual Place of Abode** |

- Ms. Olsen will argue that her sister's house was not her usual place of abode.
- Ms. Olsen will argue that she was not actually living at Ms. Webster's house and that, therefore, Ms. Webster's house was not her usual place of abode.
- Ms. Olsen can make three arguments to support her assertion that her sister's house was not her usual place of abode. First . . . .

| EXAMPLE 2 | **Three Ways of Setting Out the State's General Assertion Relating to Usual Place of Abode** |

- In response, the State will argue that Ms. Webster's house was Ms. Olsen's usual place of abode.
- The State will counter by arguing that Ms. Olsen was actually living at her sister's house.
- The State can make three arguments to support its assertion that the service was made at Ms. Olsen's usual place of abode.

In addition to setting out each side's general assertion, you should also introduce and set out each side's subassertions. For example, if you have decided to organize the arguments around types of arguments, introduce each of these types of arguments, asserting that the plain language, the analogous cases, and the policies underlying the statute or rule support your general assertion. Likewise, if you are organizing your arguments around factors or lines of arguments, include a sentence introducing each of these subassertions.

| EXAMPLE | **Sentences Introducing Subassertions** |

- First, Ms. Olsen can argue that under the plain language of the statute her sister's house was not her usual place of abode.
- The first factor supports Ms. Olsen's position: . . . .
- Ms. Olsen can argue . . . . In the alternative, Ms. Olsen can argue . . . .

It is not, however, enough to just set out general assertions and subassertions. You also need to show the attorney how each side will support those assertions. One way to do this is to picture yourself standing in front of a judge. If you are making a plain language argument, what facts would you use, and how would you characterize those facts? If you are making an analogous case argument, what cases would you use, and how would you characterize and use those cases? If you are making a policy argument, what policies would you rely on, and how would you use those policies? Similarly, picture the other side presenting its arguments. How would its attorney use the facts, cases, and policies to support its position?

The following example is a poor draft because the writer has not supported her assertions. For instance, in the first paragraph, the writer asserts that Ms. Olsen's sister's house was not Ms. Olsen's usual place of abode because the halfway house was her usual place of abode. The writer does not, however, back up this assertion with facts: she does not point out the Ms. Olsen had been a full-time resident of the halfway house for several months and that she was still spending four nights a week there. Similarly, although the writer asserts that Ms. Olsen's case is more like *Torres* and *Alvarez* than it is like *Heffernan*, she does not support this assertion by comparing and contrasting the facts in those cases to the facts in Ms. Olsen's case. Finally, although the writer sets out a rule relating to the burden of proof, she does not explain why or how that rule will produce a just result.

P R A C T I C E

POINTER

While almost every attorney wants citations to authority in the rule and analogous case sections of memos, not all attorneys want them in the argument sections. Thus, before you draft your memo, determine which approach the attorney that you are working for prefers. (In the following examples, we did not include citations in the argument section.)

EXAMPLE 1   Poor Draft: Writer Has Set Out Assertions but Has Not Supported Those Assertions

In this case, Ms. Olsen can make three arguments to support her assertion that the summons and complaint were not left at her usual place of abode. First, she can argue that her sister's house was not her usual place of abode because the halfway house was her usual place of abode. Second, she can use the cases to support her position. Her case is more like *Torres* and *Alvarez* than *Heffernan*. Finally, she can argue that as a matter of public policy the party seeking to invoke the jurisdiction of the court has the burden of proving that the service was valid.

In response, the defendant will argue that the summons and complaint were left at Ms. Olsen's usual place of abode. The facts establish that Ms. Olsen was, in fact, living at her sister's house at the time the summons and complaint were served. Thus, this case is like *Heffernan*. In addition, the defendant will distinguish *Torres* and *Alvarez* on the basis that, in those cases, the defendant was not spending any time at the house where the service was made. Finally, the defen-

General assertion

First subassertion

Second subassertion

Third subassertion

General assertion

First subassertion

Second subassertion

dant can argue that the service was valid because the defendant's sister's house was the place where she was most likely to receive notice.	Third subassertion

The following example, while not perfect, is much better. In addition to setting out his assertions, the writer has supported those assertions.

EXAMPLE 2   **Improved Draft: Writer Has Set Out Assertions and Support for Those Assertions**

Ms. Olsen can make three arguments to support her assertion that her sister's house was not her usual place of abode. First, Ms. Olsen will argue that, under the plain language of the rule, her sister's house was not her usual place of abode. When a defendant has more than one residence, the service must be made at the place where the defendant was actually living at the time the summons and complaint were served. In this case, Ms. Olsen had more than one residence: during the week she lived at the halfway house and on weekends she visited her sister. Because the summons and complaint were served on a Wednesday, a weekday, the service was not made at the place where Ms. Olsen was actually living.	Ms. Olsen's general assertion Ms. Olsen's first subassertion Facts that support Ms. Olsen's first subassertion
Second, Ms. Olsen will argue that this case is more like *Torres* than it is *Heffernan*. Like Mr. Torres, who only visited his mother and who was not at his mother's house when service was made, Ms. Olsen only visited her sister and was not at her sister's house when the summons and complaint were served. However, while Mr. Torres's mother's statement that Mr. Torres "would be home soon" suggested that Mr. Torres would be returning to his mother's house that day, Ms. Olsen's sister told the process server that Ms. Olsen "isn't here today." In addition, while the plaintiff in *Torres* had tried on a number of occasions to serve Mr. Torres at his New York house, in Olsen's case we do not know whether the defendant tried to serve Ms. Olsen personally or at the halfway house. Finally, *Heffernan* can be distinguished in two ways: (1) while Mr. Heffernan had been at his family's apartment only an hour before the summons and complaint were served, Ms. Olsen had not been at her sister's house for several days; and (2) while in *Heffernan* the summons and complaint were served on the defendant's wife, in Olsen's case the summons and complaint were served on her sister. It is also impor-	Ms. Olsen's second subassertion Explanation of how cases support Ms. Olsen's second subassertion

tant to note that, since *Heffernan*, the courts have interpreted the service process statutes more narrowly.

Finally, Ms. Olsen can argue that, as a matter of public policy, the court should hold that the summons was not left at Ms. Olsen's usual place of abode. The courts have repeatedly held that the service of process statutes should be strictly construed and that service on a relative is not, by itself, enough. *Shurman v. A. Mortg. & Inv. Corp.*, 795 So. 2d 952, 953-54 (Fla. 2001). In addition, in this case, Ms. Olsen did not receive notice.

Ms. Olsen's third subassertion

Policies supporting Ms. Olsen's third subassertion

In response, the State will argue that Ms. Olsen was served at one of her usual places of abode. In this case, Ms. Olsen was actually living at her sister's house at the time the summons and complaint were served. The courts have not required that the plaintiff be living at the house on the day on which the summons was served. Instead, they require only that the defendant be living there "at the time of service." Therefore, while Ms. Olsen may not have been at her sister's house on the day that the summons and complaint were served, she had been there the previous weekend, and she was there the following weekend. In addition, Ms. Olsen had possessions at her sister's house, and she listed her sister's address as her own address when she applied for a driver's license.

State's main assertion
State's first subassertion

Facts that support State's first subassertion

Thus, the State will argue that the facts in this case are much stronger than the facts in *Heffernan*. While in *Heffernan*, Mr. Heffernan visited his family only "twice during the season," Ms. Olsen lived at her sister's house three days a week. In addition, while Mr. Heffernan had another permanent residence, Ms. Olsen was staying at a halfway house, which is by definition only a temporary residence. Finally, while in *Heffernan* there was no indication that Mr. Heffernan listed the Florida address on any documents, Ms. Olsen listed her sister's address on her driver's license and there is evidence indicating that Ms. Olsen received other types of mail at her sister's house.

State's second subassertion

Case that supports State's second subassertion

The State will use these same facts to distinguish *Torres*. While in *Torres*, Mr. Torres presented evidence establishing that his permanent residence was in New York, Ms. Olsen did not have a permanent residence. In the five months before service, she had been an inpatient in a treatment facility, she had lived at the halfway house, and she had lived with her sister. The State can also distinguish *Shurman* and *Thompson*.

Case that supports State's second subassertion

While in *Shurman* and *Thompson* the record indicated that the defendants had not lived at the house where service had been made for months or years, in this case, Ms. Olsen admits that she had stayed at her sister's house on the weekend before her sister was served.

Finally, the State will argue that, because the return was regular on its face, Ms. Olsen has the burden of proving, by clear and convincing evidence, that her sister's house was not her usual place of abode. In this instance, Ms. Olsen has not met that burden. In addition, when there is evidence that the defendant was in fact living at the house where service was made, the courts should not require States to determine which house the defendant was living at on any particular day.

State's third subassertion

Policies supporting State's third subassertion

§ 9.4.4 Predict How the Court Will Decide the Element

The final piece of information you need to include is your prediction about how a court is likely to decide the element. Is it more likely that the court will find that the element is met, or is it more likely that the court will decide that the element is not met?

In writing this section, you must once again change roles. Instead of playing the role of reporter describing the rules and analogous cases or advocate making each side's arguments, you must play the role of judge. You must put yourself in the position of the particular court that would decide the issue—the trial court, appellate court, state court, federal court—and decide how that court is likely to rule.

At least initially, you may be uncomfortable making such predictions. How can you predict how the court might rule? The good news is that with time, and experience, you will get better and better at making predictions. In the meantime, read the statutes and cases carefully, and critically evaluate each side's arguments. Careful reading and careful consideration of arguments, plus common sense, will help you make reliable predictions. Remember, too, that you are predicting, not guaranteeing, an outcome.

In setting out your mini-conclusion, do two things: First, set out your prediction. Second, briefly explain why you believe the court will decide the element as you have predicted. You do not have to include phrases like "I think" or "in my opinion."

In the first example below, the writer has set out her prediction but not her reasoning. In the second, the writer has set out both his prediction and his reasoning.

| EXAMPLE 1 | Poor Draft: Writer Has Set Out the Prediction but Not the Reasoning |

While both sides have strong arguments, the court will probably conclude that the summons was not left at Ms. Olsen's usual place of abode.

| EXAMPLE 2 | Better Draft: Writer Has Set Out Both the Prediction and Reasoning |

While both sides have strong arguments, the court will probably conclude that the summons was not left at Ms. Olsen's usual place of abode. In the more recent cases, the courts have strictly construed the statute, holding that the service was not made at the defendant's usual place of abode when the defendant had a more permanent place of abode. Thus, because the halfway house was Ms. Olsen's more permanent residence, the court will probably conclude that it was Ms. Olsen's usual place of abode. In addition, the court may be influenced by two key facts: the record does not indicate that the State tried to serve Ms. Olsen at the halfway house, and Ms. Olsen states that she did not receive notice.

§ 9.5 Checklist for Critiquing a Discussion Section Written Using a Script Format

A. Content

Introduction

- The writer has included a sentence or paragraph introducing the governing statute or common law rule.
- The writer has set out the general rule, quoting the applicable statutory sections and quoting or paraphrasing the common law rule.
- The writer had set out any other general rules.
- When appropriate, the writer has briefly described the policies underlying the statute or common law rule.
- The writer has included a roadmap.
- The writer has not included rules or information that the attorney does not need.
- The rules are stated accurately and objectively.
- For each rule stated, the writer has included a citation to authority.

Discussion of Undisputed Elements

- The writer has identified the element and, when there are specific rules, set out those specific rules.
- The writer has applied the rules to the facts of the client's case, explaining why the element is not in dispute.

Discussion of Disputed Elements

- For each disputed element, the writer has set out the specific rules, described cases that have interpreted and applied those rules, set out each side's arguments, and predicted how the court will decide the element.
- The writer has included all of the applicable specific rules and set out those rules accurately and objectively.
- The writer has introduced each group of analogous cases, telling the attorney what rule or principle the cases illustrate.
- The case descriptions illustrate the rule or principle and are accurate and objective.
- In setting out the arguments, the writer has set out both assertions and support for those assertions.
- The analysis is sophisticated: The writer has set out more than the obvious arguments.
- The writer has predicted how each element will be decided and given reasons to support those predictions.

B. Large-Scale Organization

- The writer has presented the information in the order in which the attorney expects to see it. For example, the writer begins the discussion section with an introductory section in which he or she sets out the general rules.
- The writer then walks the attorney through each of the elements, raising and dismissing the undisputed elements and doing a more complete analysis of the disputed elements.

C. Writing

- The attorney can understand the discussion with just one reading.
- The paragraph divisions are logical, and the paragraphs are neither too long nor too short. (See Chapter 3 in *Just Writing, 2d ed.*)
- Transitions and dovetailing have been used to make the connection between ideas clear. (See section 13.1 in this book and Chapter 4 in *Just Writing, 2d ed.*)
- In most sentences, the writer has used the actor as the subject of the sentence, and the subject and verb are close together.

(See section 13.2.1 in this book and Chapter 5 in *Just Writing, 2d ed.*)

- The writer has varied the length of the sentences and the sentence patterns so that each sentence flows smoothly from the prior sentence. (See section 13.2 in this book and Chapter 5 in *Just Writing, 2d ed.*)
- The writing is concise and precise. (See sections 13.2.2 and 13.2.3 in this book and Chapter 6 in *Just Writing, 2d ed.*)
- The writing is grammatically correct and correctly punctuated. (See section 13.2.4 in this book and Chapters 8 and 9 in *Just Writing, 2d ed.*)
- The discussion section has been proofread. (See section 13.3 in this book and Chapter 1 in *Just Writing, 2d ed.*)

10

Drafting the Discussion Section Using an Integrated Format

While some people prefer symphonies, others prefer rock concerts or raves. Similarly, while some attorneys prefer a script format, others prefer one of the more integrated formats.

Note: This chapter presumes that you have read Chapter 9.

§ 10.1 The Integrated Format

The script and integrated formats have much in common. For example, when the problem involves an elements analysis, the large-scale organization is the same. Regardless of whether you use a script or integrated format, you will begin the discussion section with an introductory section in which you set out the general rules, and you will then walk the attorney through the elements, element by element. In addition, regardless of whether you use a script or an integrated format, your discussion of the undisputed elements will be the same. You will set out the applicable tests, rules, or definitions and then apply them to the facts of your client's case. Finally, regardless of whether you use a script or an integrated format, your discussion of the disputed elements will include the same types of information: rules, descriptions of analogous cases, arguments or analysis, and conclusions. The only difference between the script and an integrated format is the way in which you package your discussion of the disputed elements. When you use an integrated format, you present the information in a different order and from a different perspective.

The following chart, Chart 10.1, illustrates the ways in which the script and integrated formats are similar. For the purposes of the chart, presume that there are three elements, that the first element is not in dispute, and that the second and third elements are in dispute.

Chart 10.1 — Discussion Section for a Problem Involving an Elements Analysis

Script Format

Introductory Section

- If one or both sides will make a policy argument, describe the policies underlying the statute or rule.
- Introduce and set out the applicable statute(s) or common law rule.
- Explain which side has the burden of proof and what that burden is.
- Set out any other rules that apply to all of the elements.
- End the introduction by providing the attorney with a roadmap for the rest of the discussion.

A. First Element *[not in dispute]*
- Set out and apply applicable rule.

B. Second Element *[in dispute]*
- Specific rules for second element.
- Examples of how specific rules. have been applied in analogous cases.
- Arguments
  o Party with burden of proof's arguments.
  o Responding party's arguments.
- Mini-conclusion for second element.

C. Third Element *[in dispute]*
- Specific rules for third element.
- Examples of how specific rules have been applied in analogous cases.

Integrated Format

Introductory Section

- If one or both sides will make a policy argument, describe the policies underlying the statute or rule.
- Introduce and set out the applicable statute(s) or common law rule.
- Explain which side has the burden of proof and what that burden is.
- Set out any other rules that apply to all of the elements.
- End the introduction by providing the attorney with a roadmap for the rest of the discussion.

A. First Element *[not in dispute]*
- Set out and apply applicable rule.

B. Second Element *[in dispute]*
- Specific rules for second element.
- Examples of how specific rules have been applied in analogous cases.
- Mini-conclusion/prediction.
- Reasoning.
Note: Instead of setting out the cases in a separate section, you can integrate them into the reasoning.

C. Third Element *[in dispute]*
- Specific rules for third element.
- Examples of how specific rules have been applied in analogous cases.

(continues)

Continued

- Arguments
  - o Party with burden of proof's arguments.
  - o Responding party's arguments.
- Mini-conclusion for third element.

- Mini-conclusion/prediction.
- Reasoning.

Note: Instead of setting out the cases in a separate section, you can integrate them into the reasoning.

§ 10.1.1   Inductive Reasoning vs. Deductive Reasoning

When you use the script format, you use a form of inductive reasoning. You set out the specific rules, you illustrate how those rules have been applied in analogous cases, you set out each side's arguments, and you set out your conclusion. In contrast, when you use an integrated format, you use a form of deductive reasoning. You set out your conclusion near the beginning and then set out your reasoning. See Chart 10.2.

Chart 10.2   **Inductive vs. Deductive Reasoning**

Script Format Inductive Reasoning	Integrated Format Deductive Reasoning
Specific Rules	Specific Rules
Descriptions of Analogous Cases	Descriptions of Analogous Cases
Moving Party's Arguments	Mini-conclusion/Prediction
• First Argument	Reasoning
• Second Argument	• First Reason (Summarize and evaluate each side's arguments)
• Third Argument	• Second Reason (Summarize and evaluate each side's arguments)
Responding Party's Arguments	• Third Reason (Summarize and evaluate each side's arguments)
• First Argument	
• Second Argument	
• Third Argument	
Rebuttal (if any)	
Mini-conclusion/Prediction	

§ 10.1.2   Script Writer vs. Judge

When you write a discussion section using a script format, you assume the perspective of a script writer. In contrast, when you write a memo using a more integrated format, you assume a perspective that is similar to that of a judge drafting an opinion. After setting out the applicable law and analogous cases, you set out your conclusion and then your reasoning. In doing so, you do what most judges do. You summarize each side's arguments and then explain why one side's arguments are more persuasive than the other side's.

§ 10.1.3 Advantages and Disadvantages

The script format has a number of advantages. From the reader's perspective, the most significant advantage is that, with the script format, it is easy to see what each is likely to argue: all of the plaintiff's arguments are together, and all of the defendant's arguments are together. From the writer's perspective, the most significant advantage is that the format forces the writer to be objective. Even though you may think that one side's arguments are stronger than the other side's, you still have to set out both sides' arguments. In addition, it is easier to write a discussion section using the script format than it is to write a discussion section using a more integrated format. Topic sentences are easier to write because, in most instances, they are just a party's main assertion or one of its sub-assertions. In addition, other sentences are easier to write because you do not need to use as many dependent clauses. The disadvantage of the script format is that the discussion is usually longer, and the format may produce what reads like a laundry list of arguments.

The advantage of the integrated format is that the discussion of the disputed element is shorter and, when done well, the analysis may appear to be more sophisticated. The disadvantage is that it can be difficult to write a good integrated discussion: it can be difficult to give appropriate weight to each side's arguments, and it can be difficult to write sentences that are easy to read and understand.

PRACTICE POINTER   The discussion of a disputed element written using the integrated format should contain the same information as a discussion of that element written using the script format. If you are leaving out information, you are doing something wrong.

---

§ 10.2 The Specific Rule Section

The specific rule section is the same regardless of whether you use the script or the integrated format. Set out more general rules before more specific rules and exceptions, do more than just string together a series of quotes, and include a citation to authority for each rule that you set out. (For more on setting out the specific rules, see section 9.4.1.) Chart 10.3, which is based on the sample memo set out in section 6.4.3, illustrates that the specific rule section is the same regardless of whether you use the script format or the integrated format.

Chart 10.3	Specific Rule Section for a Discussion Section Written Using the Script Format and for a Discussion Section Written Using an Integrated Format

Specific Rules— Script Format	Specific Rules— Integrated Format
D. Hostile	D. Hostile
While before 1984, the Washington courts considered the claimant's subjective intent in determining whether its use of the land was hostile, since 1984 the claimant's subjective intent has been irrelevant. *Chaplin,* 100 Wn.2d at 860-61, 676 P.2d 431(1984) (overruling cases in which the courts considered the claimant's subjective intent.) Thus, under current Washington law, the claimant must prove only that it used the land as if it were its own for the statutory period. *Id.; Miller v. Anderson*, 91 Wn. App. 822, 828, 964 P.2d 365 (1998). If the claimant proves that it used the land as if it were its own, the use was hostile unless the true owner can prove that it gave the claimant permission to use the land. *Id.* Permission can be express or implied. *Miller v. Anderson*, 91 Wn. App. at 829, *citing Granston v. Callahan*, 52 Wn. App. 288, 759 P.2d 462 (1988) (case dealt with a prescriptive easement and not adverse possession). The courts infer that the use was permissive when, under the circumstances, it is reasonable to assume that the use was permitted. *Id.* If there was permission, the party claiming adverse possession bears the burden of proving that permission terminated either because (1) the servient estate changed hands through death or alienation or (2) the claimant has asserted a hostile right. *Id.*	While before 1984, the Washington courts considered the claimant's subjective intent in determining whether its use of the land was hostile, since 1984 the claimant's subjective intent has been irrelevant. *Chaplin,* 100 Wn.2d at 860-61, 676 P.2d 431(1984) (overruling cases in which the courts considered the claimant's subjective intent.) Thus, under current Washington law, the claimant must prove only that it used the land as if it were its own for the statutory period. *Id.; Miller v. Anderson*, 91 Wn. App. 822, 828, 964 P.2d 365 (1998). If the claimant proves that it used the land as if it were its own, the use was hostile unless the true owner can prove that it gave the claimant permission to use the land. *Id.* Permission can be express or implied. *Miller v. Anderson*, 91 Wn. App. at 829, *citing Granston v. Callahan*, 52 Wn. App. 288, 759 P.2d 462 (1988) (case dealt with a prescriptive easement and not adverse possession). The courts infer that the use was permissive when, under the circumstances, it is reasonable to assume that the use was permitted. *Id.* If there was permission, the party claiming adverse possession bears the burden of proving that permission terminated either because (1) the servient estate changed hands through death or alienation or (2) the claimant has asserted a hostile right. *Id.*

In setting out citations to authority, you can use parentheticals to provide the attorney with additional information about the cases. For instance, in the preceding example, the writer used a parenthetical to tell the attorney that, in *Chaplin*, the Washington Supreme Court overruled those cases in which the courts had considered the claimant's subjective intent in determining whether the claimant's use was hostile. Similarly, the writer used a parenthetical to tell the attorney that, while the *Miller* court cited *Granston* as authority, *Granston* involved a prescriptive easement and not adverse possession.

§ 10.3 The Analogous Case Section

The specific rules section is not the only section that is the same under the script and integrated formats. If you set out the descriptions of analogous cases in a separate analogous case section, that section will be the same regardless of whether you use a script or an integrated format.

While most of the time you will want to set out the cases in a separate analogous case section, if the case descriptions are very short, you may want to integrate the case descriptions into your reasoning. The following example is taken from the memo set out in section 6.4.3.

EXAMPLE   Case Description Integrated into Reasoning

In addition, DNWC's use and maintenance of the campsites, fire area, outhouse, and dock are probably enough to establish that its possession was uninterrupted. In all of the cases in which the claimants maintained and used permanent structures, the courts have held that the use was uninterrupted. In addition, in *Howard v. Kunto*, 3 Wn. App. 393, 397-98, 477 P.2d 210 (1970), the court held that the claimants' use was continuous even though they only used the property during the summer. As the court noted in that case, "the requisite possession requires such possession and dominion 'as ordinarily marks the conduct of owners in general in holding, managing, and caring for property of like nature and condition.'" *Id.* at 397. Thus, while Mr. Garcia might be able to argue that the DNWC's use of the land was not uninterrupted because it only used the land during the summer months, this argument is a weak one. Because the land is recreational land, DNWC's use of the land in the summer is consistent with how the owners of similar land hold, manage, and care for their property.

In drafting the analogous case section, remember why you are including descriptions of analogous cases. You are not including them to prove that you read cases. Instead, you are including them to provide the attorney with examples of how the specific rules have been applied in cases that are factually similar to your case. As a consequence, to write the analogous cases section for a discussion section written using an integrated format, you need to go through the same process that you went through in drafting the analogous case section for a discussion section using a script format: (a) identify the analogous cases; (b) sort the analogous cases, for example, putting the cases in which the element was met in one stack and the cases in which the element was not met in another stack; (c) go through the cases in both stacks, analyzing each case and then synthesizing each group of cases; (d) draft a sentence introducing each group of cases; and (e) draft your case descriptions. (For more on each of these steps, see section 9.4.2.)

Chart 10.4 shows analogous case sections for both script and integrated formats.

Chart 10.4	Analogous Case Section for a Discussion Section Written Using the Script Format and for a Discussion Section Written Using an Integrated Format

Analogous Case Section Script Format	Analogous Case Section Integrated Format
In deciding whether the claimant was using the land as if it were its own, the courts consider whether the claimant made improvements to the land, whether the claimant maintained the property, and whether the claimant used the land on a regular basis. *See e.g. Chaplin*, 100 Wn.2d at 855-56; *Timberlane*, 79 Wn. App at 310-11. For example, in *Chaplin*, the court held that the claimants were using the land as if it were their own when the claimants built a road across the disputed land, cleared and maintained the disputed land, installed utility lines, and used the area for recreational activities. *Id.* at 855-56. Similarly, in *Timberlane*, the court held that claimants had used land belonging to the homeowners' association as if it was their own when they built and maintained a fence and a concrete patio and the claimants' children played on the land. *Id.*	In deciding whether the claimant was using the land as if it were its own, the courts consider whether the claimant made improvements to the land, whether the claimant maintained the property, and whether the claimant used the land on a regular basis. *See e.g. Chaplin*, 100 Wn.2d at 855-56; *Timberlane*, 79 Wn. App at 310-11. For example, in *Chaplin*, the court held that the claimants were using the land as if it were their own when the claimants built a road across the disputed land, cleared and maintained the disputed land, installed utility lines, and used the area for recreational activities. *Id.* at 855-56. Similarly, in *Timberlane*, the court held that claimants had used land belonging to the homeowners' association as if it was their own when they built and maintained a fence and a concrete patio and the claimants' children played on the land. *Id.*
In deciding whether the claimants' use was permissive, the courts consider whether the parties are related or have	In deciding whether the claimants' use was permissive, the courts consider whether the parties are related or have

(continues)

Continued

Analogous Case Section Script Format	**Analogous Case Section Integrated Format**
a friendly relationship, whether the improvements benefited both the claimants' and the title owners' property, and whether the title owners allowed the claimants to use the land as a neighborly accommodation. *See e.g. Lingvall v. Bartmess*, 97 Wn. App. 245, 256, 982 P.2d 690 (1999); *Granston v. Callahan*, 52 Wn. App. 288, 759 P.2d 462 (1988); *Miller v. Jarman*, 2 Wn. App. 994, 471 P.2d 704 (1970). For instance, in *Granston*, the court held that the claimants' use was permissive because the original owners of the two parcels were brothers who worked together to build driveways, walkways, and other improvements that benefited both properties. *Id*. at 294-95. Likewise, in *Miller,* the court held that the use was permissive because the title owners had allowed the claimants, who were their neighbors, to use their driveway as a neighborly accommodation. *Id*. at 996. In contrast, in *Lingvall* the court held that the antagonistic relationship between two brothers negated a finding that the claimant's use of the land was permissive. *Id*. at 256.	a friendly relationship, whether the improvements benefited both the claimants' and the title owners' property, and whether the title owners allowed the claimants to use the land as a neighborly accommodation. *See e.g. Lingvall v. Bartmess*, 97 Wn. App. 245, 256, 982 P.2d 690 (1999); *Granston v. Callahan*, 52 Wn. App. 288, 759 P.2d 462 (1988); *Miller v. Jarman*, 2 Wn. App. 994, 471 P.2d 704 (1970). For instance, in *Granston*, the court held that the claimants' use was permissive because the original owners of the two parcels were brothers who worked together to build driveways, walkways, and other improvements that benefited both properties. *Id*. at 294-95. Likewise, in *Miller,* the court held that the use was permissive because the title owners had allowed the claimants, who were their neighbors, to use their driveway as a neighborly accommodation. *Id*. at 996. In contrast, in *Lingvall* the court held that the antagonistic relationship between two brothers negated a finding that the claimant's use of the land was permissive. *Id*. at 256.

PRACTICE POINTER   Remember to introduce each group of cases. For example, include a topic sentence that tells the attorney what principle or point you are using a group of cases to illustrate. In addition, use a transition to tell the attorney whether a second case illustrates the same or different point from the first case.

§ 10.4 The Mini-conclusion or Prediction

The first subsection that is different is the mini-conclusion, or prediction. Because the script format is based on inductive reasoning, when you use the script format the mini-conclusion goes after the arguments and contains both your evaluation of each side's arguments and your prediction about how the court will decide the disputed element. In contrast, because the integrated formats use deductive reasoning, the mini-conclusions are integrated into your reasoning. Chart 10.5 illustrates the differences.

Chart 10.5	Mini-conclusion for a Discussion Section Written Using the Script Format and for a Discussion Section Written Using an Integrated Format
Mini-conclusion Script Format	**Mini-conclusion Integrated Format**
D. Hostile	**D. Hostile**
Specific Rules *[not shown]*	Specific Rules *[not shown]*
Analogous Cases *[not shown]*	Analogous Cases *[not shown]*
Arguments *[not shown]*	Mini-conclusion
Mini-conclusion	In this case, the court will probably conclude that the DNWC has met its burden of proving that its use of the Garcia land was hostile.
In this case, the DNWC appears to have the stronger arguments. First, although the DNWC has the burden of proof, it will probably be able to prove that it used Mr. Garcia's land as if it were its own when it maintained and used the campsites, the fire area, the outhouse, and the dock during the peak season. Second, the DNWC will probably be able to prove that its use was not permissive. Although it is possible that initially the DNWC was using the land with Mr. Garcia's grandfather's permission, that permission terminated when Mr. Garcia's grandfather died and left the property to Mr. Garcia. In addition, even though DNWC asked for permission to continue using the property, Mr. Garcia never responded to that request, and DNWC did an act that indicated its hostile intent when it posted the no trespassing sign and continued to use	First, the court will probably conclude that the DNWC has met its burden of proving that it used the land as if it were its own. *[Rest of the reason 1 goes here.]* Second, the court will probably conclude that the DNWC's use of the Garcia land was not permissive. *[Rest of reason 2 goes here.]* Finally, the court will probably conclude that Mr. Garcia did not allow the DNWC to use his land as a neighborly accommodation. *[Rest of reason 3 goes here.]*

(continues)

Mini-conclusion Script Format	Mini-conclusion Integrated Format

Continued

the property as its own. Third, it seems unlikely that a court would conclude that Mr. Garcia allowed the DNWC to use his land as a neighborly accommodation. Although it may not be uncommon for farmers to allow a neighbor to use a driveway, it is uncommon for owners of recreational land to allow a neighbor to use their land through the peak season. Thus, because the DNWC used the property as its own and did an act that would have terminated the permission, the court will probably hold that it has proven that its use was hostile.

PRACTICE POINTER   When you use an integrated format, you can use your mini-conclusion both to set out your conclusion and as a roadmap for the paragraphs setting out your reasoning.

In this case, the court will probably conclude that the DNWC's use of Mr. Garcia's land was hostile for two reasons: (1) the DNWC was using the land as if it were its own and (2) the DNWC's use of Mr. Garcia's land was not permissive.

First, the court will probably conclude that the DNWC has met its burden of proving that it used the land as if it were its own. *[Rest of the analysis goes here.]*

Second, the court will probably conclude that the DNWC's use of Mr. Garcia's land was not permissive. *[Rest of the analysis goes here.]*

---

§ 10.5 The Arguments

When you set out the arguments using the script format, you organize the arguments by party. You set out all of the party with the burden of proof's arguments and then all of the responding party's arguments. In contrast, when you use an integrated format, you organize the arguments, or analysis, around "reasons." You set out the mini-conclusion and then the first reason, the second reason, and so on. See Chart 10.6.

Chart 10.6	Outline Showing Organizational Scheme for Arguments Presented Using a Script Format and Using an Integrated Format

Script Format (arguments organized by party)	Integrated Format (arguments organized by reasons)
Moving Party's Arguments	Mini-conclusion

• Moving party's general assertion
• Moving party's first sub-assertion and support for that sub-assertion
• Moving party's second sub-assertion and support for that sub-assertion
	Reason 1
	  • Integrated discussion of moving and responding parties' arguments
	Reason 2
	  • Integrated discussion of moving and responding parties' arguments

Responding Party's Arguments	Reason 3
• Responding party's first sub-assertion and support for that sub-assertion • Responding party's second sub-assertion and support for that sub-assertion	• Integrated discussion of moving and responding parties' arguments

Chart 10.7 illustrates the differences between the script and integrated formats.

Chart 10.7	Argument Section for a Discussion Section Written Using the Script Format and for a Discussion Section Written Using an Integrated Format

Arguments Script Format	Conclusions and Reasoning Integrated Format
The DNWC can argue that its use of Mr. Garcia's land was hostile because it treated Mr. Garcia's land as its own and because, since 1994, it did not have either express or implied permission to use the land. The DNWC will begin by arguing that it used the land as if the land were its own. Like the claimants in *Chaplin* and *Timberla*ne, the DNWC maintained the disputed land: not only did it maintain the campsites and fire area, but it also maintained the outhouse and	The court will probably conclude that the DNWC's use of Mr. Garcia's land was hostile. First, the court will probably conclude that the DNWC used Mr. Garcia's land as if it were the true owner. Although the DNWC did not build any new structures on Mr. Garcia's land, it maintained the campsites, the fire area, the outhouse, and the dock. In addition, although the DNWC did not use the property year round, it did use the property during

(continues)

Continued

Arguments **Script Format**	**Conclusions and Reasoning** **Integrated Format**

the dock. In addition, like the claimants in *Chaplin* and *Timberlane*, the DNWC used the property on a regular basis by holding campouts on the land several nights a week for eight weeks every summer.

The DNWC will also argue that its use was not permissive. Unlike *Granston*, in which the parties were related, in this case there are no facts indicating that any of the DNWC's members are related to Mr. Garcia. In addition, unlike the title owners in *Miller,* who allowed their neighbors to use their driveway, owners of recreational property do not typically allow their neighbors to use their land throughout the summer months.

In contrast, Mr. Garcia can argue that the DNWC was not using the property as if it were its own or, even if it was, it was using the land with his implied permission.

Mr. Garcia will argue that the facts do not support a conclusion that the DNWC was using the land as if it were its own. Although the DNWC maintained the campsites, fire area, outhouse, and dock, it did not build any new structures. In addition, although it used the land, it did so for only a few days a week during the summer. Thus, the facts in this case can be distinguished from the facts in *Chaplin* and *Timberlane*. While in both of those cases, the claimants made substantial improvements to the land, for example, building a road or building a fence and a patio, in this case the DNWC did not build anything new.

In the alternative, Mr. Garcia can argue that even if the DNWC was using

the summer, which is how a typical owner would have used the land. Thus, this case is similar to *Chaplin* and *Timberlane,* in which the claimants maintained and used the disputed land as a true owner would have used it. While in *Chaplin* and *Timberlane* the claimants built new structures (in *Chaplin*, the claimants built a road and, in *Timberlane*, they built a fence and a patio), the courts have held that the claimant does not have to do everything that a title owner might do.

Second, the court will probably conclude that the DNWC's use of Mr. Garcia's land was not permissive. Unlike *Granston*, in which the parties were related and had a close relationship, there is no evidence that the members of the DNWC are related to Mr. Garcia. In addition, unlike *Miller*, in which the title owners allowed the claimants, their neighbors, to use their driveway, the typical owner of recreational land does not allow a neighboring property owner to use its land several days a week during the peak season.

While Mr. Garcia can argue that the letter that DNWC sent to him establishes that the DNWC's use of the land was permissive, the court will probably reject this argument. First, the court will conclude that if Mr. Garcia's grandfather gave the DNWC permission to use his land, that permission terminated when his grandfather died. In addition, the court will probably conclude that even if the DNWC used Mr. Garcia's land with Mr. Garcia's implied permission from the time of his grandfather's death until it sent the letter in February of 1994, that

(continues)

Continued

the land as if it were its own, it was doing so with his permission. In its 1994 letter to Mr. Garcia, the DNWC acknowledged that it was using the land with Mr. Garcia's permission, and it requested permission to continue using the land. Because Mr. Garcia did not revoke his permission, it is reasonable to assume that the DNWC used the land with Mr. Garcia's implied permission. Consequently, this case is more similar to *Miller* than it is to *Lingvall.* Like the title owners in *Miller*, who allowed the claimants to use their driveway as a neighborly accommodation, Mr. Garcia allowed the DNWC to use his land as a neighborly accommodation. In addition, unlike *Lingvall* in which there was an antagonistic relationship between the parties, in this case there was not.

In response, the DNWC can argue that even if its initial use was permissive, that permission would have terminated when Mr. Garcia's grandfather died. *See Granston*, 52 Wn. App. at 294-95. Likewise, even if the DNWC had Mr. Garcia's implied permission to use the land, that permissive use ended in 1994 when, after not receiving a response from Mr. Garcia, the DNWC posted a no trespassing sign on the dock and continued to use the property as if it were its own.

permission terminated in the summer of 1994 when the DNWC posted the no trespassing sign and continued to use the property as its own.

§ 10.6 Common Problems

The two most common problems writers encounter when using an integrated format are (1) how to give appropriate weight to each side's arguments and (2) how to write sentences that are easy to read.

§ 10.6.1 Give Appropriate Weight to Each Side's Arguments

In drafting the argument section, constantly remind yourself that you are writing an objective memo. Thus, even though you begin the argument section by setting out your conclusion, you still need to give appropriate weight to each side's arguments. The attorney needs to know what each side is likely to argue and why one set of arguments is more persuasive than another set. Compare the following examples.

EXAMPLE   **Poor Example: Writer Sets Out Only Those Arguments that Support Her Conclusion**

First, the court will probably conclude that the DNWC used Mr. Garcia's land as if it were the true owner. The DNWC maintained the campsites, the fire area, the outhouse, and the dock. In addition, the DNWC used the land for eight weeks each summer, which would be typical for that type of property. Consequently, this case is similar to *Chaplin* and *Timberlane* in which the claimants maintained and used the disputed land as if it were their own.

EXAMPLE   **Better Example: Writer Sets Out Both Sides' Arguments**

First, the court will probably conclude that the DNWC used Mr. Garcia's land as if it were the true owner. Although the DNWC did not build any new structures on Mr. Garcia's land, it maintained the campsites, the fire area, the outhouse, and the dock. In addition, although the DNWC did not use the property year round, it did use the property during the summer, which is how a typical owner would have used the land. Therefore, this case is similar to *Chaplin* and *Timberlane*, in which the claimants maintained and used the disputed land as a true owner would have used the land. While in *Chaplin* and *Timberlane* the claimants built new structures (in *Chaplin*, the claimants built a road and in *Timberlane*, they built a fence and a patio), the courts have held that the claimant does not have to do everything that a title owner might do.

PRACTICE POINTER   In switching from the script format to an integrated format, you should not lose any content: if you set out an argument when you wrote the discussion section using a script format, you should also set out that argument when you write the discussion section using an integrated format. The only things that change when you switch from the script to an integrated format are the organizational scheme and point of view. When you use the script format you set out one side's arguments and the other side's arguments, and you play the role of a script writer. In contrast, when you use an integrated format you assume a role that is similar to the role a judge plays in writing an opinion: you set out your conclusion and then your reasoning, which should refer to both sides' arguments.

§ 10.6.2   Write Sentences that Are Easy to Read

Writing sentences that give appropriate weight to each side's arguments can be difficult. In attempting to write sentence that set out both sides' arguments, some writers end up writing sentences that are difficult to read or that contain grammatical errors. If you are having trouble with a sentence, try one of the following strategies.

Strategy 1:   Put the weaker argument in a dependent clause and the stronger argument in the main clause.

One of the easiest ways to give appropriate weight to each side's argument is to put the weaker argument in a dependent clause and the stronger argument in the main clause. A dependent clause is a clause that begins with a word like "although," "even though," or "while." A main clause is a clause that could stand by itself as a complete sentence.

Although [weaker argument], [stronger argument]_____.

EXAMPLE **Weaker Argument in the Dependent Clause and Stronger Argument in the Main Clause**

(The dependent clause is underlined, and the main clause is in boldface type.)

<u>Although the DNWC did not build any new structures on Mr. Garcia's land</u>, **it maintained not only the campsites and the fire area but also the outhouse and the dock.** In addition, <u>although the DNWC did not use the property year round</u>, **it did use the property during the summer, which is how a typical owner would have used the land.**

The problem, of course, is that if you use this construction too often your writing becomes monotonous. Sometimes you can solve the problem by changing the word that you use to introduce the dependent clause. Instead of using "although," you can use "even though," or "while." At other times, though, you will need to break the pattern by using another strategy.

P R A C T I C E   Most attorneys think that the word "though" is too informal for use in a formal memo or a brief. Instead, use the more formal "although" or "even though."

Strategy 2: Use a "this and not that" sentence structure.

Another strategy that can work well is a "this and not that" sentence. When you use this strategy, remember to include a sentence that explains why your case is more like Case A than it is Case B.

EXAMPLE   "This but not that" Sentence Structure

Thus, Mr. Garcia's case is more like *Granston* than *Lingvall*.

Strategy 3: Set out one side's argument in one sentence or set of sentences and the other side's argument in a second sentence or set of sentences.

When you use an integrated format, you do not need to set out both sides' arguments in a single sentence. When the arguments are complicated, set out one side's arguments in one sentence or set of sentences and the other side's arguments in a separate sentence or set of sentences. Note that it is often a good idea to start the other side's argument with a transitional word or phrase that signals to the reader the shift in perspective.

EXAMPLE   Each Side's Arguments Set Out in Separate Sentences

---

(Mr. Garcia's argument is underlined, and the DNWC's argument is in boldface type.)

Mr. Garcia has paid all of the taxes and assessments on the disputed piece of property. **Nevertheless, the courts have consistently found that payment of taxes and assessments is not enough to defeat an adverse possession claim.**

EXAMPLE   Each Side's Arguments Set Out in Separate Sentences

---

(Mr. Garcia's arguments are underlined, and the DNWC's arguments are in boldface type.)

Some actions taken by DNWC and Mr. Garcia suggest that both sides knew the property was his. In about February 1994, DNWC wrote Mr. Garcia asking whether it could continue using his land for campouts. In August of 2006, Mr. Garcia visited the property with the intent of spending a few days camping on the lake. When he discovered that there were children and their counselors on the property, he went to the camp's headquarters and talked to the director. Arguably, these actions suggest that Mr. Garcia was asserting his rights as an owner. Other actions, however, suggest that the DNWC was successfully asserting its adverse claim. First, when Mr. Garcia did not respond to the DNWC letter, the DNWC put up a no trespassing sign. There is no evidence that Mr. Garcia had ever put up a no trespassing sign, nor is there evidence that he removed the DNWC's no trespassing sign. Second, when Mr. Garcia found children and counselors on the property, he did not tell them to leave. Instead he was the one who left, returning only the following evening after they had gone.

Strategy 4: Use the "plaintiff will argue, defendant will argue" language.

It is also not wrong to include an occasional "the plaintiff will argue" or "the defendant will respond." Just make sure to organize the arguments around the lines of argument and not each side's arguments

---

EXAMPLE   **Using the Phrase the "Plaintiff Will Argue" and "the Defendant Will Respond" to Set Out the Arguments**

We can argue that the letter that the DNWC sent to Mr. Garcia establishes that the DNWC's use of the land was permissive. However, the court will probably reject this argument on the ground that even though Mr. Garcia did not respond, DNWC continued using his land for more than ten years.

P R A C T I C E

POINTER

In reading cases, pay attention to the ways in which the courts present each side's arguments. In particular, note which types of sentences are easy to read and understand and which are more difficult. You can then use some of the easy-to-read sentence patterns in your own writing.

---

§ 10.7 Another Example

Charts 10.8 sets out an additional example, which is taken from a memo in which the issue was whether the State could prove that the defendant had constructive knowledge that a pinball machine found in a house where he was house-sitting was stolen property. The first column sets out a discussion of "knowledge" using a script format: the specific rules are set out first, the descriptions of analogous cases are set out second, the State's arguments are set out third, the defendant's arguments are set out fourth, and the mini-conclusion is at the end. In contrast, the second and third columns show you how to write the same discussion section using an integrated format. In the middle column, the specific rules are set out first, the analogous cases are set out second, the conclusion is set out third, and the reasons are set out at the end. In the last column, the discussion section is integrated even more. Instead of setting out the analogous cases in a separate analogous case section, the writer integrates the case descriptions into the arguments.

Chart 10.8	Analysis of "Knowledge" Using a Script Format and Two Different Integrated Formats	
Script Format	**Integrated Format: State's and Defendant's Arguments Integrated**	**Integrated Format: Descriptions of the Analogous Cases Integrated into the Arguments**
Knowledge	Knowledge	Knowledge
Knowledge is defined in RCW 9A.O8.01(1)(b) as follows.	Knowledge is defined in RCW 9A.O8.01(1)(b) as follows.	Knowledge is defined in RCW 9A.O8.01(1)(b) as follows.
(b) Knowledge. A person knows or acts knowingly or with knowledge when: (i) he is aware of a fact, facts, or circumstances or result described by a statute defining an offense; or (ii) he has information which would lead a reasonable man in the same situation to believe that facts exist which facts are described by a statute defining an offense.	(b) Knowledge. A person knows or acts knowingly or with knowledge when: (i) he is aware of a fact, facts, or circumstances or result described by a statute defining an offense; or (ii) he has information which would lead a reasonable man in the same situation to believe that facts exist which facts are described by a statute defining an offense.	(b) Knowledge. A person knows or acts knowingly or with knowledge when: (i) he is aware of a fact, facts, or circumstances or result described by a statute defining an offense; or (ii) he has information which would lead a reasonable man in the same situation to believe that facts exist which facts are described by a statute defining an offense.
In applying this statute, the courts have stated that the first subsection sets out the test for actual knowledge and that the second subsection sets out the test for constructive	In applying this statute, the courts have stated that the first subsection sets out the test for actual knowledge and that the second subsection sets out the test for constructive	In applying this statute, the courts have stated that the first subsection sets out the test for actual knowledge and that the second subsection sets out the test for constructive

(continues)

Continued

knowledge. *See e.g. State v. Shipp*, 93 Wn.2d 510, 517, 610 P.2d 1322 (1980); *State v. Jennings*, 35 Wn. App. 216, 219, 666 P.2d 381 (1983). In this case, the State will not be able to prove that Richardson had actual knowledge because Richardson has not admitted that he knew the pinball machine was stolen property, and there is no other evidence to prove that he had actual knowledge. The State may, however, be able to prove that Richardson had constructive knowledge that the machine was stolen.

Although subsection (ii) appears to set out an objective standard, the Washington Supreme Court has held that such a test is unconstitutional. *See Shipp*, 93 Wn.2d at 514-15. Instead, the court has said that subsection (ii) must be interpreted as permitting, but not requiring, the jury to infer that the defendant had knowledge when a reasonable person in the same circumstances would have known that the property was stolen. *Id.* Thus, to prove that Richardson had

(continues)

Continued

constructive knowledge, the State will have to prove that the facts and circumstances were sufficient to put Richardson on notice that the pinball machine was stolen. *See State v. Rye*, 2 Wn. App 920, 927, 47 P.2d 96 (1970).

In the cases in which the courts determined that there was sufficient evidence to support a finding that the defendant had constructive knowledge, the defendants had possession of the property but gave questionable explanations about how they came into possession of the property. Although these cases were decided before *Shipp*, they demonstrate facts from which knowledge may be inferred. In *State v. Rye*, 2 Wn. App. 920, 471 P.2d 96 (1970), the defendant told the police that he was storing the items for a friend who had acquired the property from a pawnshop. However, the defendant knew that the friend had been convicted of theft, and the items were not the types of items that would typically be found in a pawnshop. *Id*. at 927-28. In addition, the items were found in

constructive knowledge, the State will have to prove that the facts and circumstances were sufficient to put Richardson on notice that the pinball machine was stolen. *See State v. Rye*, 2 Wn. App 920, 927, 47 P.2d 96 (1970).

In the cases in which the courts determined that there was sufficient evidence to support a finding that the defendant had constructive knowledge, the defendants had possession of the property but gave questionable explanations about how they came into possession of the property. Although these cases were decided before *Shipp*, they demonstrate facts from which knowledge may be inferred. In *State v. Rye*, 2 Wn. App. 920, 471 P.2d 96 (1970), the defendant told the police that he was storing the items for a friend who had acquired the property from a pawnshop. However, the defendant knew that the friend had been convicted of theft, and the items were not the types of items that would typically be found in a pawnshop. *Id*. at 927-28. In addition, the items were found in

constructive knowledge, the State will have to prove that the facts and circumstances were sufficient to put Richardson on notice that the pinball machine was stolen. *See State v. Rye*, 2 Wn. App 920, 927, 47 P.2d 96 (1970).

In our case, absent additional information that Coming or another individual told Richardson that the pinball machine was stolen or evidence that Richardson played the pinball machine, it is unlikely that a jury will find that the facts and circumstances were sufficient to put either Richardson or a reasonable person on notice that the pinball machine was stolen.

First, it is unlikely that a jury will find that the nature of the property or its location was sufficient to put Richardson on notice that the pinball machine was stolen. In *State v. Rye*, 2 Wn. App. 920, 471 P.2d 96 (1970), the court found that the nature and location of the property indicated that the defendant knew that the property was stolen. In that case, the defendant told the police

(continues)

Continued

places in the defendant's residence that indicated that the items were being used rather than stored. *Id*. The court found that these facts were sufficient to put a reasonable person on notice that the property was stolen.

Similarly, in *State v. Rockett*, 6 Wn. App. 399, 493, P.2d 321 (1972), the defendant first explained that he had the car seats shipped from California. *Id*. at 401. However, when he was unable to provide bills of lading for that shipment, the defendant said that he brought them up with him when he came from California. *Id*. Later, the defendant said that the seats had been shipped from California through an Oregon establishment and that from there they had been shipped to a wrecking company in Seattle. *Id*. at 401-02. The court found that because the defendant gave a number of contradictory and unverifiable explanations, "there was sufficient evidence from which the jury could find that the defendant knew that the bucket seats in the instant case were stolen, or that the defendant had

places in the defendant's residence that indicated that the items were being used rather than stored. *Id*. The court found that these facts were sufficient to put a reasonable person on notice that the property was stolen.

Similarly, in *State v. Rockett*, 6 Wn. App. 399, 493, P.2d 321 (1972), the defendant first explained that he had the car seats shipped from California. *Id*. at 401. However, when he was unable to provide bills of lading for that shipment, the defendant said that he brought them up with him when he came from California. *Id*. Later, the defendant said that the seats had been shipped from California through an Oregon establishment and that from there they had been shipped to a wrecking company in Seattle. *Id*. at 401-02. The court found that because the defendant gave a number of contradictory and unverifiable explanations, "there was sufficient evidence from which the jury could find that the defendant knew that the bucket seats in the instant case were stolen, or that the defendant had

that he was storing the items for a friend who had acquired the property from a pawnshop. However, the items— household items and clothing— were not the types of items that would typically be found in a pawnshop. *Id*. at 927-28. In addition, the items were found in places in the defendant's residence that indicated that the items were being used rather than stored. *Id*. The court found that these facts were sufficient to put a reasonable person on notice that the property was stolen. While it may be uncommon for an individual to purchase clothing and other personal items from a pawnshop, it is not uncommon for college students to purchase a used pool table or a pinball machine and place it their living room.

Second, it is likely that the jury will find that the condition of the pinball machine was sufficient to put Richardson on notice that the pinball machine was stolen. Although Richardson has admitted that he had been house-sitting for ten days, at this point there is no evidence

(continues)

Continued

knowledge of facts sufficient to put him on notice that the bucket seats were stolen." *Id.* at 403.

In our case, the State will argue that the facts and circumstances are sufficient to establish that Richardson had constructive knowledge that the pinball machine was stolen property. First, the State will argue that, as in *Rye*, in this case, the nature and location of the property should have put Richardson on notice that the pinball machine was stolen. Just as it is unlikely that an individual would purchase clothing and other personal items from a pawnshop, it is unlikely that a college student would purchase a commercial pinball machine and place it in his or her living room.

Second, the State will argue that the condition of the pinball machine should have put Richardson on notice that it was stolen. Because the pinball machine was found in the family room of the residence in which Richardson had been staying for ten days, more likely than not he saw both the partially

knowledge of facts sufficient to put him on notice that the bucket seats were stolen." *Id.* at 403.

In our case, absent additional information that Coming or another individual told Richardson that the pinball machine was stolen or evidence that Richardson played the pinball machine, it is unlikely that a jury will find that the facts and circumstances were sufficient to put either Richardson or a reasonable person on notice that the pinball machine was stolen.

First, it is unlikely that a jury will find that the nature of the property or its location was sufficient to put Richardson on notice that the pinball machine was stolen. While it may be uncommon for an individual to purchase clothing and other personal items from a pawnshop, it is not uncommon for college students to purchase a used pool table or a pinball machine and place it their living room.

Second, it is unlikely that the jury will find that the condition of the pinball

that he inspected or played the pinball machine. As a result, a jury may believe him when he says that he never noticed the partially scratched off label or the altered coin box.

Third, even if Richardson admits that he inspected or played the machine, the jury may believe him if he explains that he believed that Coming had purchased the pinball machine from the Last Chance Tavern. Such an explanation would be by far more reasonable than the explanations that the defendants gave in *Rye* and *State v. Rockett*, 6 Wn. App. 399, 493, P.2d 321 (1972). In *Rockett*, the defendant first explained that he had the car seats shipped from California. *Id.* at 401. However, when he was unable to provide bills of lading for that shipment, the defendant said that he brought them up with him when he came from California. *Id.* Later, the defendant said that the seats had been shipped from California through an Oregon establishment and that from there they had been shipped to a wrecking company in

(continues)

Continued

scratched off owner identification label and the altered coin box.

Third, the State will argue that, just as Rye's relationship with his cellmate made it more likely that Rye knew that the property was stolen, Richardson's relationship with Comings makes it more likely that he knew that the pinball machine was stolen. Because Richardson and Comings had been friends for four years, it is reasonable to assume that they had talked about the pinball machine and how Comings acquired it. The State will argue that, taken together, these facts and circumstances are sufficient to establish that Richardson knew that the pinball machine was stolen. Richardson will argue that the facts and circumstances were not sufficient to put him on notice that the pinball machine was stolen. First, he will argue that the nature and location of the pinball machine did not put him on notice that it was stolen. It is not uncommon for college students to purchase used pool tables and pinball machines and place them in their living rooms.

machine was sufficient to put Richardson on notice that the pinball machine was stolen. Although Richardson has admitted that he had been house-sitting for ten days, at this point there is no evidence that he inspected or played the pinball machine. As a result, a jury may believe him if he says that he never noticed the partially scratched off label or the altered coin box.

Third, even if Richardson admits that he inspected or played the machine, the jury may believe him if he explains that he believed that Coming had purchased the pinball machine from the Last Chance Tavern. Such an explanation would be by far more reasonable than the explanations that the defendants gave in *Rye* and *Riggs*. In addition, if the jury believes Richardson's explanation, it might also find that it would have been reasonable for Richardson to believe that, after purchasing the pinball machine, Coming altered the coin box and tried to scratch off the label.

Fourth, the jury is likely to find that there is nothing in Richardson and

Seattle. *Id*. at 401-02. The court found that because the defendant gave a number of contradictory and unverifiable explanations, "there was sufficient evidence from which the jury could find that the defendant knew that the bucket seats . . . were stolen, or that the defendant had knowledge of facts sufficient to put him on notice that the bucket seats were stolen." *Id*. at 403.

In addition, if the jury believes Richardson's explanation, it might also find that it would have been reasonable for Richardson to believe that, after purchasing the pinball machine, Coming altered the coin box and tried to scratch off the label.

Fourth, the jury is likely to find that there is nothing in Richardson and Coming's relationship that should have put Richardson on notice that the pinball machine was stolen. Unlike *Rye* in which the defendant's friend had four theft convictions and had been the defendant's cellmate, Coming does not have a criminal record.

Finally, as a matter of

(continues)

Continued

Second, he will testify that the condition of the machine did not put him on notice that the pinball machine was stolen. He may make either of two arguments. He may testify that although he saw the pinball machine in the living room, he did not inspect or play it. As a result, he did not see the partially scratched-out identification label or notice that the coin box had been altered. In the alternative, he may argue that although he saw the label and coin box, they were not sufficient to put him on notice that the machine was stolen. If Coming had purchased the pinball machine from the tavern, it would have been reasonable for him to try to scratch off the label and to disable the coin box.

Third, Richardson may testify that, unlike Mr. Rye's friend, Coming does not have a criminal record. As a result, Richardson had no reason to suspect that the pinball machine was stolen.

Fourth, unlike the defendants in *Rye* and *Rockett*, Richardson can probably offer a reasonable explanation.

Coming's relationship that should have put Richardson on notice that the pinball machine was stolen. Unlike Rye's friend who had four theft convictions, Coming does not have a criminal record.

Finally, as a matter of public policy, the jury will probably be reluctant to convict a person who is only house-sitting of possessing stolen property found in the house. Although some of the jurors may be persuaded by the State's argument that a person who has reason to know that the property is stolen and does not report the property to the police is aiding and abetting theft, most of the jurors will probably be reluctant to make a person criminally liable, particularly when it requires a house sitter to inspect a friend's property and to report that friend.

public policy, the jury will probably be reluctant to convict a house sitter of possessing stolen property found in the house. Although some of the jurors may be persuaded by the State's argument that a person who has reason to know that the property is stolen and does not report the property to the police is aiding and abetting theft, most of the jurors will probably be reluctant to make a person criminally liable, particularly when it requires the house sitter to inspect a friend's property and to report that friend.

(continues)

Continued

If he testifies, he may state that he presumed that Coming had purchased the used pinball machine from the tavern.

Finally, Richardson will argue that, as a matter of public policy, we do not want to discourage individuals from house-sitting by making them criminally liable for any stolen property that might be in the house. In addition, Richardson may try to trade on the sympathies of the jury. Unless he had actual knowledge that the property was stolen, he should not be required to report his friend to the police.

In response, the State will argue that it is not inappropriate to hold a house sitter criminally liable when the house sitter has reason to know that the property is stolen and does not report the stolen property to the police. In such a situation, the house sitter is aiding and abetting those who steal or receive stolen property.

Absent additional information, for example, evidence that Coming or another person told Richardson that the

(continues)

Continued

pinball machine was
stolen or evidence that
Richardson played the
pinball machine, it is
unlikely that the State will
be able to prove, beyond
a reasonable doubt, that
the facts and
circumstances were
sufficient to put
Richardson or a
reasonable person on
notice that the pinball
machine was stolen.

§ 10.8   Checklist for Discussion Section Written Using an Integrated Format

A. Content

Introduction

- The writer has included a sentence or paragraph introducing the governing statute or common law rule.
- The writer has set out the general rule, quoting the applicable statutory sections and quoting or paraphrasing the common law rule.
- The writer had set out any other general rules.
- When appropriate, the writer has briefly described the policies underlying the statute or common law rule.
- The writer has included a roadmap.
- The writer has not included rules or information that the attorney does not need.
- The rules are stated accurately and objectively.
- For each rule stated, the writer has included a citation to authority.

Discussion of Undisputed Elements

- The writer has identified the element and, when there are specific rules, set out those specific rules.
- The writer has applied the rules to the facts of the client's case, explaining why the element is not in dispute.

Discussion of Disputed Elements

- For each disputed element, the writer has set out the specific rules, described cases that have interpreted and applied those rules, stated his or her conclusion or prediction, and summarized his or her reasoning.
- The writer has included all of the applicable specific rules and set out those rules accurately and objectively.
- The writer has introduced each group of analogous cases, telling the attorney what rule or principle the cases illustrate.
- The case descriptions illustrate the rule or principle and are accurate and objective.
- In setting out the reasoning, the writer has given appropriate weight to each side's arguments.
- The analysis is sophisticated.

B. Large-Scale Organization

- The writer has presented the information in the order in which the attorney expects to see it. For example, the writer begins the discussion section with an introductory section in which he or she sets out the general rules.
- The writer then walks the attorney through each of the elements, raising and dismissing the undisputed elements and doing a more complete analysis of the disputed elements.

C. Writing

- The attorney can understand the discussion with just one reading.
- The paragraph divisions are logical, and the paragraphs are neither too long nor too short. (See Chapter 3 in *Just Writing, 2d ed.*)
- Transitions and dovetailing have been used to make the connection between ideas clear. (See section 13.1 in this book and Chapter 4 in *Just Writing, 2d ed.*)
- In most sentences, the writer has used the actor as the subject of the sentence, and the subject and verb are close together. (See section 13.2.1 in this book and Chapter 5 in *Just Writing, 2d ed.*)
- The writer has varied the length of the sentences and the sentence patterns so that each sentence flows smoothly from the prior sentence. (See section 13.2.1 in this book and Chapter 5 in *Just Writing, 2d ed.*)
- The writing is concise and precise. (See sections 13.2.3 and 13.2.3 in this book and Chapter 6 in *Just Writing, 2d ed.*)

- The writing is grammatically correct and correctly punctuated. (See section 13.2 in this book and Chapters 8 and 9 in *Just Writing, 2d ed.*)
- The discussion section has been proofread. (See section 13.3 in this book and Chapter 1 in *Just Writing, 2d ed.*)

Drafting a Discussion Section for an Issue of First Impression

While the majority of legal issues require an elements analysis, occasionally you will encounter an issue that requires a different type of analysis. For example, the issue may require you to balance competing interests or it may involve an issue of first impression, that is, an issue that has not yet been decided by your jurisdiction's courts.

In this chapter, we describe how to organize a discussion section for problems that involve an issue of first impression. Although the techniques used in this chapter can be used in an objective memo written by one member of a law firm for another member of the same law firm, the example we have used comes from a bench memo written for a United States District Court judge for the Southern District of Florida. In the bench memo, the judge's law clerk analyzes an issue raised in a case pending before the District Court: whether providing a tsunami warning system to the Liberation Tigers of Tamil Eelam (LTTE), a group that has been designated as a terrorist organization, violates the Antiterrorism and Effective Death Penalty Act. A copy of the bench memo is set out in section 6.4.5.

§ 11.1 Organizational Plans for Issues of First Impression

When it comes to organizing an issue of first impression, you have a number of options. If other jurisdictions have decided the issue but taken different approaches, you can organize your discussion section around these different approaches. In the alternative, you can organize your discussion section around types of arguments, for example, in one section you can set out plain language arguments, in another section legislative history arguments, and so on. The following examples outline these two approaches.

EXAMPLE 1   Organizing the Discussion of an Issue of First Impression Using the Approaches Taken in Other Jurisdictions as the Organizing Principle

Discussion

Introduction

- Introduce "rule" that the court has been asked to interpret, for example, the statute that the court has been asked to interpret.
- Introduce the approaches that other jurisdictions have taken.

Part I: Approach 1

- Describe approach.
- Set out reasons courts have given for adopting this approach.
- Set out other reasons that support the adoption of this approach.

Part II: Approach 2

- Describe approach.
- Set out reasons courts have given for adopting this approach.
- Set out other reasons that support the adoption of this approach.

Part III: Evaluation

- Critique and evaluate the two approaches.
- Recommend approach and reasons that support recommendation.

PRACTICE POINTER   While most often the courts will split, taking two different approaches, sometimes there are more than two approaches. If the courts have taken three, four, or five different approaches, add subsections so that you have a subsection for each approach. In addition, distinguish the various approaches, setting out the reasons the courts have given for adopting each approach, summarizing other reasons that support the adoption of each approach, and critiquing and evaluating each approach.

EXAMPLE 2	**Organizing the Discussion of an Issue of First Impression Using the Types of Arguments as the Organizing Principle**

Discussion

Introduction

- Introduce the "rule" that the court has been asked to interpret, for example, the statute that the court has been asked to interpret.
- Briefly describe the possible approaches.
- Include a roadmap that identifies the types of arguments the parties are likely to make.

I. Plain Language Arguments

- Set out and critique the plain language arguments using an integrated format.

II. Legislative History Arguments

- Set out and critique the legislative history arguments using an integrated format.

III. Analogous Case Arguments

- Set out and critique arguments based on the case law using an integrated format.

IV. Policy Arguments

- Set out and evaluate the policy arguments using an integrated format.

PRACTICE POINTER   You will not always set out all four types of arguments, For example, if your problem involved the interpretation of a constitutional provision and not a statute, there would not be any legislative history arguments. Similarly, if there are no cases, either in your jurisdiction or any other jurisdiction, that discuss the issue, you would not have any arguments based on the cases unless one or both sides can use cases that discuss a related issue. In addition, you may not always set out the arguments in the order that they are listed in Example 2. Although in general courts look to the plain language of a statute before they consider other arguments, if there is another argument that is determinative, start your discussion with that argument.

Depending on the issue, there may also be other ways to organize the discussion. Thus, before deciding on an organizational scheme, think about other possible organizational schemes. Is there another scheme that might work better than the ones set out above? If there is, use it. However, make sure that the organizational scheme that you choose works not just for you but also for your readers.

If a court in another jurisdiction has discussed the issue that you have been asked to analyze, look at how that court organized its opinion. If that court's opinion was easy for you to follow, think about adopting its organizational plan. If, however, you found the other court's opinion confusing, determine whether the organizational scheme was the culprit. If it was, pick a different plan.

§ 11.2 The Introduction

Most of the time, start your discussion section with an introductory section. If you are writing an office memo, use this section to tell the attorney for whom you work that the issue is one of first impression and to provide the attorney with the background information that he or she will need to understand the issue and to evaluate the various approaches and arguments. In contrast, if you are writing a bench memo, use the introductory section to provide your judge with background information.

In deciding what information to include, think about your reader. How much does your reader know about this area of law? If the reader knows very little, you may need to place the issue into a larger context. How does your issue fit with related issues and doctrines? Why and when was the statute enacted? If, however, your reader is familiar with the area of law, your introductory section can be much shorter: just provide your reader with the information he or she needs to understand the particular issue that you were asked to research and analyze. In other words, give your reader what he or she needs: nothing less and nothing more.

You are not expected to be a mind reader. Thus, when you get an assignment, ask questions. Is the attorney or judge who assigned the memo familiar with the area of law? Does the attorney or judge like a lot of background information, or does he or she prefer just a brief overview?

EXAMPLE 1 **Introduction for a Judge Who Is Not Familiar with the Area of Law**

In response to the Oklahoma City bombing, Congress enacted the *Antiterrorism and Effective Death Penalty Act of 1996*, Pub. L. No. 104-132, 110 Stat. 1214 (1996) (AEDPA), to combat terrorist financing and support. *See* 142 Cong. Rec. S3352 (daily ed. Apr. 16, 1996) (statement of Sen. Hatch). The AEDPA authorizes the Secretary of State to designate an organization as a Foreign

Terrorist Organization (FTO), *see* 8 U.S.C. § 1189(a) (West, WESTLAW current through P.L. 109-4), and prohibits the provision of material support to these designated FTOs. *See* 18 U.S.C. § 2339B(a)(1) (West, WESTLAW current through P.L. 109-4). Under the current version of § 2339B,

> *[w]hoever knowingly provides material support or resources to a foreign terrorist organization*, or attempts or conspires to do so, shall be fined under this title or imprisoned not more than 15 years, or both, and, if the death of any person results, shall be imprisoned for any term of years or for life.

18 U.S.C. § 2339B(a)(1) (emphasis added).

The term "material support or resources" (material support) is defined in § 2339B's sister statute, 18 U.S.C. § 2339A (West, Westlaw current through P.L. 109-4). Section 2339A defines "material support or resources" as follows:

> (1) the term *"material support or resources" means* any property, tangible or intangible, or service, including currency or monetary instruments or financial securities, financial services, lodging, training, expert advice or assistance, safehouses, false documentation or identification, *communications equipment*, facilities, weapons, lethal substances, explosives, personnel (1 or more individuals who may be or include oneself), and transportation, except medicine or religious materials;
>
> (2) the term "training" means instruction or teaching designed to impart a specific skill, as opposed to general knowledge;

18 U.S.C. § 2339A(b)(1) (emphasis added).

Congress enacted § 2339A two years prior to enacting § 2339B, as part of the *Violent Crime Control and Law Enforcement Act of 1994*, Pub. L. No. 103-322, 108 Stat. 1796, 2022 (1994). Unlike § 2339B, § 2339A criminalizes the provision of material support only when the defendant knows or intends that the support will be used by the recipient to further its terrorist agenda (the recipient need not be designated an FTO). The relevant wording of the current version of § 2339A follows:

> *Whoever provides material support or resources* or conceals or disguises the nature, location, source, or ownership of material support or resources, *knowing or intending that they are to be used in preparation for, or in carrying out [terrorist activities]*. . . .

18 U.S.C. § 2339A(a) (emphasis added).

On its face, § 2339B does not require that the provider of material support know or intend that the support would further the FTO's unlawful ends. Instead, § 2339B requires only that the defendant know that the recipient of the support was an FTO or that the recipient had engaged in terrorist activities. *See id*. In this case, the Tamil Welfare and Human Rights Committee (TWHRC) argues that the statute requires proof that a person not only provided material support to an FTO but also intended to further the FTO's unlawful ends. Although it can make plain language, legislative history, and analogous case arguments, TWHRC's strongest argument is a policy argument. In response, the Government argues that the plain language of the statute, its legislative history, and the Ninth Circuit's decision establish that Congress did not intend that the statute require proof of intent. In addition, the Government has a strong policy argument.

EXAMPLE 2   Introduction for Reader Who Is Familiar with the Area of Law

In 1994, Congress enacted what is now 18 U.S.C. § 2339A as part of the Violent Crime Control and Law Enforcement Act of 1994. Pub. L. No. 103-322, § 120005, 108 Stat. 1796 (1994). Section 2339A makes it a crime to provide "material support or resources" knowing or intending that they will be used "in preparation for, or in carrying out" crimes of terrorism. 18 U.S.C. § 2339A (2000). "Material support or resources" is defined very broadly; the current definition reads as follows:

> (1) the term "material support or resources" means any property . . . or service, including currency or monetary instruments . . . , lodging, training, expert advice or assistance, . . . *communications equipment*, facilities, weapons, lethal substances, explosives, personnel (1 or more individuals who may be or include oneself), and transportation, except medicine or religious materials . . . .

18 U.S.C.A. § 2339A (West, Westlaw through P.L. 109-4) (emphasis added).

In 1996, Congress enacted 18 U.S.C. § 2339B as part of the Antiterrorism and Effective Death Penalty Act (AEDPA). Like § 2339A, § 2339B made it a crime, punishable by a ten-year imprisonment, to knowingly provide "material support or resources"; unlike § 2339A, § 2339B encompassed a broad range of behavior, criminalizing all knowing provisions of material support to any organization that had been designated as a "foreign terrorist organization" by the Secretary of State, whether the provider intended that the support be used for terrorist purposes or for humanitarian (or any other) purposes. Section 2339B uses the same broad definition of "material support or resources" as § 2339A.

In 2001, Congress amended the USA PATRIOT Act of 2001, increasing the prison term to fifteen years and adding a life sentence if any death resulted from the violation. Pub. L. 107-56, § 810(d), 115 Stat. 272 (2001). Two years later, the Ninth Circuit Court of Appeals struck down portions of § 2339B on First and Fifth Amendment grounds. *See Humanitarian Law Project v. United States Dept. of Justice* 352 F.3d 382, 403 (9th Cir. 2003), *vacated by* 393 F.3d 902 (9th Cir. 2004) (*Humanitarian* 2003). In response, Congress enacted the Intelligence Reform and Terrorism Prevention Act of 2004, which clarified the definition of "material support or resources" and made the intent requirement more explicit. Pub. L. 108-458, § 6603, 118 Stat. 3638 (2004). The relevant portion of the current version of § 2339B reads as follows:

> § 2339B. Providing material support or resources to designated foreign terrorist organizations
>> (a) Prohibited activities.
>>> (1) Unlawful conduct. Whoever knowingly provides material support or resources to a foreign terrorist organization, or attempts or conspires to do so, shall be fined under this title or imprisoned not more than 15 years, or both, and, if the death of any person results, shall be imprisoned for any term of years or for life. *To violate this paragraph, a person must have knowledge that the organization is a designated terrorist organization . . . that the organization has engaged or engages in terrorist activity. . . , or that the organization has engaged or engages in terrorism . . . .*
>
> ....
>
>> (g) Definitions. As used in this section—
>
> ....
>
>>> (4) the term "material support or resources" has the same meaning given that term in section 2339A (including the definitions of "training" and "expert advice or assistance" in that section);
>
> ....
>
>>> (i) Rule of construction. *Nothing in this section shall be construed or applied so as to abridge the exercise of rights guaranteed under the First Amendment to the Constitution of the United States.*

18 U.S.C.A. § 2339B (West, Westlaw through P.L. 109-3) (emphasis added).

This memo analyzes the plain language of § 2339B, its legislative history, the cases from other jurisdictions that have interpreted § 2339B, and each side's policy arguments.

§ 11.3   Identifying, Setting Out, and Evaluating the Arguments

Regardless of how you decide to organize the arguments (majority/minority, type of argument) you need to provide the reader with a thorough but concise summary and evaluation of each side's arguments. In doing so, your analysis needs to be sophisticated, and your writing needs to be clear, precise, and engaging.

§ 11.3.1 Identify the Arguments

Start by making sure that you have identified all of the arguments. One way to make sure that you have identified all of the possible arguments is to walk through the "standard moves" using a chart like Chart 11.1.

	TWHRC's Arguments	Government's Arguments
Chart 11.1 — Chart for Recording Arguments		
Plain Language Arguments		
Legislative History Arguments		
Analogous Case Arguments		
Policy Arguments		
Constitutional Concerns		

Finally, think beyond the boxes. Are there other ways to approach the issue? Other arguments that could be made? Assumptions that need to be challenged?

§ 11.3.2 Identifying and Presenting Plain Language Arguments

The canons of statutory construction, that is, the rules that the courts use in interpreting statutes, say that the courts should begin their analysis of a statute by looking at the statute's language. If that language is unambiguous, the analysis stops there. The courts simply apply the statute's "plain language." If, however, the statute's language is ambiguous or would produce an absurd result, for example, a statute that is unconstitutional on its face, the courts continue their analysis, looking at the statute's legislative history, at how other courts have applied the statute or similar statutes, and at the policies underlying the statute.

PRACTICE POINTER The canons of statutory construction can, however, be a double-edged sword: if you use one canon, you come up with one result, but if you use a different canon, you come up with a different result. See, for example, Karl N. Llewellyn, *Remarks On the Theory of Appellate Decision and the Rules or Canons About How Statutes Are to Be Construed*, 3 Vand. L. Rev. 395, 401 (1950).

Because courts usually begin their analysis by looking at the language used in the statute, you will usually start your discussion by setting out any plain language arguments the parties may have. If you have organized your arguments by approach, start by telling the reader whether the statute's plain language supports that approach. If, however, you are organizing the arguments as we have chosen to do—by type—set out and evaluate each side's plain language arguments. In doing so, make sure that your analysis is objective and sophisticated and that your writing is clear and concise.

Compare the following examples. While in the first example, the writer provides the reader with the basic information, the analysis is not particularly sophisticated. The second and third examples are better.

EXAMPLE 1 **Writer Provides Reader with Basic Information but the Analysis Is Not Particularly Sophisticated**

A. Plain language arguments

In interpreting a statute, the courts look first at the plain language of the statute.

> The writer sets out one of the applicable canons of statutory construction but does not include a citation to authority.

In this case, § 2339B's plain language establishes that Congress did not want to require proof of specific intent to further the terrorist activities of an FTO. Neither the original nor the amended version of § 2339B includes language requiring the government to prove that the defendant intended to further an FTO's terrorist activities. Instead, the plain language requires only two things: (1) that the defendant knowingly provide material support and (2) that the defendant knows that the group has been designated as an FTO.

> The writer sets out her conclusion.
>
> The writer includes some support for her conclusion. The analysis is, however, very basic.

EXAMPLE 2 **Analysis Is More Sophisticated**

A. Plain language arguments

In interpreting a statute, the courts look first to the statute's plain language. *Boim v. Quranic Literacy Inst.*, 291 F.3d 1000, 1009 (7th Cir. 2002). Unless that language is ambiguous or its application would produce an absurd result, the analysis ends with the statute's plain language. *Id.*

> Instead of setting out only one of the applicable canons of statutory construction, the writer sets out two. Because the writer works

for a Seventh Circuit District Court judge, the writer cites a Seventh Circuit Court of Appeals case as authority.

In this case, the government will argue that § 2339 is not ambiguous. While § 2339B requires proof that the person knew that he or she was providing material support or resources to a group that has been designated as an FTO, it does not require proof that the person intended to further the FTO's illegal activities.

(a) Prohibited activities.

(1) Unlawful conduct. *Whoever knowingly provides material support or resources to a foreign terrorist* organization, or attempts or conspires to do so, shall be fined under this title or imprisoned not more than 15 years, or both . . . . To violate this paragraph, *a person must have knowledge that the organization is a designated terrorist organization . . . , that the organization has engaged or engages in terrorist activity. . . , or that the organization has engaged or engages in terrorism . . . .*

18 U.S.C. § 2339B (emphasis added.)

Although the writer presents the arguments using the script format, the focus is on the two competing canons of statutory construction: The government uses the first canon to support its position, and the TWHRC uses the second canon to support its position.

Note how the writer has used italics to emphasize the key terms in the statute. The writer has also added a parenthetical following the citation (emphasis added) to let the reader know that he has added the italics.

The TWHRC will respond by arguing that a plain language interpretation of § 2339B produces an absurd result: a statute that is unconstitutional. Thus, the TWHRC will argue that this Court has two choices: Either it can hold that 18 U.S.C. § 2339B is unconstitutional, or it can apply the rule set out by the United States Supreme Court in cases like *Jones v. United States*, 526 U.S. 227 (1999), and *United States v. X-Citement Video*, 513 U.S. 64 (1994), and interpret the statute in such a way to avoid constitutional difficulties. While TWHRC's first choice would be for the Court to hold that the statute is unconstitutional, its second choice would be for the Court to read an intent requirement into the statute: to obtain a conviction the government

The writer uses a topic sentence to let the reader know that he is moving from the government's argument to TWHRC's arguments. Note that in setting out TWHRC's arguments, the writer tells the reader (1) that the TWHRC is asking for alternative forms of relief and (2) which of these forms the TWHRC prefers.

would have to prove that the person intended to further the FTO's illegal activities.

While in this example the writer's analysis is more sophisticated, he has not evaluated each side's arguments or reached a conclusion. While the writer does not need to put that evaluation and conclusion in this subsection, he does need to put it somewhere, for example, at the end of the discussion/analysis section or in the conclusion/recommendation.

EXAMPLE 3   **Analysis Is Even More Sophisticated**

A. Plain language arguments

The plain language of § 2339B indicates that the government does not have to prove that the defendant intended to further the FTO's illegal activities.

The writer begins the plain language arguments subsection with a mini-conclusion.

The current version of § 2339B requires only that a person knowingly provide material support or resources to an FTO with the "knowledge that the organization is a designated terrorist organization" or that the organization has engaged or engages in terrorist activity. Although the Court could interpret this phrase to mean that the person must *know* or believe that the organization is likely to use such support to further its terrorist activities, such an interpretation is tenuous at best.

In setting out the plain language arguments, the writer uses an integrated approach. For example, in this paragraph the writer sets out both an argument that supports the government's position and an argument that supports TWHRC's position. Note that the writer evaluates TWHRC's argument, saying that it is "tenuous at best."

Three facts support the conclusion that Congress did not want to require the government to prove that the defendant intended to further the

The writer uses this paragraph to introduce three arguments that

FTO's illegal activities. First, in enacting § 2339B's sister statute, § 2339A, Congress included the language "knowing or intending."

18 U.S.C. § 2339A

(a) Offense. — Whoever provides material support or resources or conceals or disguises the nature, location, source, or ownership of material support or resources, *knowing or intending* that they are to be used in preparation for, or in carrying out, a violation of . . . .

In contrast, in enacting 18 U.S.C. § 2339B, Congress did not include the "knowing or intending" language.

18 U.S.C. § 2339B

(a) Prohibited activities.
  (1) Unlawful conduct. *Whoever knowingly provides material support or resources to a foreign terrorist organization,* or attempts or conspires to do so, shall be fined under this title or imprisoned not more than 5 years, or both . . . . To violate this paragraph, *a person must have knowledge that the organization is a designated terrorist organization . . . that the organization has engaged or engages in terrorist activity . . . , or that the organization has engaged or engages in terrorism . . . .*

Second, although Congress amended § 2339B to clarify the knowledge requirement, it did not add an intent requirement. Subsection (a)(1) of the 2004 amendments inserted the following language: "To violate this paragraph, a person must have knowledge that the organization is a designated terrorist organization (as defined in subsection (g)(6)), that the organization has engaged or engages in terrorist activity (as defined in section 212(a)(3)(B) of the Immigration and Nationality Act), or that the organization has engaged or engages in terrorism (as defined in section 140(d) (2) of the Foreign Relations Authorization Act, Fiscal Years 1988 and 1989)."

support the government's position and to set out the first of those three arguments.

Note that the writer introduces the statutes, has edited out irrelevant language, and has italicized the key terms.

The writer uses a signpost ("second") to let the reader know that she is moving from the first of the three arguments to the second of the three arguments.

Although this second argument is, arguably, a legislative history argument, the writer has placed it in her plain language section. When appropriate, you can cross reference or even combine your discussion of the plain language and legislative history arguments.

Third, in enacting § 2339B, Congress found that "foreign terrorist organizations that engage in terrorist activity are so tainted by their criminal conduct that *any contribution* to such an organization facilitates that conduct." Pub. L. No. 104-132, § 301(a)(7), 110 Stat. 1214, 1247 (emphasis added). This finding strongly suggests that Congress did not want to require proof of intent.

The writer uses a signpost ("Third,") to let the reader know that she is moving from the second argument to the third and last argument.

The United States Supreme Court has held, however, that, when possible, the courts should interpret statutes to avoid constitutional difficulties. *United States v. X-Citement Video*, 513 U.S. 64 (1994). *See also* 18 U.S.C. § 2339B(i), which states that "[n]othing in this section shall be construed or applied so as to abridge the exercise of rights guaranteed under the First Amendment to the Constitution of the United States." Thus, if § 2339B is unconstitutional without an intent requirement, the Court could read an intent requirement into the statute.

In the topic sentence for this paragraph, the writer uses the word "however" to alert the reader to the fact that she is moving to an argument that supports the TWHRC's position. The writer sets out one of the possible contingencies.

Although the writer sets out her conclusion at the very beginning and, in the first paragraph, evaluates one of TWHRC's arguments, she does not explain why, taken as a whole, the government's arguments are stronger than TWHRC's arguments.

§ 11.3.3   Identifying and Presenting Legislative History Arguments

In setting out the legislative history, you have several options: You can present the legislative history as a history, describing the events in the order in which they occurred, or you can set out that part of the legislative history that supports one reading of the statute and then the legislative history that supports the other reading of the statute. Compare the following examples.

EXAMPLE 1   Analysis Is Weak

When introducing the bill that included the language that now makes up § 2339B, Senator Hatch stated,

> This bill also includes provisions making it a crime to knowingly provide material support to the terrorist functions of foreign groups designated by a Presidential finding to be engaged in terrorist activities. [N]othing in the Constitution provides the right to engage in violence against fellow citizens or foreign nations. Aiding and financing foreign terrorist bombings is not constitutionally protected activity. . . . I have to believe that honest donors to any organization want to know if their contributions are being used for such scurrilous terrorist purposes. We are going to be able to tell them that after this bill. . . . I am convinced we have crafted a narrow but effective designation provision which meets these obligations while safeguarding the freedom to associate, which none of us would willingly give up.

142 Cong. Rec. S3354 (daily ed. April 16, 1996).

Section 2339B has been amended twice since it became law; the first amendment increased the penalties associated with violation of the statute, and the second amendment clarified the definitions of training and personnel, as well as adding language to clarify the general intent requirement. 18 U.S.C. § 2339B (2000) (amended 2001 and 2004).

Although Senator Hatch's statement may support the TWHRC's argument, Congress's failure to amend the statute to require proof of specific intent is evidence that Congress does not want to require proof of intent.

In this example, the writer jumps, feet first, into the statute's legislative history.

The writer begins the legislative history section by setting out a long quote from the *Congressional Record*. However, because the writer has not introduced the quote or highlighted the key language, the reader does not know why the writer included the quote or what to look for in reading the quote. For example, which approach does this quote support? The government's position? TWHRC's position?

Unexpectedly, the writer moves from Senator Hatch's statement to a discussion of the amendments.

EXAMPLE 2   **Analysis Is More Sophisticated**

B. Legislative History Arguments

Like the plain language, 2339B's legislative history suggests that Congress did not intend to require proof that a defendant intended to further an FTO's illegal activities.

The writer begins this subsection both with a subheading that tells the reader that this subsection contains the legislative history arguments and with a topic sentence that connects this subsection to the prior subsection and then set out the writer's conclusion, all in thirty words, which includes the subheading.

In introducing the Senate Conference Report on the AEDPA, Senator Hatch, who cosponsored the bill, stated, "This bill also includes provisions making it a crime to knowingly provide material support *to the terrorist functions* of foreign groups designated . . . to be engaged in terrorist activities." 142 Cong. Rec. S3354 (daily ed. April 16, 1996) (statement of Sen. Hatch) (emphasis added). Although Senator Hatch's statement seems to imply that Congress only wanted to prohibit contributions that are intended to further an FTO's terrorist functions, Senator Hatch immediately went on to say, "I am convinced we have crafted a narrow but effective designation provision which meets these obligations while safeguarding the freedom to associate, which none of us would willingly give up." *Id.*

The writer sets out the legislative history using a chronological organizational scheme. In doing so, the writer integrates a description of the history with a discussion and evaluation of each side's arguments. For example, note the sentence that begins with "Although Senator Hatch's statement . . . ." In this sentence the writer sets out the weaker argument in the dependent clause, and then sets out and evaluates the stronger argument in the main or independent clause.

This second sentence alters the context in which the first sentence should be interpreted, making it less likely that Senator Hatch was speaking about scienter and more likely that he was speaking about the distinction between punishing mere association with an FTO (which would likely

In this paragraph and the following paragraphs, the writer provides the reader with an integrated discussion of whether Congress could abridge a right granted by the First Amendment) and punishing the conduct of providing material support to an FTO (which would have fewer constitutional implications). These statements do, however, provide evidence that Congress intended to craft a statute that did not criminalize an overly broad range of behavior and did not abridge any constitutionally protected rights.

On the same day that Senator Hatch made his comments, Senator Snowe said, "this bill . . . will cut off the ability of terrorist groups . . . to raise huge sums in the United States for supposedly 'humanitarian' purposes, where in reality a large part of those funds go toward conducting terrorist activities." 142 Cong. Rec. S3380 (daily ed. April 16, 1996) (statement of Sen. Snowe). This statement can be interpreted at least two ways. On one hand, this comment provides some evidence that Congress intended to cut off *all* support from the United States to FTOs, regardless of the ostensible purpose of the donation. On the other hand, this comment could also be read as evidence that Congress intended to prohibit only support for terrorist activities that was cloaked behind a fraudulent façade of humanitarianism. It is not clear from Senator Snowe's statement whether Congress intended to criminalize donations of support that *in reality* go towards conducting humanitarian activities. The Congressional statement of findings and purpose regarding § 2339B provides some clarification on this point: "foreign organizations that engage in terrorist activity are so tainted by their criminal conduct that *any contribution* to such an organization facilitates that conduct." Antiterrorism and Effective Death Penalty Act of 1996, Pub. L. No. 104-132, § 301, 110 Stat 1214 (1996) (emphasis added).

This finding provides unequivocal evidence that Congress did in fact intend to criminalize all donations made to FTOs, regardless of the intent of the donor or of the actual use to which the support would be put. Supporting this interpretation, the House Conference Report for the Comprehensive Antiterrorism Act of 1995 (a predecessor of the AEDPA) provides further evidence of Congress's approach to controlling contributions to terrorist organizations:

have intended to deviate from standard practice and enacted a criminal statute that does not require proof of specific intent. Note how the writer provides the reader with both information and analysis.

There is no other mechanism, other than an *outright prohibition on contributions*, to effectively prevent such organizations from using funds raised in the United States to further their terrorist activities abroad. . . . The prohibition is absolutely necessary to achieve the government's compelling interest in protecting the nation's safety from the very real and growing terrorist threat.

H.R. Rep. No. 104-383 at 45 (emphasis added).

In conclusion, the *Congressional Record* contains some support for a holding that § 2339B has a scienter requirement. However, less equivocal evidence in the record supports a holding that to convict under § 2339B, the government would need only to prove that defendants knew they were providing material support to an organization that they knew had been designated as an FTO.

The writer ends his discussion of legislative intent by setting out a mini-conclusion.

§ 11.3.4   Identifying and Presenting Arguments Based on Case Law

If the issue you have been asked to research is an issue of first impression, there are, by definition, no controlling cases. The only cases will be cases from other jurisdictions or cases that discuss analogous statutes or issues.

If there are cases from other jurisdictions, you will usually want to tell the reader about those cases. In doing so, your focus will not be on the facts of those cases; rather, your focus will be on the rule that the courts in the other jurisdictions applied. What rule did the court apply, and why did it apply that rule rather than some other rule? If you note a problem with the court's reasoning, tell the reader about that problem.

In the following example, Example 1, the writer has forgotten why he is describing the court's decision in *Al-Arian*: Instead of focusing on what the court did and why, the writer devotes most of the description to a summary of the facts, which, although interesting, are not relevant.

EXAMPLE 1   Poor Analogous Case Description

C. Analogous case arguments

TWHRC will ask the court to take the approach that the United States District Court for Middle District of Florida took in *United States v. Al-Arian*, 308 F. Supp. 2d 1322 (M.D. Fla. 2004).

The writer's heading and topic sentence are good: the heading tells the reader the topic, and the topic sentence tells the reader that the writer is setting out TWHRC's arguments.

In *Al-Arian*, the government filed criminal charges against members of the Palestinian Islamic Jihad-Shiqaqi Faction (the "PIJ"), who purportedly operated and directed fundraising and other organizational activities in the United States for almost twenty years. The PIJ is a foreign organization that uses violence, principally suicide bombings, and threats of violence to pressure Israel to cede territory to the Palestinian people. Count 1 of the Indictment alleged a wide ranging pattern of racketeering activity beginning in 1984 lasting through February 2003, including murder, extortion, and money laundering. The indictment detailed some 256 overt acts, ranging from soliciting and raising funds to providing management, organizational, and logistical support for the PIJ. The overt act section of the indictment detailed numerous suicide bombings and attacks by PIJ members causing the deaths of over 100 people, including two American citizens, and injuries to over 350 people, including seven American citizens.

In this paragraph the writer sets out the facts, which are, we agree, interesting. Unfortunately, this is not the information the reader needs. While the reader needs a quick summary of the facts, the focus needs to be on the court's reasoning.

In its decision, the court concluded that to convict a defendant under Section 2339B(a)(1), the government had to prove beyond a reasonable doubt that the defendant knew that (a) the organization was an FTO or had committed unlawful activities that caused it to be so designated and (b) what he was furnishing was "material support." In addition, the court concluded that government also had to prove that the defendant had a specific intent that the support would further the illegal activities of an FTO. *See Al-Arian*, 329 F. Supp at 1297.

Although the writer tells the reader what the court concluded, he does not tell the reader why the court reached that conclusion.

EXAMPLE 2   Better Example

While the court's decision in *United States v. Al-Arian*, 329 F. Supp. 2d 1294 (M.D. Fla. 2004), supports the Government's position, the court's reasoning is no longer sound.

The writer begins his discussion with his conclusion.

In *Al-Arian*, the United States District Court for the Middle District of Florida read an intent requirement into 18 U.S.C. § 2339B. *Id.* In concluding that the government had to prove that the defendants intended to further the FTO's illegal activities, the court stated that "where a statute is susceptible of two constructions, by one of which grave and doubtful constitutional questions arise and by the other of which such questions are avoided, our duty is to adopt the latter." *Id.* at 1299 (quoting *Jones v. United States*, 526 U.S. 227, 239 (1999)).

> The writer then describes *Al-Arian*. In doing so, the writer focuses on that part of the decision that is relevant to the issue that he was asked to research: whether the statute requires proof of intent.

Although the version of § 2339B that the *Al-Arian* court interpreted may have been susceptible to a construction requiring specific intent, the amended version is not. Before Congress amended § 2339B, there were multiple ways to interpret the statute. The statute could have been read as providing for a strict liability offense. Alternatively, it could have been read to require knowledge that the organization was a designated FTO or knowledge of the organization's conduct to give rise to its designation as an FTO. Finally, it is even feasible that the statute implied that the person providing material support must at least know or believe that the FTO was likely to use such support for terrorist activities, which seems to be the construction accepted by the *Al-Arian* court. However, the recent amendment makes it clear that, in order to violate the statute, a person must only have knowledge of the organization's designation or the activities that gave rise to the designation. Although Congress could have taken the approach that the court took in *Al-Arian*, it adopted the approach taken by the Ninth Circuit in *Humanitarian II*.

> In this paragraph the writer does a sophisticated analysis of the court's decision in *Al-Arian*.

While in our example problem there were cases from other jurisdictions that were on point, you may come across a situation in which there are no cases, either in your jurisdiction or in any other jurisdiction. If such situations, include a sentence telling the reader that there are no cases on point.

EXAMPLE | **Sentence Telling Reader that There Are No Cases**

To date, there are no reported cases involving (include reference to statute).

In other situations you may be asked to work on an issue in which the other side has cited a case that you have determined is not on point. When this happens, tell the reader that the case is not on point and explain why.

EXAMPLE **Paragraph Telling Reader that the Cases the Other Side Relied on Are Not on Point**

Although the TWHRC uses *Smith v. Jones* to support its argument, that case is not on point. While the present case involves a criminal statute, that case involves a civil statute. Similarly, although the Government cites *United States v. Morgan* as authority, that case applied a statute that has since been repealed.

---

§ 11.3.5   Identifying and Presenting Arguments Based on Policy

When a case involves an issue of first impression, the most persuasive arguments are often policy arguments. Thus, identify each side's policy arguments, and then briefly summarize them. In doing so, look both at what would be "just" in the case that is currently before the court and at the bigger picture. In future cases, what rule would be the best rule?

EXAMPLE **Good Discussion of Policy Arguments**

In deciding how to interpret § 2339B, the courts must balance the United States' interest in providing humanitarian aid against its interest in protecting its citizens against terrorism.

The writer begins her discussion of the policy arguments by identifying the competing interests.

In this case, the TWHRC will argue that the United States' interest in allowing it to provide a tsunami warning system to the LTTE far outweighs any risks to the United States or its citizens. In the event of another tsunami, the warning system could save thousands if not hundreds of thousands of lives and, the LTTE presents little or no threat to the United States. Although the LTTE has been designated as a foreign terrorist organization, organizations like the LTTE "often do much more than commit terrorist acts. They also undertake important and worthwhile charitable, humanitarian, educational, or political activities." Randolph N. Jonakait, *The Mens Rea For the Crime of Providing Material Resources to a Foreign Terrorist Organization,*

In this paragraph, the writer sets out the TWHRC's policy arguments.

56 Baylor L. Rev. 861, 873 (2004). If the court holds that § 2339B has no scienter requirement, charitable giving that ought to be encouraged by a rich country like the United States will have taken on previously unknown risks, because donors who seek only to support an FTO's humanitarian agenda could be subjected to criminal penalties. *Id.*

In response the government will argue that the allowing the TWHRC to donate the equipment to a known terrorist organization undermines Congress's goal of combating terrorism. *See* H.R. Rep. No. 104-383 at 45. In addition, any exemption for humanitarian aid would be extremely difficult to administer so as to ensure that the humanitarian aid was not subverted to further the FTO's terrorist agenda. Terrorist organizations do not maintain organizational structures or "firewalls" to prevent resources donated for humanitarian purposes from being used to commit or support terrorist acts.

In this paragraph, the writer sets out the government's policy arguments.

P R A C T I C E

Sometimes it works better to integrate the policy arguments into your legislative history arguments or into the arguments based on cases from other jurisdictions. If you do integrate the arguments into another section, you do not need a separate section for policy arguments.

---

§ 11.4 Checklist for a Discussion Section Involving an Issue of First Impression

A. Content

Introduction

- The writer has included a sentence or paragraph introducing the governing statute or common law rule.
- The writer has told the reader that the issue is one of first impression.
- If other jurisdictions have decided the issue, the writer has briefly described those approaches.

Analysis

- The writer has set out all of the applicable arguments. For example, the writer has set out plain language arguments, legislative history arguments, arguments based on analogous cases, policy arguments, and constitutional arguments.
- The analysis is balanced: the writer has given appropriate consideration to the various approaches.
- The analysis is sophisticated: the writer has critically analyzed each of the possible approaches.

B. Large-Scale Organization

- The writer has organized the discussion around the various approaches other jurisdictions have taken, by type of argument, or by party.

C. Writing

- The reader can understand the discussion with just one reading.
- The paragraph divisions are logical, and the paragraphs are neither too long nor too short. (See Chapter 3 in *Just Writing, 2d ed.*)
- Transitions and dovetailing have been used to make the connection between ideas clear. (See section 13.1 in this book and Chapter 4 in *Just Writing, 2d ed.*)
- In most sentences, the writer has used the actor as the subject of the sentence, and the subject and verb are close together. (See section 13.2.1 in this book and Chapter 5 in *Just Writing, 2d ed.*)
- The writer has varied the length of the sentences and the sentence patterns so that each sentence flows smoothly from the prior sentence. (See section 13.2.1 in this book and Chapter 5 in *Just Writing, 2d ed.*)
- The writing is concise and precise. (See sections 13.2.3 and 13.2.3 in this book and Chapter 6 in *Just Writing, 2d ed.*)
- The writing is grammatically correct and correctly punctuated. (See section 13.2 in this book and Chapters 8 and 9 in *Just Writing, 2d ed.*)
- The discussion section has been proofread. (See section 13.3 in this book and Chapter 1 in *Just Writing, 2d ed.*)

Drafting the Formal Conclusion

You are not doing anything wrong. In drafting a formal memo, you do set out your conclusions in more than one place. If you included a brief answer, you set out your conclusion there. In addition, if your problem required an elements analysis, you set out mini-conclusions for each disputed element. And yes, you will now, once again, set out your conclusion, this time in a formal conclusion.

While some attorneys think that the typical memo has too many conclusions, other attorneys believe that each conclusion serves a useful purpose. The brief answer is exactly that: a brief answer. If the client is on the phone and the attorney has not had time to read the full memo, he or she can read the brief answer. The mini-conclusions serve a different purpose. They are part of the analysis and help the attorney understand which elements will be easy to prove and which may be more difficult to prove. The formal conclusion serves still a different purpose. It is the place where you pull all of the pieces together.

§ 12.1 Formal Conclusion in a One-Issue Memo

In a one-issue memo, the formal conclusion is used to summarize the analysis of that one issue. For example, in the service of process memo set out in section 6.4.2, the writer used the formal conclusion to tell the attorney that he thinks that the service of process is invalid. Note the writer begins by answering the question set out in the issue statement. The writer does not, however, stop there. In addition to answering the question, he goes through the elements, element by element. In the second paragraph, the writer tells the attorney that Ms. Olsen will have to concede that the summons was left with a person of suitable age and discretion and that, more likely than not, the court will probably conclude that the process server told Ms. Olsen's sister about the contents. In the third paragraph, the writer talks about the last element, usual place of abode, briefly explaining why he thinks that Ms. Olsen can prove that the summons was not left at her usual place of abode.

EXAMPLE   **Formal Conclusion for a Single-Issue Memo**

Conclusion

Because of the strong public policy in favor of ensuring that defendants receive notice of actions that have been filed against them, the court will probably decide that the substituted service of process was not valid and set aside the order terminating Ms. Olsen's parental rights.

Ms. Olsen will have to concede that her sister, Ms. Webster, is a person of suitable age and that Ms. Webster was residing at the house where the service was made. In addition, because the process server told Ms. Webster that Ms. Olsen needed to go to court, it seems unlikely that Ms. Olsen will be able prove that Ms. Webster was not informed of the contents.

Ms. Olsen may, however, be able to prove that the summons and complaint were not served at her usual place of abode. In the more recent cases, the courts have strictly construed the usual place of abode requirement, holding that the service was not made at the defendant's usual place of abode when the defendant had a more permanent residence. Thus, because the halfway house was Ms. Olsen's more permanent residence, the court will probably conclude that it was Ms. Olsen's usual place of abode. In addition, the court may be influenced by two key facts: the record does not indicate that the plaintiff tried to serve Ms. Olsen at the halfway house, and Ms. Olsen states that she did not receive notice.

PRACTICE POINTER   The easiest way to draft the formal conclusion is to set out your answer to the issue in the first sentence or paragraph. Then cut and paste your mini-conclusions for each element into your formal conclusion. Finally, revise your draft so that each paragraph flows smoothly from the prior paragraph.

§ 12.2 Formal Conclusion for a Multi-issue Memo

When the memo discusses several issues, use your formal conclusion to summarize your analysis of each issue and to explain the relationships among the issues. In the following example, which is taken from the memo set out in section 6.4.4, the writer begins her formal conclusion by setting out her conclusions. Then, in the next three paragraphs, she goes through the issues, one by one, summarizing her analysis.

EXAMPLE	Formal Conclusion for a Multi-issue Memo

Although Elder Care is a covered employer and Ms. Smith is a covered employee, Ms. Smith did not provide Elder Care with the required notice. In addition, it seems unlikely that Ms. Smith will be able to prove that she had a serious health condition as that term is defined under the FMLA.

Elder Care is a covered employer because it is engaged in commerce and employs fifty or more employees. We should, however, verify that at least fifty of these employees work within a seventy-five-mile radius. It also appears that Ms. Smith is a covered employee. We should, though, check Elder Care's records to make sure that Ms. Smith worked at least 1,250 hours during the previous twelve months and that she has not already used twelve weeks of FMLA leave.

The court will probably determine that Ms. Smith's email was not sufficient to put Elder Care on notice that Ms. Smith was requesting or was entitled to FMLA leave. While in her email Ms. Smith stated that she had been at the hospital and that she needed to take care of some family matters, she did not say why she had been at the hospital or what type of family matters she needed to take care of. Although as a matter of public policy the courts may not want to require that employees tell their employers that they have been a victim of domestic violence, employers should not be required to investigate every employee absence to determine whether the employee is entitled to FMLA leave.

If, however, the court determines that Ms. Smith did give Elder Care adequate notice, Ms. Smith will have to prove that she had a "serious health condition," which is defined as "an illness, injury, impairment, or physical or mental condition that involves (A) inpatient care in a hospital, hospice, or residential medical care facility or (B) continuing treatment by a health care provider." Because no court has held that domestic violence is a serious health condition, this case would present an issue of first impression. Although Ms. Smith missed more than three weeks of work, she may have a difficult time proving that she was unable to work. In addition, because she was treated at the emergency room, she will have a difficult time proving that she received inpatient care or that she received continuing treatment.

Although it appears unlikely that Ms. Smith will be able to prove that Elder Care violated the FMLA, litigation can be expensive. Therefore, we should talk to Elder Care about settling. For example, if turnover is high, it may be possible for Elder Care to reinstate Ms. Smith sometime in the near future.

> **PRACTICE POINTER**
>
> By convention, most writers do not include citations to authority in the formal conclusion. For example, in the above example, the author quotes but does not cite the applicable statute.

§ 12.3 Advice

While some attorneys just want conclusions, others may want you to go one step further and offer advice. What are the client's options? What action should the attorney take next? Is this the type of case that the firm should, or wants to, handle? When you are asked to include this type of information in the conclusion, add a paragraph like the following.

EXAMPLE 1   Paragraph Setting Out Advice

If it appears that Ms. Olsen might win on the merits, I recommend that we move to quash the service of process and vacate the order terminating her parental rights.

EXAMPLE 2   Paragraph Setting Out Advice

Although it appears unlikely that Ms. Smith will be able to prove that Elder Care violated the FMLA, litigation can be expensive. Thus, we should talk to Elder Care about settling. For example, if turnover is high, it may be possible for Elder Care to reinstate Ms. Smith sometime in the near future.

EXAMPLE 3   Paragraph Setting Out Advice from a Memo about Constructive Eviction of a Business

Although we may be able to prove that Ms. Walter was constructively evicted, we should warn her that litigation is expensive and that there are no guarantees. In addition, we should make sure that she understands her options.

Option 1: Stay and pay rent.

Although this option avoids the expense and stress of litigation, Ms. Walter may lose her right to claim that she has been constructively evicted. One of the requirements for constructive eviction is that the tenant move out within a reasonable time.

Option 2: Sublease the space to another business.

Although Ms. Walter's lease requires that she obtain Valley Antiques' approval before subletting her space, the courts have said that a landlord cannot withhold approval except for good cause. The risk associated with this option is that Ms. Walter may be liable for unpaid rent if the new tenant fails to make payments.

Option 3: Try to negotiate an early termination of the lease.

Ms. Walter can try to negotiate an early termination of the lease on the grounds that Valley Antiques has violated the lease by leasing to the arcade and second-hand stores.

§ 12.4 Checklist for Formal Conclusion

A. Content

- In a one-issue memorandum, the conclusion is used to predict how the issue will be decided and to summarize the reasons supporting that prediction.
- When appropriate, the writer includes not only the conclusion but also strategic advice.

B. Organization

- The information is organized logically.

C. Writing

- The attorney can understand the conclusion with just one reading.
- The paragraph divisions are logical, and the paragraphs are neither too long nor too short. (See Chapter 3 in *Just Writing, 2d ed.*)
- Transitions and dovetailing have been used to make the connections between ideas clear. (See section 13.1 in this book and Chapter 4 in *Just Writing, 2d ed.*)
- In most sentences, the writer has used the actor as the subject of the sentence, and the subject and verb are close together. (See section 13.2 in this book and Chapter 5 in *Just Writing, 2d ed.*)
- The writer has varied the length of the sentences and the sentence patterns so that each sentence flows smoothly from the prior sentence. (See section 13.2 in this book and Chapter 5 in *Just Writing, 2d ed.*)
- The writing is concise and precise. (See section 13.2 in this book and Chapter 6 in *Just Writing, 2d ed.*)
- The writing is grammatically correct and correctly punctuated. (See section 13.2 in this book and Chapters 8 and 9 in *Just Writing, 2d ed.*)
- The discussion section has been proofread. (See section 13.3 in this book and Chapter 1 in *Just Writing, 2d ed.*)

13

Revising, Editing, and Proofreading

Yes, there are times when, because of time or money restraints, you will have to turn in a first draft of an in-house memo. You should not, however, get in the habit of submitting first drafts to your supervising attorney, and you should never submit a first draft to a court, opposing counsel, or your client. Unlike a speech, which disappears as soon as the words are spoken, written words remain: while well-written documents can enhance your reputation, poorly written ones can destroy it.

§ 13.1 Revising

Revising is the process of "re-visioning" what you have drafted. During this re-visioning process, step back from your draft and look at it through the eyes of the attorney or attorneys who will be reading it. Have you given the attorney all of the information that he or she needs? Have you presented that information in the order that the attorney expects to see it?

During the revising stage, you need to be willing to make major changes. If, in reviewing your draft, you realize that you did not need to include one part of your discussion, you need to delete that part, no matter how many hours you spent drafting it. Similarly, if in reviewing your draft, you realize that you did not research or discuss a major point, you must go back and do that research, analysis, and writing. Finally, if in reviewing your draft, you realize that your organizational scheme just does not work, start over, reorganizing one section or even the entire statement of facts or discussion section.

 As a general rule, writers do a better job revising when they print out a draft and lay out the pages side by side. Problems that were not apparent when you looked at your draft on your computer screen may become apparent when you look at the draft in hard copy.

§ 13.1.1 Content

In revising a draft, look first at its content. If there are problems with content, that has to be your first priority.

(a) Have You Given the Attorney the Information He or She Needs?

The first question that you should ask yourself is whether you have given the attorney the information that he or she requested. Did you research the assigned issue or issues? Did you locate all of the applicable statutes, regulations, and cases? Did you identify and present the arguments that each side is likely to make? Did you evaluate those arguments and predict how the court is likely to rule?

(b) Have You Made Any Errors?

In law, small errors can have serious consequences. The failure to cite check to make sure that a case is still good law, the omission of a "not," or writing "or" when you should have written "and" can make the difference between your client winning and losing, between competent lawyering and malpractice.

As a consequence, in writing the memo, you must exercise care. Because the attorney is relying on you, your research must be thorough. Make sure that you have located the applicable statutes, regulations, and cases, and make sure those statutes, regulations, and cases are still good law. In addition, make sure your analysis is sound. Did you read the statutes, regulations, and cases carefully? Is the way in which you put the pieces together sound? Finally, make sure you have presented the statutes, regulations, and cases accurately and fairly. Did you correctly identify the issue in the analogous cases? Did you take a rule out of context? Did you misrepresent the facts or omit a key fact? Unless the attorney reads the statutes, regulations, and cases that you cite, she may not see an error until it is too late.

§ 13.1.2 Large-Scale Organization

The next step is to check the discussion section's large-scale organization. Has the information been presented in the order the attorney expects to see it?

One way to check large-scale organization is to prepare an after-the-fact outline. To create such an outline, go through your draft, labeling the subject matter of each paragraph and then listing those labels in outline form. See Chart 13.1.

Chart 13.1	**Excerpt from an After-the-Fact Outline for Usual Place of Abode Memo**
A. Usual Place of Abode	First disputed element
If a defendant has more than one residence, the defendant's usual place of abode is the place where the defendant was actually living at the time of service. *Shurman v. A. Mortg. & Inv. Corp.*, 795 So. 2d 952, 953-54 (Fla. 2001). It is not enough that the summons and complaint are left with a relative. *Torres v. Arnco Const., Inc.*, 867 So. 2d 583, 586 (Fla. 5th DCA 2004).	Specific rules
The only case in which the Florida courts have held that the service was made at the defendant's usual place of abode is *State ex rel. Merritt v. Heffernan*, 195 So. 145 (Fla. 1940). In that case, the defendant was on a train enroute to his permanent residence in Minnesota when his wife was served at the family's apartment in Florida where the defendant had visited "twice during the season." *Id.* at 146. In its decision, the court stated that when a person has more than one residence, the summons and complaint must be served at the dwelling house in which the defendant is living at the time when the service is made. *Id.* In applying this rule to the facts of the case, the court concluded that the defendant was "not within the classification of persons who had at the time of service lost one place of residence and had not yet established another." *Id.* at 148. Thus, the court determined that, at the time of service, the defendant's then place of abode was still the family's apartment in Florida. *Id.* at 147.	Analogous case in which the court held that the element was met
In contrast, in most of the cases in which the courts have held that the summons was not left at the defendant's usual place of abode, the defendant had not lived at the house where service was made for a substantial period of time. *See e.g. Thompson v. State, Dept. of*	Analogous cases in which the court held that the element was not met

(continues)

Continued

Revenue, 867 So. 2d 603, 605 (Fla. 1st DCA 2004); *Shurman,* 795 So. 2d at 953-54. For example, in *Shurman,* the court held that the service had not been made at the defendant's usual place of abode when the summons was left with the defendant's wife at the family home but the defendant had been incarcerated for at least nine months. *Id.* at 955. Similarly, in *Thompson,* the court held that the summons had not been left at the defendant's usual place of abode when the summons was left with the defendant's wife at the family home. *Id.* at 605. In reaching its decision, the court relied on the defendant's affidavit in which the defendant stated that he was separated from his wife, that he had not resided at that address for over three years, and that he did not authorize anyone to accept service of process on his behalf. *Id.* at 605.

The only Florida case in which the summons was left with a relative with whom the defendant was visiting is *Torres,* 867 So. 2d at 585-86. In that case, the plaintiff tried, for more than a month, to serve Mr. Torres at the New York apartment where Mr. Torres had lived for thirteen years. *Id.* Although all attempts at service were unsuccessful, the New York process server indicated in his affidavit that he had "verified" with a neighbor that "Mr. Torres lived at the New York address, but that he was often out of town, and was expected to return in two weeks." *Id.* Because it could not serve the defendant in New York, the plaintiff served Mr. Torres's mother at her residence in Florida. In his affidavit, the Florida process server stated that Mr. Torres's mother told him that "he (presumably Mr. Torres) would be home soon." *Id.* Mr. Torres stated that he never received notice. In holding that the service was not valid, the court noted that while the standard of review was gross abuse of discretion, the trial court had not heard live testimony, and the plaintiff had the burden of establishing that the service was valid. *Id.* at 587. It then went on to note that the evidence tended to support Mr. Torres's position that his usual place of abode was in New York and that Mr. Torres's mother's statement that Mr. Torres would be home soon was, at best, ambiguous. *Id.*

> Another analogous case in which the element is not met

Ms. Olsen can make three arguments to support her assertion that her sister's house was not her usual place of abode. First, Ms. Olsen will argue that, under the plain language of the statute, her sister's house was not her

> Ms. Olsen's arguments

(continues)

Continued

usual place of abode. When a defendant has more than one residence, the service must be made at the place where the defendant was actually living at the time summons and complaint were served. In this case, Ms. Olsen had more than one residence: During the week she lived at the halfway house and on weekends she visited her sister. Because the summons and complaint were served on a Wednesday, a weekday, the service was not made at the place where Ms. Olsen was actually living.

Ms. Olsen's plain language arguments

Second, Ms. Olsen will argue that the facts in her case are more like the facts in *Torres* than the facts in *Heffernan*. Like Mr. Torres, who was only visiting his mother and who was not at his mother's house when service was made, Ms. Olsen only visited her sister and was not at her sister's house when the summons and complaint were served. However, while Mr. Torres's mother's statement that Mr. Torres "would be home soon" suggested that Mr. Torres would be returning to his mother's house that day, Ms. Olsen's sister told the process server that Ms. Olsen "isn't here today." In addition, while the plaintiff in *Torres* had tried on a number of occasions to serve Mr. Torres at his New York house, in our case we do not know whether the defendant tried to serve Ms. Olsen personally or at the halfway house. Finally, *Heffernan* can be distinguished in two ways: (1) While Mr. Heffernan had been at his family's apartment only an hour before the summons and complaint were served, Ms. Olsen had not been at her sister's house for several days; and (2) while in *Heffernan* the summons and complaint were served on the defendant's wife, in the Olsen case the summons and complaint were served on Ms. Olsen's sister. It is also important to note that, since *Heffernan*, the courts have interpreted the service process statutes more narrowly.

Ms. Olsen's analogous case arguments

Finally, Ms. Olsen can argue that, as a matter of public policy, the court should hold that the summons was not left at Ms. Olsen's usual place of abode. The courts have repeatedly held that the service of process statutes should be strictly construed and that service on a relative is not, by itself, enough. *Shurman,* 795 So. 2d at 953-54. In addition, in this case, Ms. Olsen did not receive notice.

Ms. Olsen's policy arguments

In response, the State will argue that Ms. Olsen was served at one of her usual places of abode. In this case,

The State's arguments

(continues)

Continued

Ms. Olsen was actually living at her sister's house at the time the summons and complaint were served. The courts have not required that the plaintiff be living at the house on the day on which the summons was served. Instead, they only require that the defendant be living there "at the time of service." Therefore, while Ms. Olsen may not have been at her sister's house on the day that the summons and complaint were served, she had been there the previous weekend, and she was there the following weekend. In addition, Ms. Olsen had possessions at her sister's house, and she listed her sister's address as her own address when she applied for a driver's license.	The State's plain language arguments

[The rest of the discussion is omitted.]

After you have completed your after-the-fact argument, compare it to the outline that you created before you began writing. See Chart 13.2.

Chart 13.1   Initial Outline vs. After-the-Fact Outline

Initial Outline	After-the-Fact Outline
A. Usual Place of Abode (disputed element)	First disputed element
1. Specific rules	Specific rules
2. Examples of how specific rules have been applied in analogous cases	Analogous case in which the court held that the element was met
	Analogous cases in which the court held that the element was not met
	Another analogous case in which the element is not met

3. Arguments
• The State's arguments
	• Ms. Olsen's arguments
	  • Ms. Olsen's plain language arguments
	  • Ms. Olsen's analogous case arguments
	  • Ms. Olsen's policy arguments

• Ms. Olsen's arguments	• The State's arguments
	  • The State's plain language arguments
	  • The State's analogous case arguments
	  • The State's policy arguments

4. Mini-conclusion	• Mini-conclusion

If there are differences, decide whether your initial outline was better or whether the way that you wrote the draft is better. In the example set out above, the writer decides that the way she wrote the draft is better. Although in preparing her initial outline she thought that she would set out the State's arguments first, once she did the research she realized that Ms. Olsen would have the burden of proof. Thus, because Ms. Olsen has the burden of proof, her arguments should go first.

For more on after-the-fact outlines, see section 1.42 in *Just Writing, 2d ed.*

§ 13.1.3 Roadmaps, Signposts, Topic Sentences, Transitions, and Dovetailing

Once you have revised for content and large-scale organization, shift your focus to small-scale organization: in particular, turn your focus to your use of roadmaps, signposts, topic sentences, transitions, and dovetailing.

(a) Roadmaps

A roadmap is just what the term implies: a "map" that provides the reader with an overview of the document. In most memos you will want to put a roadmap at the end of your introductory section: in this roadmap, tell the attorney which elements are likely to be in dispute and which elements are not likely to be in dispute.

EXAMPLE **Roadmap Telling the Attorney Which Elements Will Be in Dispute and Which Elements Will Not Be in Dispute**

In this case, Ms. Olsen will have to concede that the summons was left with a person 15 years or older who was residing at the house where the summons and complaint were served. In addition, it is unlikely that Ms. Olsen will be able to prove that the her sister was not informed of the contents of the documents. Ms. Olsen may, however, be able to present clear and convincing evidence that the summons was not left at her usual place of abode.

In addition, if the analysis of a particular element is complex, you may want to include a roadmap that provides the reader with a summary or overview of that analysis. The following example is taken from the discussion section of the memo set out in section 6.4.4. Before discussing an alternative argument, the writer tells the reader that she is setting out an alternative argument and lists the requirements.

| EXAMPLE | **Roadmap Introducing the Discussion of an Alternative Argument** |

In the alternative, Ms. Smith can try to prove that she received continuing treatment. To do this, she will have to prove that she was incapacitated for three or more days and at least one of the following: (i) she received treatment two or more times by a health care provider, by a nurse or physician's assistant under direct supervision of a health care provider, or by a provider of health care services under orders of, or on referral by, a health care provider; or (ii) she received treatment by a health care provider on at least one occasion that results in a regimen of continuing treatment under the supervision of the health care provider; or (iii) she suffered from a chronic health condition. 29 C.F.R. § 825.800(1)(iii).

Note that in both of the above examples the roadmap is substantive in nature. Instead of saying, "First I will discuss this and then I will discuss that," the writer has stated who can prove what. For more on roadmaps, see section 2.2.1 in *Just Writing, 2d ed.*

(b) Signposts, Topic Sentences, and Transitions

Signposts, topic sentences, and transitions serve the same function that directional signs serve on a freeway. They tell readers where they are, what to expect, and how the pieces are connected. See section 2.2.2 (signposts), section 3.5 (topic sentences) and Chapter 4 (transitions) in *Just Writing, 2d ed.* While these directional signs may not be particularly important in some types of writing or in some cultures, they are essential in legal writing. In writing to a United States attorney, you need to make the connections between paragraphs and the connections between sentences clear.

Compare Example 1 below, in which the writer has not included topic sentences, signposts, or transitions with Example 2. In Example 2, the topic sentences, signposts, and transitions are in boldface type.

| EXAMPLE 1 | **Writer Has Not Included Topic Sentences, Signposts, or Transitions** |

When a defendant has more than one residence, the service must be made at the place where the defendant was actually living at the time the summons and complaint were served. Ms. Olsen had more than one residence: During the week she lived at the halfway house, and on weekends she visited her sister. Because the summons and complaint were served on a Wednesday, a weekday, the service was not made at the place where Ms. Olsen was actually living.

Like Mr. Torres, who only visited his mother and who was not at his mother's house when service was made, Ms. Olsen only visited her sister and was not at her sister's house when the summons and complaint were served. While Mr. Torres's mother's statement that Mr. Torres "would be home soon" suggested that Mr. Torres would be returning to his mother's house that day, Ms. Olsen's sister told the process server that Ms. Olsen "isn't here today." While the plaintiff in *Torres* had tried on a number of occasions to serve Mr. Torres at his New York house, we do not know whether the defendant tried to serve Ms. Olsen personally or at the halfway house. While Mr. Heffernan had been at his family's apartment only an hour before the summons and complaint were served, Ms. Olsen had not been at her sister's house for several days and, while in *Heffernan* the summons and complaint were served on the defendant's wife, in our case the summons and complaint were served on Ms. Olsen's sister. Since *Heffernan*, the courts have interpreted the service process statutes more narrowly.

The courts have repeatedly held that the service of process statutes should be strictly construed and that service on a relative is not, by itself, enough. *Shurman v. A. Mortg. & Inv. Corp.*, 795 So. 2d 952, 953-54 (Fla. 2001). Ms. Olsen did not receive notice.

EXAMPLE 2 Writer Has Included Topic Sentences, Signposts, and Transitions

Ms. Olsen can make three arguments to support her assertion that her sister's house was not her usual place of abode. First, Ms. Olsen will argue that, under the plain language of the rule, her sister's house was not her usual place of abode. When a defendant has more than one residence, the service must be made at the place where the defendant was actually living at the time summons and complaint were served. **In this case,** Ms. Olsen had more than one residence: during the week she lived at the halfway house, and on weekends she visited her sister. Because the summons and complaint were served on a Wednesday, a weekday, the service was not made at the place where Ms. Olsen was actually living.

Second, Ms. Olsen will argue that this case is more like *Torres* than it is *Heffernan*. Like Mr. Torres, who only visited his mother and who was not at his mother's house when service was made, Ms. Olsen only visited her sister and was not at her sister's house when the summons and complaint were served. **However,** while Mr. Torres's mother's statement that Mr. Torres "would be home soon" suggested that Mr. Torres would be returning to his mother's house that day, Ms. Olsen's sister told the process server that Ms. Olsen "isn't here today." **In addition,** while the plaintiff in *Torres* had tried on a number of occasions to serve Mr. Torres at his New York house, **in the Olsen case** we do not know whether the defendant tried to serve Ms. Olsen personally or at the halfway house. **Finally, *Heffernan* can be distinguished in two ways: (1)** While Mr. Heffernan had been at his family's apartment only an hour before the summons and complaint were served, Ms. Olsen had not been at her sister's house for several days; and **(2)** while in *Heffernan* the summons and complaint were served on the defendant's wife, in our case the summons and complaint were served on Ms. Olsen's sister. **It is also important to note that,** since *Heffernan*, the courts have interpreted the service process statutes more narrowly.

Third, Ms. Olsen can argue that, as a matter of public policy, the court should hold that the summons was not left at Ms. Olsen's usual place of abode. The courts have repeatedly held that the service of process statutes should be strictly construed and that service on a relative is not, by itself, enough. *Shurman v. A. Mortg. & Inv. Corp.*, 795 So. 2d 952, 953-54 (Fla. 2001). **In addition,** in this case, Ms. Olsen did not receive notice.

(c) Dovetailing

Another technique that you can use to make the connections between ideas clear is dovetailing. You use dovetailing when you refer back to a point made in the prior sentence or paragraph.

A   B   Reference to B   C

————————————————— . —————————————————— .

     Sentence 1   *Sentence 2*

In the following two examples, the writer has used dovetailing to make clear the connections between the first and second sentences. The language in bold is the dovetail.

EXAMPLE 1   **Dovetailing Used to Connect First and Second Sentences**

During July and August 2006, Ms. Olsen spent weeknights at the halfway house and Friday, Saturday, and Sunday nights at her **sister's house. Because she was spending time at her sister's house**, she moved some of her clothing and personal effects into her sister's house.

EXAMPLE 2   **Dovetailing Used to Connect First and Second Sentences**

Although the party seeking to invoke the jurisdiction of the court has the burden of proving that service was proper, the courts presume that the service was valid if the return is regular on its face. *Thompson v. State, Dept. of Revenue,* 867 So. 2d 603, 605 (Fla. 1st DCA 2004); *Magazine v. Bedoya*, 475 So. 2d 1035, 1035 (Fla. 3d DCA 1985). **In such instances**, the party challenging the service has the burden of presenting clear and convincing evidence that the service was invalid. *Id.*

While in the above examples dovetailing was used to make clear the connections between sentences, in the next example it is used to make clear the connections between paragraphs. The first sentence in the second paragraph refers back to the information at the end of the first paragraph.

| EXAMPLE 3 | **Dovetailing Used to Connect Paragraphs** |

Thus, the State will argue that the facts in this case are much stronger than the facts in *Heffernan*. While in *Heffernan*, Mr. Heffernan visited his family only "twice during the season," Ms. Olsen lived at her sister's house three days a week. In addition, while Mr. Heffernan had another permanent residence, Ms. Olsen was staying at a halfway house, which is by definition, only a temporary residence. Finally, while in *Heffernan* there was no indication that Mr. Heffernan listed the Florida address on any documents, Ms. Olsen listed her sister's address on her driver's license, and there is evidence indicating that Ms. Olsen received other types of mail at her sister's house.

The State will use these same facts to distinguish *Torres*. While in *Torres*, Mr. Torres presented evidence establishing that his permanent residence was in New York, in our case, Ms. Olsen did not have a permanent residence. In the five months before service, she had been an inpatient in a treatment facility, she had lived at the halfway house, and she had lived with her sister. The plaintiff can also distinguish *Shurman* and *Thompson*. While in *Shurman* and *Thompson* the record indicated that the defendants had not lived at the house where service had been made for months or years, in this case, Ms. Olsen admits that she has stayed at her sister's house on the weekend before her sister was served. Thus, the plaintiff will argue that the facts in this case are much stronger than the facts in *Heffernan*. While in *Heffernan*, Mr. Heffernan visited his family only "twice during the season," Ms. Olsen lived at her sister's house three days a week. In addition, while Mr. Heffernan had another permanent residence, Ms. Olsen was staying at a halfway house, which by definition, is only a temporary residence. Finally, while in *Heffernan* there was no indication that Mr. Heffernan listed the Florida address on any documents, Ms. Olsen listed her sister's address on her driver's license.

For more on dovetailing, see section 4.3.1 in *Just Writing, 2d ed.*

| PRACTICE  | While roadmaps, topic sentences, signposts, transitions, and dovetailing are more important in legal writing than in many other types of writing, do not overuse them. For example, do not use dovetailing to connect all of your sentences or all of your paragraphs. |

---

§ 13.2 Editing

The work is now almost done. When you step back from the memo and look at it through the attorney's eyes, you are pleased with its content and organization. You do, however, still need to edit your memo.

Like revising, editing requires that you look at your work through fresh eyes. At this stage, however, the focus is not on the larger issues of content

and organization but on sentence structure, conciseness, precision, grammar, and punctuation. The goal is to produce a professional product that is
easy to read and understand.

§ 13.2.1 Sentences

Most writers can substantially improve their sentences by following
four suggestions.

1. Make the actor the subject of most sentences.
2. Keep the subject and verb close together.
3. Put old information at the beginning of the sentence and new
   information at the end.
4. Vary sentence length and pattern.

Suggestion 1: Make the Actor the Subject of Most Sentences

By making the actor the subject of most of your sentences, you can
eliminate many of the constructions that make legal writing hard to understand: overuse of the passive voice, most nominalizations, expletive constructions, and many modifier problems.

(a) Passive Constructions

In a passive construction, the actor appears in the object rather than
in the subject slot of the sentence, or it is not named at all. For example,
in the following sentence, although the jury is the actor, the word "jury" is
used as the object of the preposition "by" rather than as the subject of the
sentence.

EXAMPLE   Passive Voice

A verdict was reached by the jury.
Subject   Verb   Object of the preposition

In the following example, the actor, "jury," is not named at all.

EXAMPLE   Passive Voice

A verdict was reached.
 Subject   Verb

To use the active voice, simply identify the actor—that is, the person or
entity or object that is doing the action—and use it as the subject of the

sentence. If you are having trouble identifying the actor, ask who is doing the action. For instance, in our example, ask who is it that reached the verdict? The answer, "the jury," is the actor.

EXAMPLE   **Active Voice**

The jury reached a verdict.
Subject   Verb   Object

As a general rule, the active voice is better unless the passive voice improves the flow of sentences or the writer wants to de-emphasize what the actor did.

Now read the following sentences, marking the subjects and verbs and deciding whether the writer used actors as subjects. If the writer did not use the actor as the subject of the sentence, decide whether the sentence should be rewritten.

EXAMPLE   **Sample Sentences**

Ms. Webster's testimony will include her statement that the summons was never given to her sister. Believing the paper related to some of Ms. Olsen's unpaid bills, the summons was simply put in a shoebox in the kitchen with a stack of Ms. Olsen's other mail.

Sentence 1:

Ms. Webster's testimony will include her statement that the summons was never given to her sister

Sentence 1 is written using a nominalization and the passive voice. In the main clause, the subject is "testimony" and the verb is "will include." In the dependent clause, the subject is "summons" and the verb is "was given." Because the passive voice does not improve the flow of the sentences and because the author does not need to de-emphasize what the actor did, it would be better to rewrite the sentence using the active voice.

Sentence 1: revised so actor is the subject in the main and dependent clauses

Ms. Webster will testify that she never gave the summons to her sister.
Subject   Subject

Note that in the main clause when the real actor (*Ms. Webster*) is put in the subject slot, that edit naturally changes the nominalization (*testimony*) to an active verb (*will testify*). See section b below. Note that in the dependent clause when the real actor (*she*) is put in the subject slot, that edit naturally changes the verb from passive voice (*was never given*) to active voice (*never gave*).

Sentence 2:

Believing the paper related to some of Ms. Olsen's unpaid bills, the summons was simply put in a shoebox in the kitchen with a stack of Ms. Olsen's other mail.

This second sentence is also written in the passive voice: in the main clause, the subject is "summons" and the verb is "was simply put." Because the author did not have a good reason for using the passive voice, it would be better to rewrite the sentence using the active voice.

Sentence 2: revised so actor is the subject and sentence is active voice

Believing the paper related to some of Ms. Olsen's unpaid bills, Ms. Webster simply put the summons in a shoebox in the kitchen with a stack of Ms. Olsen's other mail.

Note that in the second sentence, editing the sentence so that it is in active voice and has the actor (Ms. Webster) in the subject slot also corrects the earlier grammatical error—a dangling modifier problem. Before the sentence was edited, the phrase "believing the paper related to some of Ms. Olsen's unpaid bills" was a dangling modifier because the noun it should modify (Ms. Webster) was not in the sentence.

 **PRACTICE POINTER**   Be sure to distinguish between the passive voice and past tense. A sentence written in the past tense may or may not use the passive voice.

For more on the active and passive voice, see section 5.1 in *Just Writing, 2d ed.*

(b) Nominalizations

You create a nominalization when you turn a verb or an adjective into a noun. Although there are times when you will want to use a nominalization, overusing nominalizations can make your writing harder to read and understand. In the following sentence, "presumption" is a nominalization.

EXAMPLE   Nominalization

If the return is regular on its face, there is a **presumption** that the service is valid.

To make this sentence better, identify the real actor (in this case, the court) and then, in the verb, specifically state what action that actor has taken or will take. Note that "presumption" becomes "presume."

EXAMPLE   Rewrite without Nominalization

If the return is regular on its face, the courts **presume** that the service is valid.

(c) Expletive Constructions

In an expletive construction, phrases such as "it is" or "there are" are used as the subject and verb of the sentence. Although it is sometimes necessary to use such a construction (note the use of an expletive construction in this sentence), such a construction gives the reader almost no information. Therefore, when possible, use a concrete subject and action verb—that is, a subject and verb that describe something the reader can "see" in his or her mind. For more on concrete subjects and action verbs, see sections 5.2 and 5.3 in *Just Writing, 2d ed.*

EXAMPLE   Expletive Constructions

However, if the return is regular on its face, <u>there is</u> a presumption that the service is valid.

<u>It is</u> Ms. Duncan's argument that . . . .

EXAMPLE   Rewrites Without Expletives

If the return is regular on its face, the <u>courts presume</u> that the service is valid.

Ms. <u>Olsen will argue</u> that . . . .

PRACTICE

Note that expletive constructions and nominalizations often go hand in hand. Using an expletive construction forced the writer to use a nominalization:

If the return is regular on its face, <u>there is</u> a **presumption** that the service is valid.

(d) Dangling Modifiers

A dangling modifier is a modifier that does not reasonably modify anything in the sentence. For example, in the following sentence, the modifying phrase "Applying this test" does not reasonably modify anything in the sentence. It is not "it was held" that is doing the "applying."

EXAMPLE	**Dangling Modifier**

Applying this test, it was held that the summons and complaint were not left at the defendant's usual place of abode.

The dangling modifier can be eliminated if the actor is used as the subject of the sentence.

EXAMPLE	**Rewrite Without Dangling Modifier**

Applying this test, the **court** held that the summons and complaint were not left at the defendant's usual place of abode.

Now the phrase "Applying this test" modifies something in the sentence: the court. For more on dangling modifiers, see section 8.6.2 in *Just Writing, 2d ed.*

Suggestion 2: Keep the Subject and Verb Close Together

Researchers have established that readers cannot understand a sentence until they have located both the subject and the verb. In addition, readers have a difficult time remembering the subject if there are more than seven words between the subject and verb. The lesson to be learned from this research is that, as a writer, you should try to keep your subject and verb close together. In the following examples, the subject and verb are underlined.

EXAMPLE 1	**Subject and Verb Are Too Far Apart**

In such instances, the <u>burden</u> of presenting clear and convincing evidence that the service was invalid <u>is</u> on the party challenging the service.

EXAMPLE 2	**Rewrite with Subject and Verb Closer Together**

In such instances, the <u>party</u> challenging the service <u>has</u> the burden of presenting clear and convincing evidence that the service was invalid.

For more on subject-verb distance, see section 5.4 in *Just Writing, 2d ed.*

Suggestion 3: Put Old Information at the Beginning of the Sentence and New Information at the End

Sentences, and the paragraphs they create, make more sense when the old information is placed at the beginning and the new information is placed

at the end. When this pattern is used, the development progresses naturally from left to right without unnecessary backtracking.

> **EXAMPLE**   **Old Information Is at the Beginning of the Sentence, and New Information Is at the End**
>
> The only Florida case in which the summons was left with a relative with whom the defendant was visiting is *Torres*, 867 So. 2d at 585-86. In that case, the plaintiff tried, for more than a month, to serve Mr. Torres at the New York apartment where Mr. Torres had lived for thirteen years. *Id*. Although all attempts at service were unsuccessful, the New York process server indicated in his affidavit that he had "verified" with a neighbor that "Mr. Torres lived at the New York address, but that he was often out of town, and was expected to return in two weeks." *Id*. Because it could not serve the defendant in New York, the plaintiff served Mr. Torres's mother at her residence in Florida. In his affidavit, the Florida process server stated that Mr. Torres's mother told him that "he (presumably Mr. Torres) would be home soon." *Id*. Mr. Torres stated that he never received notice. In holding that the service was not valid, the court noted that while the standard of review was gross abuse of discretion, the trial court had not heard live testimony, and the plaintiff had the burden of establishing that the service was valid. *Id*. at 587. It then went on to note that the evidence tended to support Mr. Torres's position that his usual place of abode was in New York and that Mr. Torres's mother's statement that Mr. Torres would be home soon was, at best, ambiguous. *Id*.

In the paragraph set out above, the first sentence acts as a topic sentence, telling the attorney that there is only one Florida case that has similar facts to the facts in the client's case. That first sentence ends with a reference to the new information, which is the name of the case: "*Torres*." In the second sentence, the name of the case is now the old information, and the second sentence begins with a reference back to that old information. The second sentence then ends with the new information: that the plaintiff had tried, on a number of occasions, to serve the defendant in New York. In the third sentence, the old information is that the plaintiff had tried to serve the defendant in New York. Thus, the author uses this old information to start the third sentence, putting the new information, that the neighbor had told the process server that the defendant was out of town, at the end of the third sentence.

Suggestion 4: Vary Sentence Length and Pattern

Even if writing is technically correct, it is not considered good if it is not pleasing to the ear. Read the following example aloud.

EXAMPLE 1 **All Sentences Are About the Same Length and Use the Same Pattern**

A process server went to Ms. Webster's house on Wednesday, July 26, 2006. The process server asked for Elaine Olsen. Ms. Webster told the process server that "Elaine isn't here today." The process server then handed the summons and complaint to Ms. Webster. The process server told Ms. Webster that Ms. Olsen "needed to go to court."

In the Example 1, the writing is not pleasing because the sentences are similar in length and all follow the same pattern. Although short, uncomplicated sentences are usually better than long, complicated ones, the use of too many short sentences results in writing that sounds choppy and sophomoric. As Example 2 illustrates, the passage is much better when the writer varies sentence length and pattern.

EXAMPLE 2 **Sentences Are Varied in Length and Sentence Pattern**

On Wednesday, July 26, 2006, a process server went to Ms. Webster's house and asked for Elaine Olsen. When Ms. Webster told the process server that "Elaine isn't here today," the process server handed the summons to Ms. Webster and told her that Ms. Olsen "needed to go to court."

For more on sentence construction, see Chapter 5 in *Just Writing, 2d ed.*

§ 13.2.2 Writing Concisely

Although writing sentences with strong subject-verb units eliminates much unnecessary language, you also need to edit out such throat-clearing expressions as "it is expected that . . ." and "it is generally recognized that . . ." and redundancies like "combined together" and "depreciate in value." In the following examples, the first draft has seventy-two words, and the edited draft has fifty-four words.

EXAMPLE 1 **First Draft (Seventy-Two Words)**

It is generally recognized that a claimant can satisfy the open and notorious element by showing one of two things. The claimant can show either (1) that the title owner had real and actual notice of the claimant's use of the land throughout the statutory period or (2) that the claimant used the land in such a way that any reasonable person would have thought or believed that the claimant owned it.

| EXAMPLE 2 | **Revised Draft (Fifty-Four Words)** |

A claimant can prove that its possession was open and notorious by showing either (1) that the title owner had actual notice of the adverse use throughout the statutory period or (2) that the claimant used the land in such a way that any reasonable person would have thought that the claimant owned it.

In the preceding examples, some simple editing allowed the writer to reduce the number of words by 25 percent. By using the same editing techniques throughout the draft, the writer could get a ten-page draft down to seven-and-a-half pages. For more on writing concisely, see section 6.2 in *Just Writing, 2d ed.*

§ 13.2.3 Writing Precisely

In addition to writing concisely, you also want to be precise. Make sure that you use correct terms, that you use those terms consistently, that you pair the right subject with the right verb, and that you compare or contrast like things.

(a) Select the Correct Term

In the law, many words have specific meanings. For example, the words "**held**," "**found**," and "**ruled**" have very different meanings. Use "held" in describing the appellate court's answer to the issue raised on appeal; "found" in referring to the trial court's or jury's findings of fact, and "ruled" when talking about the court's ruling on a motion or objection.

Compare the following four examples. In Example 1, the writer used "held" incorrectly. Because the writer is describing facts, "held' is incorrect. In contrast, in Example 2, the writer has used "held' correctly. Similarly, in Example 3, the writer uses "found" correctly. Because the writer is describing the court's findings of fact, "found" is correct. Finally, in Example 4, the writer uses "ruled" correctly.

| EXAMPLE 1 | **"Held" Used Incorrectly** |

In *Chaplin*, the court **held** that the claimants had built a road across the disputed land, cleared and maintained the disputed land, installed utility lines, and used the disputed land for recreational activities.

| EXAMPLE 2 | **"Held" Used Correctly** |

In *Chaplin*, the court **held** that the claimants had used the disputed land as their own when they built a road across the disputed land, cleared and maintained the disputed land, installed utility lines, and used the disputed land for recreational activities.

EXAMPLE 3   "Found" Used Correctly

In *Chaplin,* the court **found** that the claimants had built a road across the disputed land, cleared and maintained the disputed land, installed utility lines, and used the disputed land for recreational activities.

EXAMPLE 4   "Ruled" Used Correctly

The court **ruled** that the evidence was inadmissible.

(b) Use Terms Consistently

In addition to making sure that you use the correct term, make sure that you use terms consistently. If something is an "element," continue referring to it as an element. Do not switch and suddenly start calling it a "factor" or a "requirement."

EXAMPLE 1   Inconsistent Use of Terms

To prove adverse possession, the claimant must prove five **elements**: that its possession was (1) exclusive, (2) actual and uninterrupted, (3) open and notorious, and (4) hostile for the statutory period. *ITT Rayonier, Inc. v. Bell,* 112 Wn.2d 754, 757, 774 P.2d 6 (1989); *Chaplin v. Sanders,* 100 Wn.2d 853, 857, 676 P.2d 431 (1984). In this case, the statutory period is ten years. RCW 4.16.020(1). Whether a particular **factor** is met is a mixed question of law and fact. *Chaplin,* 100 Wn.2d at 863. Whether the essential facts exist is for the trier of fact to decide; but whether the facts, as found, satisfy the **requirement** is for the court to determine as a matter of law. *Id.*

EXAMPLE 2   Consistent Use of Terms

To prove adverse possession, the claimant must prove five **elements**: that its possession was (1) exclusive, (2) actual and uninterrupted, (3) open and notorious, and (4) hostile for the statutory period. *ITT Rayonier, Inc. v. Bell,* 112 Wn.2d 754, 757, 774 P.2d 6 (1989); *Chaplin v. Sanders,* 100 Wn.2d 853, 857, 676 P.2d 431 (1984). In this case, the statutory period is ten years. RCW 4.16.020(1). Whether a particular **element** is met is a mixed question of law and fact. *Chaplin,* 100 Wn.2d at 863. Whether the essential facts exist is for the trier of fact to decide; but whether the facts, as found, satisfy the **element** is for the court to determine as a matter of law. *Id.*

PRACTICE
POINTER

Some legal writers mistakenly believe that they will bore legal readers if they use the same term every time they mean the same thing. This belief may come from their undergraduate or high school writing days when they might have been encouraged to use a number of synonyms for key concepts that appeared frequently in a paper. Because of their training in reading statutes, legal readers, unlike the general reading public, are inclined to assume that a switch in terms signals a switch in concept, not a writer's effort to keep them entertained. Consequently, for clarity's sake, legal writers should use consistent terms for key terms, such as "element." With other kinds of words that are not key terms, such as transitions, it is still a good idea to use a little variety.

(c) Pair the Right Subject with the Right Verb

In addition to making sure that you have selected the right word and used it consistently, also make sure the subjects of your sentences can do the actions described by the verb. For instance, while courts "state," "find," "rule," "hold," "reason," "conclude," and so forth; they do not "argue." It is the parties who present arguments. (For a list of subjects and verbs that go together in legal writing, see Exhibit 6.1 on page 115 in *Just Writing, 2d ed.*) In the following example, the subject and verb do not go together.

EXAMPLE 1   **Subject Does Not Do Action Described by Verb**

The **court** can **argue** that DNWC was not using the land as if it were its own.

EXAMPLE 2   **Subject Can Do Action Described by Verb**

Mr. Garcia argued that DNWC was not using the land as if it were its own.

or

The **court concluded** that DNWC was not using the land as if it were its own.

(d) Compare or Contrast Like Things

In setting out the arguments, you will often want to show how your case is similar to or different from other cases. For instance, you will want to compare or contrast the facts in your case to the facts in another case. In making these comparisons, make sure you are "comparing apples with apples and oranges with oranges." For example, compare an analogous case to your case, one of the parties in the analogous case to one of the parties in your case, or one of the facts in the analogous case to the comparable fact in your case.

In most instances, it works best to put the reference to the analogous case before the reference to your case.

In the first example that follows, the author has not compared similar things. She compared a case (*Crites*) to a person (Mr. Garcia). In the second example, the author compared like things.

EXAMPLE   **Author Has Not Compared Like Things**

Unlike *Crites,* in which the title owner allowed the claimants to use his land as a neighborly accommodation, **Mr. Garcia** did not allow the DNWC to use his land as a neighborly accommodation.

EXAMPLE   **Author Has Compared Like Things**

Unlike *Crites,* in which the title owner allowed the claimants to use his land as a neighborly accommodation, **in this case**, Mr. Garcia did not allow the DNWC to use his land as a neighborly accommodation.

Remember that when a name is italicized, the reference is to case, but when a name is not italicized, the reference is to a person. Thus, in the following sentence, "*Crites*" is a reference to the court's decision in *Crites v. Koch*, and the reference to "Crites" is a reference to the plaintiff, Mr. Crites. For example:

In *Crites,* the court held that Koch allowed Crites to use his land as a neighborly accommodation.

For more on writing precisely, see section 6.1 in *Just Writing, 2d ed.*

§ 13.2.4 Grammar and Punctuation

For a moment, imagine that you have received the following letter from a local law firm.

EXAMPLE   **Example:**

Dear Student:

Thank you for submitting an application for a position as a law clerk with are firm. Your grades in law school are very good, however, at this time we do not have any positions available. Its possible, however, that we may have a opening next summer and we therefore urge you to reapply with us then.

Sincerely,

Senior Partner

No matter how bad the job market is, most students would not want to be associated with a firm that sends out a five-line letter containing three major errors and several minor ones. Unfortunately, the reverse is also true. No matter how short-handed they are, most law firms do not want to hire someone who has not mastered the basic rules of grammar and punctuation. Most firms cannot afford a legal intern or attorney who makes careless errors or who lacks basic writing skills.

Consequently, at the editing stage you need to go back through your draft, correcting errors. Look first for the errors that potentially affect meaning (misplaced modifiers, incorrect use of "which" and "that") and for errors that educated readers are likely to notice (incomplete sentences, comma splices, incorrect use of the possessive, lack of parallelism). Then look for the errors that you know from past experience that you are likely to make.

P R A C T I C E   If you have not already done so, your professor may want you to take the online diagnostic exam for grammar and punctuation that comes with this book and with the other books in the series. You can obtain your password from your legal writing professor.

For more on grammar and punctuation, see Chapters 8 and 9 in *Just Writing, 2d ed.*

§ 13.3 Proofreading

Most writers learn the importance of proofreading the hard way. A letter, brief, or contract goes out with the client's name misspelled, with an "or" where there should have been an "and," or without an essential "not." At a minimum, these errors cause embarrassment; at worst, they result in a lawsuit.

To avoid such errors, treat proofreading as a separate step. After you have finished revising and editing, go back through your draft, looking not at content, organization, or sentence style, but for errors. Have you written what you intended to write?

Proofreading is most effective when it is done on hard copy several days (or, when that is not feasible, several hours) after you have finished editing. Force yourself to read slowly, focusing not on the sentences but on the individual words in the sentences. Is a word missing? Is a word re-peated? Are letters transposed? You can force yourself to read slowly by covering up all but the line you are reading, by reading from right to left, or by reading from the bottom of the page to the top.

PRACTICE POINTER   You can also use a free website, readplease.com, to help you proofread. Because the program reads each word, you can use it to check for double words, missing words, and incorrect words.

Also, force yourself to begin your proofreading by looking at the sections that caused you the most difficulty or that you wrote last. Because you may have been concentrating on content or were tired, these sections probably contain the most errors.

Finally, when you get into practice, do not rely on just your spelling and grammar checkers. Instead, make it a habit to have a second person proof-read your work. Not only will such a person see errors that you missed, he or she is also less likely to "read in" missing words. For more on proofread-ing, see section 1.6 in *Just Writing, 2d ed.*

§ 13.4 Citations

As a legal writer, you have an extra burden. In addition to editing and proof-reading the text, you must also edit and proofread your citations to legal authorities.

At the editing stage, focus on selection and placement of citations. Is the authority you cited the best authority? Did you avoid string cites (the citing of multiple cases for the same point)? Have you included a citation to authority for every rule stated? Did you include the appropriate signal? Have you over- or under-emphasized the citation? (You emphasize a citation by placing it in the text of a sentence; you de-emphasize it by placing it in a separate citation sentence.)

In contrast, at the proofreading stage, focus on the citation itself. Are the volume and page numbers correct? Are the pinpoint cites accurate? Have you included the year of the decision and any subsequent history? Is the spacing correct?

§ 13.5 Some Final Thoughts About Revising, Editing, and Proofreading

Given the time demands and pace of many types of law practice, it can be tempting to believe that "in house" documents such as office memoranda do not require these final steps. Before giving in to that temptation, remember that there are times when "in house" documents get shared outside of the firm. Thus, what you may have assumed was going to be an internal objective memo may become an external document. Remember too that even within the firm, you will be judged by the quality of your written work. While some supervising attorneys may forgive the occasional proofreading error or unedited sentence, most will expect consistently high-quality work.

Index

Active voice, 282–284
Advice, offered in formal conclusion, 268–269
After-the-fact outlines, 273, 276–277
Analogous cases
    arguing the application of the law, 259–260
    descriptions of, 189–200, 220–222
    illustrating court application of common law, statutes, and regulations, 68–71
    script format vs. integrated format, 221–222
    topic sentences introducing, 196–197
    using parentheticals, 199–200
Arguments, 200–211
    analogous cases, 202, 259–262
    drafting, 200–201, 206–211
    identifying, 249–250
    legislative history, 255–259
    organization of, 204–206, 224–227
    plain language, 201–202, 250–255
    policy, 202–203, 262–263
    presenting, 230–231
Assertions. See also Arguments
    not supporting, 208
    presenting, 207–208
    supporting, 209–211

Background facts, 157
Bench memos, 129–151
Binding laws, 35–36
Brief answer
    checklist, 173
    content, 171–172, 173
    formal memo involving three issues including issue of first impression, 130

formal memo sample with script format, 118
format, 173
purpose, 171

Canons of statutory construction, 250
Case law, 33
Cases, 61–95, 196–197. See also Reading statutes and cases
    analogous. See Analogous cases
    analysis of, 71, 99, 103–106
    attorneys' use of, 68–71
    binding, 61–68
    citations used for finding, 71–73
    contextualizing, 102–103
    distinguishing text of opinion from supporting material, 73–79
    purposeful reading, 105
    reading the opinion, 79–86
    relationship between statutes, regulations, and cases, 43–44
    selecting, 70
    synthesis, 101–102
Checklists
    brief answer in objective memoranda, 173
    conclusion in objective memoranda, 269–270
    discussion section in objective memoranda, 212–214, 240–242
    issue statements in objective memoranda, 170–171
    issues of first impression, 263–264
    statement of facts in objective memoranda, 161–162
Circuits, judicial, 27
Citations
    authority for rules, 184
    editing and proofreading, 294

Citations *(continued)*
     finding cases/statutes, 49–50,
          71–73
Code, 49
Common law, 33, 68–71
Comparisons/contrasts, 9, 291–292
Conciseness, 160, 288–289
Conclusion in objective memoranda,
          265–270
     advice offered in, 268–269
     bench memo involving issue of first
          impression, 149–151
     checklist, 269–270
     multi-issue memo, 267
     one-issue memo, 265–266
     predicting how court will decide the
          element, 211–212
     sample memos, 122, 128–129, 136–
          137
Consistent terminology, 290
Constitution, U.S., 46–47
Constructing arguments, 200–201,
          206–211
Court of Appeals, 27, 66
Court system
     canons of statutory construction, 250
     determining which cases are binding
          on which courts, 61–68
     state, federal, and other, 27–32

Dangling modifiers, 285–286
Discussion section in objective memo-
          randa, 175–214
     arguments, 200–211, 224–227
     balancing competing interests,
          227–230
     bench memo involving issue of first
          impression, 138–149
     checklist, 212–214, 240–242
     descriptions of analogous cases,
          189–200, 220–222
     disputed elements, 187–200, 213
     general rules, 180–185
     integrated format, 215–218
     issue of first impression, 246–264
     mini-conclusions, 222–224
     overview of, 175–176
     sample memos, 118, 124–128,
          130–136
     script format, 176–179
     specific rules, 188–189, 218–220
     undisputed elements, 185–187, 213
Disputed elements, 187–200, 213
Distance between subject and verb,
          286–287

District Courts, federal, 27
Dovetailing, 280–281

Editing, 281–293
     citations, 294
     comparisons/contrasts, 291–292
     conciseness, 288–289
     consistency of term use, 290
     grammar and punctuation, 292–293
     overview of, 281–282
     preciseness, 289
     sentences, 282–288
     subject/verb pairing, 291
Elements
     disputed, 187–200, 213
     identifying in statutes, 55
     undisputed, 185–187, 213
Emotionally significant facts, 157
Enacted law, 33–34
Executive branch
     federal government, 26
     state government, 29
Expletive constructions, 285

Facts, legally and emotionally significant,
          155–157
Federal courts, 27–28, 66–67
Federal government, 25–28, 30–33
Federal statutes
     determining which cases are binding
          on which courts,
          65–68
     as governing authority, 44–46
     overview of, 40–42
FindLaw link, 102

General rule, presenting, 180–185, 218
Grammar and punctuation, 292–293

Integrated format
     analysis of knowledge in, 232–240
     arguments in, 225–227
     checklist, 240–242
     for discussion section, 215–219
     mini-conclusions in, 223–224
     sample memo, 123–129
Issue of first impression, 243–264
     bench memo involving, 138
     checklist, 263–264
     identifying arguments, 250–262
     introduction, 246–249
     organizational plans for, 244–246
Issue statements in objective memo-
          randa
     checklist, 170–171

format, 164
multi-issue memo, 267
overview of, 163
readability of, 170
sample memos, 118, 123, 130
single-issue memo, 265–266
"under-does-when" format, 164–168
"whether" format, 168–170

Judicial branches, state and federal,
    26–30
Judicial opinions. *See* Cases
Jurisdiction, of federal, state, and local
    laws, 34–35

Legally significant facts
    issue statements, 12
    statement of facts, 155–157
Legislative branches, state and federal,
    26, 28, 31

Mandatory authority, 34–37, 64–67
Memoranda. *See* Objective memoranda
Mini-conclusions in objective memo-
        randa, 222–224
    integrated format, 223–224
    script format, 223–224
Modifiers, dangling, 285–286

Nominalizations, 284–285

Objective memoranda, 111–152
    analogous cases, 189–200, 220–222
    analyzing statutes and cases, 48–49,
        71, 99, 103–106
    audience, 112
    bench memo involving issue of first
        impression, 129–151
    brief answer, 118, 130
    compared with business memos and
        academic research
        papers, 5
    conclusion, 122, 128–129, 136–137,
        149–151
    conventions of, 112–113
    discussion section, 118–122, 124–
        128, 130–136, 138–149
    editing, 281–293
    format, 5
    headings, 54, 187, 259
    integrated format, 123–129
    issue statements, 118, 123, 130,
        138
    objectivity in, 6

proofreading, 293–294
purpose, 112
revising, 271–281
sample memos, 113–151
script format, 117–122
statement of facts, 117–118, 123–
    124, 129–130, 137–138
synthesizing statutes and cases, 101–
    102, 190–193
Objectivity, in presentation of facts, 160
Office memo
    format/conventions, 5, 11–12
    purpose of, 4–6
    reader requirements, 6–10
    writer's role, 10–11
One-issue memo, 265–266
Opinions. *See also* Cases
    advice offered in formal conclusion,
        268–269
    distinguishing text of opinion from
        supporting material, 73–79
    predicting how court will decide the
        element, 211–212
    reading, 79–86
Outlines, after-the-fact, 273, 276–277

Passive voice, 282–284
Persuasive authority, 34–37
Precision, 289
Predictions. *See* Conclusion in objective
        memoranda; Mini-conclusions in
        objective memoranda
Principle-based analysis, 195
Professionalism, 11
Proofreading, 293–294

Raise and dismiss, 185, 187
Reading statutes and cases, 97–108
    analysis and understanding, 71, 99,
        105–106
    contextualizing, 102–103
    judging/evaluating, 103–105
    purposeful approach, 105
    reading skills of lawyers, 97–99
    synthesizing, 101–102
Regulations
    cases illustrating application of,
        70–71
    challenging regulatory authority,
        47–48
    federal, 65–68
    promulgation of, 42–43
    relationship between statutes,
        regulations, and cases, 43–44

Relationship between federal and state governments, 32–33
Relationship between state and federal courts, 31–32
Research notes, 201
Revising, objective memoranda, 271–281
Roadmaps, 277–278
Rule section in objective memoranda
   citations to authority for each rule, 184–185
   general rules, 180–185, 218
   multiple statutory sections, 181
   single statutory section, 180–181
   specific rules, 188, 218–220

Sample memoranda, 113–116, 117–122, 123–129, 129–137, 137–151
Script format, 117–122, 176–179
   advantages/disadvantages, 218
   analysis of knowledge in, 232–240
   arguments in, 225–227
   for discussion section, 216
   mini-conclusions in, 223–224
   sample memos, 118, 122
   specific rule section, 219
Selecting cases, 70
Sentences, 282–288
   active and passive voices, 282–284
   dangling modifiers, 285–286
   editing techniques, 288–289
   new information at beginning, 282
   subject/verb distance, 286–287
   subject/verb pairing, 291
   "this but not that" structures, 230
   varying length and patterns, 287–288
Signposts, 278–280
Specific rules, presenting, 188, 218–220
Standard of review, 80
State courts, 29–30
State government
   branches of, 28–30
   relationship between state and federal systems, 30–33
State statutes
   analyzing, 68–71
   finding cases/statutes, 71–73
   as governing authority, 45–46
   overview of, 42

Statement of facts in objective memoranda, 153–162
   bench memo involving issue of first impression, 137–138
   checklist, 161–162
   fact selection, 155–157
   organizational schemes, 158–160
   presentation of facts, 160–161
   sample memos, 117–118, 123–124, 129–130
Statutes, 39–59. *See also* Reading statutes and cases
   analysis, 48–49
   arguments challenging, 46–48
   cases illustrating how courts have applied, 70–71
   distinguishing statute from related materials, 50–55
   elements or requirements of, 55–58
   enacting, 39–40
   federal and state, 40–42
   finding from citations, 49–50
   as governing authority, 44–46
   promulgation of regulations and, 42–43
   relationship between statutes, regulations, and cases, 43–44
   version, reading correct, 55
Subjects
   subject/verb distance, 286–287
   subject/verb pairing, 291
Supreme Court, U.S., 27–28, 66
Synthesizing statutes and cases, 101–102, 190–193

Topic sentences, 195–197, 278–280
Transitions, 194, 278–280

"Under-does-when" format, 164–168
Undisputed elements, 185–187, 213
United States Code (U.S.C.), 49–50
Unknown facts, 157

Variety, in sentence length, 287–288
Verbs
   subject/verb distance, 286–287
   subject/verb pairing, 291

"Whether" format, 168–170
Writ of certiorari, 66